Pietism and the Foundations of the Modern World

Pietism and the Foundations
of the Modern World

JUSTIN A. DAVIS

◆PICKWICK *Publications* · Eugene, Oregon

PIETISM AND THE FOUNDATIONS OF THE MODERN WORLD

Copyright © 2019 Justin A. Davis. All rights reserved. Except for brief quotations in critical publications or reviews, no part of this book may be reproduced in any manner without prior written permission from the publisher. Write: Permissions, Wipf and Stock Publishers, 199 W. 8th Ave., Suite 3, Eugene, OR 97401.

Pickwick Publications
An Imprint of Wipf and Stock Publishers
199 W. 8th Ave., Suite 3
Eugene, OR 97401

www.wipfandstock.com

PAPERBACK ISBN: 978-1-5326-6736-7
HARDCOVER ISBN: 978-1-5326-6737-4
EBOOK ISBN: 978-1-5326-6738-1

Cataloging-in-Publication data:

Names: Davis, Justin A., author.

Title: Pietism and the foundations of the modern world / by Justin A. Davis.

Description: Eugene, OR : Pickwick Publications, 2019 | Includes bibliographical references.

Identifiers: ISBN 978-1-5326-6736-7 (paperback) | ISBN 978-1-5326-6737-4 (hardcover) | ISBN 978-1-5326-6738-1 (ebook)

Subjects: LCSH: Pietism—History. | Civilization—History.

Classification: LCC BR1650.2 D19 2019 (print) | LCC BR1650.2 (ebook)

Manufactured in the U.S.A.   08/07/19

To Molly,
my dedicated wife and mother of my children

Contents

Preface | ix

Introduction | 1
  I. Ancestry of Pietism: Mysticism and Early Modernity | 8
  II. Foundational Pietism: Perkins, Arndt, and Spener | 48
  III. Institutional Pietism: Francke and Zinzendorf | 96
  IV. Denominational Pietism: Wesley and the Impact
     of Institutionalized Pietism | 141
Conclusion: Success and Impact of Halle, Moravians
    & Methodists through the Eighteenth Century | 169

Bibliography | 181

Preface

THE GUIDING FACTOR IN the construction of this work is the prominent position of experience. Experience is an important part of any religion. Yet the question always remains how the experience of the divine is understood. Should the experience itself be the judge? Or should reason interpret the experience? Should a reason based on scholastic understanding of dogmas first be articulated and then experience deduced from this point? Within Christianity as a whole, the debate about how to understand experience has taken all three positions. Eastern Orthodox, Roman Catholic, and Protestants have each possessed key leaders and movements that stressed rationalism, scholasticism, or piety. This work will focus on the Protestants' relationship to experience.

Protestantism is categorically different from the other two branches of Christianity, not in what it possesses but in what it lacks. As Protestantism developed, the authority of tradition and an ecclesial hierarchy that maintains authority evaporated. Orthodox and Catholics value tradition as one of the foundations of the church. Creeds, councils, and commentaries from saints and learned men and women all carry value as they fit within their tradition. Scripture itself is understood and interpreted through the lens of tradition. This does not mean that Protestants do not have a tradition. Lutherans point to practices as relevant because Luther followed them. The same applies to Reform with Calvin and Zwingli. The difference is that Protestants in the Reformation rejected the value of tradition. While a new tradition emerged, it is influential rather than authoritative. The same applies to an ecclesial hierarchy. Even in high church expressions of Protestantism the ecclesiastical hierarchy can be challenged or rejected by its constituent members, resulting in schism and new sect formation with greater ease than within Orthodoxy or Catholicism. The authority of Protestant bishops, when they exist, is nowhere near supreme, and nowhere is the notion of supreme pontiff present in the Protestant world.

The reason why the lack of authority in tradition and ecclesial hierarchy is important should become obvious when addressing experiences and how to interpret them. Protestants may argue that their experiences of God are interpreted through and corrected by the Bible. Still the matter of interpretation is left to the individual or at best a small community. Personal miracles and personal revelations may occur with relative frequency or not at all. Experiences of the divine are interpreted differently among different Protestants, and some interpretations actively exclude the validity of certain experiences, or experiences of outside groups. With notions of divine encounters varying and no real system set in place to determine which ones should be heralded or hated, the assortment of movements in the nineteenth, twentieth, and twenty-first centuries that emerged from experiential Protestantism is astounding. From its Protestant roots, Pietism birthed Pentecostalism, existentialism, modern liberal Protestantism, neo-liberalism, Fundamentalism, and a whole host of Christian ethics. Furthermore it provided the groundwork for neo-orthodoxy, hermeneutics, female ordination, and the Emergent Church.

Introduction

THE DEFINITION OF PIETISM is debated and is under further review and reflection by contemporary scholars such as Jonathan Strom, Peter C. Erb, Hartmut Lehman, and a whole host of others.[1] For the purposes of this study I will define Pietism in two ways. The simplest definition of Pietism that I can offer is to identify it as the experiential strand of Protestantism, or more precisely, as those Protestants who prioritize experience over scholasticism and rationalism. In many ways this definition addresses the intellectual space in which Pietists of various confessions emerge and operate. As such, there is no single unified school of Pietism with lines that demarcate fidelity, or exclude others directly. Furthermore Pietism, understood as the prioritization of experience, also serves as a corrective to the other strands of Protestant thought. More extensively, Pietism should be understood as a quasi-mystical experiential revivalist movement, found within Lutheran, Reform, and Anglican Protestantism of every age, which seeks to understand and rework their world, both inside and outside of themselves along lines of personally meaningful relationship between themselves as individuals and God, while maintaining a general antipathy or outright hostility to the greater Christian culture and religious formalism which dictates that culture's norms and practices. Many of these characteristics are not unique to Protestantism, and indeed we can find many of these same traits within Catholic and Orthodox Christianity. Nor are these features unique to the modern and early modern world, rather we have elements of these ideas in the Middle Ages and indeed within all of Christian history. While some of the particular traits are not unique among Pietists, the Protestant expression is not the same as what is found within the Catholic or Orthodox Churches. Pietism provides a unique analysis of Protestantism in general and what

1. The list of scholars intently working on a definition of Pietism and its scope in the last twenty years is extensive but includes Dale W. Brown, Christian T. Collins Winn, Christopher Gehrz, G. William Calrson, Eric Holst, Martin Brecht, Johannes Wallmann, and Douglas H. Shantz.

may occur without ecclesial restraint, as well as showing the diversity of doctrine that can emerge when experience of the divine is the primary guide rather than tradition.

While the conception of Pietism I lay out is fairly broad, the term itself also has historical weight, and not any one person or movement can, nor should be identified as Pietist. In addition to the experiential emphasis found within Lutheranism, Reform, and Anglicanism, a mode of interpretation of these experiences was developed by a series of sixteenth and seventeenth-century Pietist forefathers that include William Perkins in England and Johann Arndt in Germany. From Arndt, Philip Jakob Spener is the culmination of foundational German Pietism and often accredited founder of the movement. While he did not found the movement, his place as a foundational figure in the history of Pietism should not be overlooked. For the broader label of Pietism to be applied, an intellectual and theological legacy should be established to one of these three figures or another figure of equal theological weight and roughly contemporary with them.[2] By understanding an intellectual history, along with the experiential impulse, Pietism can begin to make sense as a movement. Once credence is given to the experiential program, an analysis of group dynamics can take shape, and Pietism can be addressed as something that helped to shape and challenge the modern world. It is also from here that nineteenth, twentieth, and twenty-first-century ideologies that serve to spur on the transformation of society can properly be understood. What concerns this study is the progression of Pietism, beginning as an outsider movement and growing into powerful institutions and denominations. Yet even the same theologians who are responsible for forming these institutions are dedicated to their experience of God and their particular calling in rejecting the larger Christian culture. This results in a fragmentation of ideologies, with some maintaining the ossified institutional forms that grew up around previous Pietist leaders, and others rejecting the newly created carapace for a new expression of experience.

Far too often discussions of the relationship between modernity and Christianity only look at the era of the Reformation and the formal systems erected by the Magisterial Reformers. The Protestant protesters are either incorrectly identified as Anabaptists or ignored for a longer discussion of denominational formation and church governance. What is lacking for these histories are those impactful voices who found homes in

---

2. Others may include many theologians who Stoeffler identifies in his work, *Rise of Evangelical Pietism*, such as Hooper, Bradford, Baxter, Bunyan, and Taylor in England; Taffin, Udemans, Tellinick, Amesius, Labadie, and Lodensteyn in the Reform churches; and Grossgebaue, Lütkemann, Müller, and Scriver in Lutheranism.

establishing denominations and worked to reshape their churches along more intimate and experiential lines. What is desperately needed is a meaningful discussion of Pietism as a historical phenomenon. Therefore it is the aim of this work to provide an in-depth yet accessible introduction to Pietism and to supplement any study of Western Christianity, especially those addressing the era of the Reformation forward. This work should also be essential to any who wish to address nineteenth-century theology, as nearly every influential Protestant theologian of the nineteenth century was impacted by or confronted Pietism or its systems.

In order to understand the impact of the Protestant Reformation upon the history of the Western world we first must understand Pietism as a historical phenomenon. To accomplish this, the work is divided into four broad sections. The first section addresses the ancestry of Pietism which includes the tradition of mysticism in Western Christianity, including Angela da Foligno, Johann Tauler, and Thomas à Kempis, all of whom directly impacted the sixteenth and seventeenth-century Pietists. This section also addresses the role Modernity has within Pietism and overviews the historical causes and individual flavors of Pietism for its Lutheran, Reform, and Anglican forms.

In the second section this work address foundational Pietism. This includes the three figures who became the architypes of Pietism for subsequent generations and who provided the theological language of Pietists. This section includes William Perkins, the father of Puritanism and the English expression of Pietism, whose work the *Golden Chain* provided much of the theological framework for the Synod of Dort. Next is Johann Arndt, whose work *True Christianity* provides the basis for both Lutheran and Reform Pietism on the continent. Following Arndt, the work turns to Philip Jakob Spener, who is often credited as the father of Pietism because of his formation of the *collegia pietatis* and the publication of *Pia Desideria*, both of which become normative in nearly all expressions of Pietism by the eighteenth century. Finally this section concludes by addressing why Pietism cannot stay just an ideology, why it must institutionalize.

The third section of the work addresses the institutionalization of Pietism by addressing August Hermann Francke and Count Nicholas Ludwig von Zinzendorf, the two inheritors of Spener's Pietism. Francke shaped Halle along his lines of Promethean Christianity, which complemented the Hohenzollerns. Together they molded the Prussian ethos, creating Prussianism and reshaping Germany. Zinzendorf's version of Pietism differs greatly with Francke's and his Moravian communities provide an invaluable counterpoint to the strict expression taking root in Prussia. Zinzendorf also illustrates the risk of prioritizing experience without the constraints of a church whose ecclesial oversight can correct heterodox teachings before they move too far.

The fourth section of the work addresses denominational Pietism and John Wesley. Wesley's theology emerges as a synthesis of English Puritanism indebted to Perkins and Zinzendorf's Moravians. It is also the most successful form of denominational Pietism, impacting both Europe and America.

The work concludes by addressing what success brings and the impact of Halle, the Moravians, and Methodists. Pietistic theology from its inception was a theology of negation, defining itself by defining the wider profane culture, and even against the more scholastic forms of Protestantism, thus understanding common theological questions along with the cultural milieu of these theologians is essential in understanding this and all revivalist and theological movements. Since Pietism lacks the ecclesial restraint of Catholic and Orthodox, and since the necessity to always place themselves as an outsider is inherent in the Pietist conception of self, Pietism tends towards producing extremes. The process is fairly gradual and contradictory with new ideas posited by leading theologians. The close of the eighteenth century anticipates the reformation of experiential Protestantism once again by nineteenth-century figures in Europe like Friedrich Schleiermacher, Soren Kierkegaard, and Georg Wilhelm Friedrich Hegel, and American theologians Charles Grandison Finney, Phoebe Palmer, and Dwight Lyman Moody, all of whom were shaped to one degree or another by Pietism and who became essential in dictating the future of Christianity in the modern world. This work contributes to the burgeoning scholarship in Pietism by clearly linking Perkins, Arndt, Spener, Francke, Zinzendorf, and Wesley together, illustrating the continuity as well as the division that exists within Pietism.

Just as there is no single definition of Pietism, the treatment of Pietism is undergoing a serious transformation. The traditional understanding, as supported by nineteenth-century theologian Albrecht Ritschl and twentieth-century theologian Karl Barth, maintains a more negative and formulaic view of Pietism. For these influential theologians, Pietism was too mystical, subjective, emotional, and individualistic. Furthermore, for these scholars there is a clear beginning of Pietism. Pietism emerged in Frankfurt during the late seventeenth century. Central to this older view of Pietism is Philipp Jakop Spener. In 1675, Spener published his central religious text, *Pia Desideria*. Spener, a young pastor, born and raised during the Thirty Years War, called for a reform of the Lutheran Church. In *Pia Desideria*, Spener displays the defects among the clergy, as well as the laity, and calls for extensive use of scriptures and religious practice in order to reform the church once again. Spener's work resonated with those who sought new avenues of intellectual and emotional piety. The traditional view is echoed by early modern German historian Rudolf Vierhaus, who contends that the Pietists were a product of their time.

The traditional view maintains that Pietism developed due to lack of confidence, with orthodox Lutherans stressing theological gnosis rather than lived piety. Pietism materialized during this period of great social change following the Thirty Years War, just as there were changes in politics, philosophy, and science. Many older scholars connect the religious changes in Europe to the political fluctuations taking place at the same time. Religion in general and Pietism specifically was simply reactionary rather than self-actuating individuals and communities who attempted to live a pious life. The scope of Pietism is further limited by focusing on its connection and opposition to orthodox Lutheranism and not examining Pietism within the Reform and Anglican machinations. For these scholars, Pietism was an opposition force to the growing power of monarchs, specifically German Lutheran monarchs. This new epoch is referred to as the Age of Absolutism, named so because of the power that monarchs possessed. While historians have challenged the doctrinaire construction of an absolutist state, very few have decoupled Pietism's growth from this narrative.

The history of Pietism changed when F. Ernest Stoeffler published his work, *The Rise of Evangelical Pietism*, in 1971. According to Stoeffler, Pietism was not simply a reaction to a growing state, rather Protestant Pietism came into existence with the Reformation. Instead of beginning his work with Spener, Stoeffler concludes his work with him. Spener stands in line with a tradition rather than breaking with it. Extreme piety, lay religious movements, and associations of those seeking to live a holy life are nothing new within the history of Christianity. The forms these take naturally look different depending on the regional, historical, and sociological events within Reform, Lutheran, Anglican, and even Catholic and Orthodox areas. Sometimes these forms work in concert with an existing power structure and sometimes they do not. Stoeffler, like other historians of Pietism, finds a simple definition of Pietism difficult, maintaining that "by its very nature the essence of Pietism cannot be completely identified with socially perceptible forms. . . . It had no one system of theology, no one integrating doctrine, no particular type of polity, no one liturgy, no geographic homogeneity. Yet as has already been mentioned, it presented a discernible historical unity."[3] In this unity Stoeffler identifies characteristics of Pietism. First it is experiential. Religion is experienced through a personally meaningful relationship of the

---

3. Stoeffler, *Rise of Evangelical Pietism*, 13.

individual with God. Second, it possesses religious idealism. Notions of sanctification, or religious perfection, created a great distaste for religious complacency and held morality as a necessary virtue. Third, Stoeffler maintains the Pietists' emphasis on the Bible. The Bible reigns supreme over tradition, councils, and even the church. This of course places greater religious authority in the hands of theologians, preachers, and charismatic devotees. Finally Pietism, like other revitalization movements, maintains an opposition to a larger society. Here Stoeffler's definition of Pietism may appear in line with the traditional view, namely that Pietism is a reactionary movement. Yet how Stoeffler constructs his definition of Pietism differs even in this explanation. Pietism is self-actuating while simultaneously being a reactionary or a revivalist movement. The desire is to be holy, to be other, to be different from the society and as such it must confront the larger culture, even if that culture is seemingly religious. Assuming that the reaction was against a greater culture, not simply the culture of the seventeenth century, forces us to reshape our understanding of Pietism. Stoeffler's work illustrates that while Pietism is opposed to forces of society, it did not emerge as a counterforce to an absolutist state, rather to a complacent society. Pietism always pushes for reform. Stoeffler's brief tome outlines the theological peculiarities of Pietism through the seventeenth century in its Anglican, Reform, and Lutheran forms.

Stoeffler's work was the first to address Pietism outside of the view put forth by Ritschl. Ritschl saw Spener as a bulwark against a period of great social change and failed to recognize the complexity and depth behind his writings. While Ritschl was right to include Pietism in his history of ideas, he failed to understand the movement itself. Following Stoeffler, other historians of Pietism have continued to investigate the depth and complexity of Pietism, its causes and effects over the centuries.

One additional note should be given when addressing the historiography of Pietism. Since Pietism is an ethos, an idea, a movement, some difficulty lies in how one should approach the development of Pietism. Traditionally Johannes Wallmann points out "the history of Pietism is essentially the history of individual leaders and tradition-building figures."[4] As such, some of the struggles and internal conflicts are lost. The character of the movement is also misrepresented by focusing on leaders, since much of the movement was lay driven. Even more noticeable is the lack of women who get elevated to this upper echelon, and often their contributions are lost, or ignored. While this work in large part remains within the traditional approach to the treatment of Pietism by looking at tradition building

---

4. Shantz, *Introduction to German Pietism*, 8.

figures, a conscious effort is made to include the contributions and critiques of not only women but also the laity when appropriate. Often subordinated women contributed greatly to the formation and continuation of Pietism, from the medieval Catholic mystic Angela da Foligno to the nineteenth-century mother of the Holiness movement, Phoebe Palmer. Pietism afforded women to become "agents of their own spirituality, meeting in non-church settings to pray, read and discuss the Bible, and to encourage one another in their faith"[5] in ways that traditional Protestantism did not.

---

5. Shantz, *Introduction to German Pietism*, 1.

I.

Ancestry of Pietism
Mysticism and Early Modernity

> "The very reason you are given a body as well as a soul is to help you to gain the favour of this outward and visible world; though at the same time you must also pray for insight into the invisible world as well, so that you may come short of nothing and the whole treasury of the Spirit may be yours."[1]
>
> — *St. Ignatius of Antioch*

No clear and universally agreed upon definition of Pietism exists. What appears universal is the myriad of Pietism definitions that proliferate in any work on the subject, as argued by Jonathan Strom.[2] In this respect I shall not differ from the established literature. It is always best to clarify terms, especially terms that are still in flux. Following Stoeffler's example I define Pietism as a quasi-mystical experiential revivalist movement, found within Lutheran, Reform, and Anglican Protestantism of every age, which seeks to understand and rework their world, both inside and outside of themselves along lines of personally meaningful relationships between themselves as individuals and God, while maintaining a general antipathy or outright hostility to the greater Christian culture and religious formalism which dictates that culture's norms and practices.

---

1. Staniforth, *Early Christian Writings*, 109.
2. Strom, "Problems and Promises," 536–54.

Key to this definition of Pietism is the belief that Pietism is not limited to German Lutheran expressions that only emerged after 1675. As such, two things stand out. First, this definition includes both Reform traditions and Anglicanism in addition to the universally agreed upon Lutheranism. Second, the emergence of Pietism is not limited to the publication of any work or the position of any particular theologian. Pietism, rather, is the generic Protestant expression of experiential Christianity. Notions of mysticism, revivalism, and antipathy towards the world and established religious culture become the standard modes in which this experiential religion is expressed. Individualism is often identified as a central tenet of both Protestantism and modernity, and as such it is also key to understanding Pietism.

Pietism is therefore shorthand for the prioritization of experience over rationalism and scholasticism for Protestants following the traditions of Arndt or Perkins. Other terms are used, but following this intellectual history the term Pietism is an expression of experiential Protestantism in general. The specific Lutheran form that Pietism is often associated with is only one strand of the interconnected tapestry. As this study will demonstrate, other terms, such as Puritanism, Moravian, Herrnhuter, and Methodist, are all expressions of this same drive toward prioritizing experience over Protestant scholastic reasoning and philosophical rationalism. These alternative terms are expressions of the same impulse that derived out of a shared history. This study will utilize each of these terms when they are most appropriate to the context of discussion, but regardless of the label, the underlying argument is the same. Each of these groups are connected and share the same drive in Protestantism.

Experiential Christianity is not limited to modern Protestants. The drive to experience God is a trait common to all forms of Christianity, and some would argue to all religion, yet Pietism is still its own undertaking. To best understand this experiential inclination, it is good to briefly look at a few pre-Protestant examples. Earlier Christian mystics set a precedent that the modern Pietists followed, though without ecclesial restraint. From this I will address the theological and cultural debates that explicitly produced ideological camps within the Protestant world, of which Pietism is just one.

THE TRADITION OF MYSTICISM IN CHRISTIANITY

> *"For the Lord is my helper, and I shall look down on mine enemies."*[3]
>
> — St. Anthony of Egypt

Pietism may be a relatively new phenomena, but its antecedents are anything but new. Key to our understanding of Pietism is the notion of experiential Christianity. Prior to the Protestant Reformation those Christians who sought after a more experiential religion are identified as mystics. Mysticism is central to historic Christianity and often the easiest place to see mystics were in monastic communities and confraternities.

There exists an interesting trend within Christianity anytime its message is accepted by a wider culture. Those Christians who want a more mystical life voluntarily remove themselves from the larger community and become monks or nuns. This is true from the days preceding Constantine promoting Christianity to the favored religion of Rome, and well before 381 when it became the official religion of the Roman Empire under Emperor Theodosius. Monastics and monastic communities begin as early as the second century in the deserts of Egypt. Early monastics retreated from the comforts of life, or set up a life where they functioned as a living martyr, whenever the potential for martyrdom was decreased. The purpose for any monk is an intimate personal and fundamentally mystical experience with the divine. Vladimir Lossky, the great twentieth-century Eastern Orthodox theologian states, "the mystical experience is a personal working out of the content of the common faith."[4] This is the entire life of the monastic. Monks and nuns serve as both individuals and as the examples for the communities of faith that surround them. The monastic ideal is the same as the mystical ideal, and monasticism should never be too distanced from the mystic.

Arguably the greatest of the early monks or "Desert Fathers" was Saint Anthony (251–356). The life of Saint Anthony illustrates a life of self-denial as well as mysticism. There are many accounts of Anthony being tempted by the devil and demons while alone in his monastic cell and while alone in the desert. Throughout these encounters Anthony becomes the example of piety, which only served to gather crowds around him. In addition to renouncing his demons, Anthony had a vision of God when he was thirty five. In the vision, God told Anthony not to fear and that he could always count on divine aid. Eventually Anthony founded a monastery. The monks

---

3. Athanasius, *Life of St. Anthony*, 8.
4. Lossky, *Mystical Theology*, 7–22.

that joined the monastery rarely if ever included any ordained clergy, yet they shaped the theological doctrines and practices of the wider church. Even today the higher clergy from the Roman Catholic and Eastern Orthodox Churches are viewed as monastics. It is largely for this reason that marriage and other prohibitions are not permitted for the ordained Priests and Bishops.[5]

Some of the greatest theologians of the church emerged from monastic communities. The degree to which monastics are mystics varies. Again Lossky maintains that "There is, therefore, no Christian mysticism without theology; but, above all, there is no theology without mysticism."[6] It is partly because of this that Saint Basil the Great (330–397), the fourth-century monastic, is also one of the three Holy Hierarchs in the Eastern Church, and whose liturgy is still celebrated today in Eastern Rite Catholic and Eastern Orthodox churches.[7] Mysticism, monasticism, and theology are made one in the life and work of Basil, and Basil is a very clear early example of how mysticism promotes and shapes the Christian church. This is as much the case for the Western Church as it is the Eastern.

The many monastic reforms, such as those from the Cluny Monastery, are examples of monks seeking to reform not only the lives of the monks but also the life of the church as a whole. The most influential theologian for the Catholic Church following Saint Augustine is Saint Thomas Aquinas. Aquinas developed his *Summa Theologica* and is the preeminent scholastic theologian. Even still, this Dominican put down his quill before finishing this work. At the feast of Saint Nicholas Mass in 1273 Aquinas experienced a mystical encounter with Christ. All the theology which preceded this moment was likened to mere straw and he would write no more.

The mystical encounters of the monastics and their theological formations produced the distinctive forms of Christianity that existed prior to the Reformation. Both Saints Thomas Aquinas and Gregory Palamas were monastics who expounded the theological expressions for their respective churches. The historical and theological developments of Christianity, both in its Roman Catholic and Eastern Orthodox forms, are shaped far more by monastic communities than the dictates of a Pope or Patriarch.

Following the Reformation, the monastic ideal is nearly lost to Protestants. With the exception of Konrade Beissel's Ephrata Society, and

---

5. Not every priest is viewed as a monastic under the Eastern Orthodox Church but the Bishops are. Many parish priests may be married, which excludes them as monastics.

6. Lossky, *Mystical Theology*, 7–22.

7. Basil's liturgy is only celebrated on special occasions. The normal liturgy for these churches is the version of Basil's liturgy edited by St. John Chrysostom.

a few converted abbeys that survived, Protestantism lost the monastic communities which produced many of their theological foundations and mystical examples. It is to Protestantism's detriment that the Ephrata Society or others were not successful, as the cache of testimony connected to experiential Christianity becomes marginalized largely to a lay movement, with the noted exceptions of some church leaders and theologians. The examples of Christianity that the mystic monastics serve in shaping Christianity in general cannot be quantified, examples to which Pietism specifically is deeply indebted.

Throughout the life and work of the foundational Pietists that are to follow in chapter two, there are references to many earlier mystical monks and nuns. Three examples of medieval mystics stand out for providing the theological underpinning of experiential Christianity for the foundational Pietists. These three are Angela da Folingo, Johann Tauler, and Thomas à Kempis. As of today only Angela da Folingo is regarded as a Saint in the Roman Catholic Church.[8] Both Tauler and à Kempis have devotees who wish to see them beatified as well. Lutherans, Reform, Anglicans, and other Protestants, as well as Catholics, regard these three as exemplars of faith.

Angela da Foligno 1248–1309.

"True and pure love, that comes from God, is in the soul and ensures that one recognizes one's own shortcomings and the divine goodness."[9]

— *Angela da Foligno*

The exact details of Angela's birth are unknown, but she was likely born in 1248 in the Italian region of Umbria, and the town of Foligno. Her father died when she was young. According to Angela her mother loved the pleasures the city had to offer. The small town had many pleasures for the thirteenth century. A center of trade and a fertile valley, continually watered by the tributaries of the Tiber, the city was wealthy and relatively safe. The city's wealth echoes the accounts of Angela's early life. Angela's mother encouraged her to indulge in the hedonistic fruit the city offered. Honoring her mother's request, Angela fell into sin and led a disorderly life. At twenty she married a wealthy man and bore him at least two sons. As a wife and mother Angela did not stop loving the disorderly life she was accustomed to.

---

8. Named a Saint by Pope Francis in 2013.
9. Benedict XVI, *Holy Women*, 44.

Some local accounts go as far as claiming she was unfaithful to her husband. We have no clear evidence of this, but Angela's own discussion of her pre-conversion sin suggests that it was sexual. Still, no real confirmation exists, and she never explicitly states that she was disloyal to her husband.

In Angela's thirties the city of Foligno underwent some devastating changes that resulted in her doing the same. The peace and stability of the region ended. A violent earthquake tore the valley in 1279, and a hurricane then followed. As if this were not enough, war broke out against Perugia with the end to hostilities nowhere to be seen. The external chaos only served to highlight Angela's own internal chaos. The weight of her own emptiness crushed her. The comforts of the world failed to fill her void. Little by little Angela became aware of her own sins, leading to her conversion in 1285. While aware of her sins for some time, she could bear the weight of them no longer. Angela called out to Saint Francis of Assisi to find her a confessor. That night she had a vision of Francis who told her, "Sister, if you would have asked me sooner, I would have complied with your request sooner. Nonetheless, your request is granted."[10]

She then went to confession and laid out her sins, with a profound fear of hell and the consequences of her sinful life. According to Pope Benedict XVI this was the real beginning of her mystical journey, "the long journey that led from her starting point, the 'great fear of hell,' to her goal, total union with the Trinity."[11] Angela continued to go to confession and longed for a monastic life, but the obligations she had as a wife and mother precluded that opportunity for three years.

In 1288, within the space of a few months, Angela was freed from these obligations, as her mother's death was followed by the death of her husband, and those of all her children. With nary a moment to waste she sold her possessions and made preparations to join the Franciscans, which she did in 1291. In rather dramatic fashion, echoing the conversion of St. Francis, Angela went to church and stood before the crucifix, stripping herself naked, and pledging herself to Christ. Following this she sold nearly all her property and clothing and gave them to the poor.

Angela de Foligno produced one major work, often simply known as her *Book*. There are two parts; the first is known as the *Memorial* and the second the *Instructions*. The *Memorial* began as Angela's confession. Angela's confessor brought a few sheets in which to record her confession following her conversion. Angela promptly responded that he needed to bring a notebook for her sins.

10. Angela of Foligno, *Complete Works*, 17.
11. Benedict XVI, *Holy Women*, 41.

The Memorial, was dictated to a friar, likely a monk known as Arnaldo, and covered her spiritual journey from 1285 to 1297. He was a relative of Angela, her confessor, and counselor. His task was to take the confessions from Angela and translate them into Latin. Of course a degree of misrepresentation could occur, as the *Memorial* is less a direct dictation than a retelling of the life of Angela, beginning when she became a monastic. At the conclusion of the work in 1297, they both agreed that it was a faithful rendering of her story. Indeed, Angela went so far as to say that "God answered me that everything which has been written is in conformity with my will and comes from me."[12] From most accounts it is clear that Arnaldo was suspicious of the mystical encounters that Angela described at the outset of this endeavor, but that dissipated as time went on.

The *Memorial* consists of thirty steps or stages along her spiritual transformation. Many of these steps repeat an early step but simply to a greater degree. For instance, of the first twenty steps, awareness of sins as the main focus occurs in step one, six, and eight. Similarly, penance is the focus of steps three and eleven, and a desire to be poor is the focus of step nine, where she stripped her clothes and renounced her possessions, as well as steps twelve and twenty. This is also a spiritual auto-biography, so the repetition of steps is understandable given the greater intimacy she proclaims throughout these steps. Later Pietists will also produce spiritual autobiographies and for Perkins, Francke, and Wesley a conversion experience is central to their message.

What is striking is not the common themes we should expect, such as sin, confession, guilt, absolution, and awareness of God, but the depth that occurs in these steps and the fluidity between the spiritual world and the material world. In many accounts Angela depicts herself standing in front of a crucifix. She then is no longer in front of a crucifix, rather standing before a living crucified Christ who points out his wounds. This focus on the wounds of Christ is later adopted by Zinzendorf and becomes one of his central theological messages. In step fourteen of Angela's *Book*, Christ even tells her to place her mouth on the blood from his side wound. In another place Angela recounts her discussions with St. John and the Virgin Mary. Angela echoes the pain they felt at Christ's passion. She also tells of her further insight into her sins, and the redemption found in Christ due to the intercession of Mary.

Angela seeks to identify herself with Mary and Jesus. Angela maintains that experiencing Jesus includes undergoing what he experienced. Most important are Christ's life of "poverty, contempt and sorrow, because, as

---

12. Angela of Foligno, *Complete Works*, 49.

she declared, 'through temporal poverty the soul will find eternal riches; through contempt and shame it will obtain supreme honor and very great glory; through a little penance, made with pain and sorrow, it will possess with infinite sweetness and consolation the Supreme Good, Eternal God.'"[13]

Following the completion of the first half of her *Book*, Angela's confessor died. Someone new received her instructions, which become the second half of the work. Likely this section was recorded by several different people and it probably underwent greater revision after her death in 1309. The point of the second half of the work was to lay out instructions for those sisters who gathered around Angela and joined themselves to her and the Franciscans in Foligno. Little is actually known about these sisters, but Angela described them as "her crown and joy in the Lord."[14]

In large measure the *Instructions* continue the rest of her biography while focusing on the same themes found in the *Memorial*. Interestingly there are very few references to specific Bible verses in Angela's *Book*, including no quotations from Psalms or the Song of Songs. These two books are common points of departure for mystics and especially medieval women mystics. Angela's mysticism, while sharing many themes with others, is her own and not simply a reproduction of what would be expected. Central to her mysticism is the love affair that Angela has with "the suffering God-man."[15] There is an example of the "passion mysticism" that is popular with Bonaventure and Suso. The idea behind passion mysticism is to see Christ's blood in his passion. This promotes deep feelings of repentance. Angela links this passion mysticism with "bridal mysticism." Not only does she focus on the blood of Christ and his passion, but this passion leads beyond repentance to a union. In this union Angela is the bride and Christ the bridegroom. The blood of Christ provides the medium for the matrimony. As one would assume, the Eucharist even more than the crucifix, becomes the central point of Angela's mysticism. Here she not only sees the blood of Christ, but takes it in herself, cementing the union.

Angela's mysticism is also an affirmation of her femininity. By connecting the body of Christ and Angela's own body through the Eucharist, Angela is remade. The product of this mystical union is a marriage and the model for women who often felt shame over their bodies, which were characterized as defiled or impure. Angela's body was united to Christ just as her heart was. Writing to one of her followers, Angela states, "My son, if

---

13. Benedict XVI, *Holy Women*, 47.
14. Angela of Foligno, *Complete Works*, 109.
15. Angela of Foligno, *Complete Works*, 85.

you were to see my heart you would be absolutely obliged to do everything God wants, because my heart is God's heart and God's heart is mine."[16]

It is also here in the *Instructions* that Angela goes into some detail on the role of temptation. Most of the work focuses on the connection of sin with penance and ultimately redemption. Angela briefly diverts from the normal focus of the work, that is, the love of Christ for her and for Christians. The diversion focuses on the continued wrath of God, connected with the persistence of temptations. A "Temptation is an instrument of God's justice, and its salutary effect is to punish us for our past sins."[17] There is a mystical connection but also a cost that is continually paid in this life by the penitent. Eventually Angela da Foligno was released from this penance when she died on January 4, 1309. Witnesses at the time of her death claim she died in peace and joy.

One may expect that upon her death her following would have grown; instead the attention for Angela's life and her book dwindled. She was little known outside of her village for a century. There existed a few miracles performed at her tomb, but the number was far less than one would expect from such a commanding mystic.[18] A century or so after her repose, it was Belgium rather than Italy that took the most interest in her work. Angela's following was localized to groups of Franciscans. Interest in Angela's mysticism grew during the fourteenth century and by the fifteenth century her book was translated into Spanish, French, and German. The likely reason for the slow following of Angela was a general fear of mystics, especially women, which existed among the elites. There was also some confusion with other women mystics who shared the theme of passion with Christ. These female mystics, like Clare of Montefalco, were interpreted as either heterodox or heretical. The safer play was to ignore them until they were explicitly approved or condemned by the church.

By the outbreak of the Protestant Reformation, Angela and her book were well known and translated into the major languages of Europe, with the exception of English. Due to the impact of Bernadino de Laredo (1482–1540), Angela's *Memorial* and *Instructions* greatly influenced the piety of St. Teresa of Avila and St. Ignatius of Loyola. St. Francis de Sales references Angela as one of a few 'superior women' who are "easier to admire than to imitate."[19] For our study, the impact of Angela de Foligno is clearly seen in Arndt's *True Christianity, Book Two*. Her influence is evident for both

---

16. Benedict XVI, "Blessed Angela of Foligno."
17. Angela of Foligno, *Complete Works*, 259.
18. Robinson, "Bl. Angela of Foligno."
19. Angela of Foligno, *Complete Works*, 114.

Catholics and Protestants after the Reformations. Only recently did Pope Francis declare her a saint by equivalent canonization.[20]

Johann Tauler 1300–1361.

"A perfect will is an abandonment of all that is not God. If a man hath not done this in works, he must do it in will if he will be perfect."[21]

— *Johann Tauler*

Likely the greatest of the medieval German mystics was Johann Tauler. Tauler was largely immune to the claims of heresy that his teacher, Meister Eckhart (d. 1328), dealt with, and his impact is greater than his fellow pupil, Henry Suso (d. 1366). Unlike Angela da Foligno, there was never a period where Tauler was unknown. During his own lifetime Tauler's works were read and widely disseminated. His success was beyond his ambitions and grew beyond the actual man, although controversies surround his legacy. Luther was enamored with Tauler, and the works attributed to Tauler. The Jesuits likewise edited and republished Tauler's sermons.[22] In the nineteenth century the mystical German language of Tauler drew Schlegel and the Romantics to his works.

Tauler's father Nikolaus was a well-to-do burgher. Unlike Angela's mother, Nikolaus Tauler was far more concerned for his own spiritual health than the temporal security his wealth might bring. Large portions of his wealth were donated to the church. Furthermore, not only would Johann accept the tonsure as a Dominican, but Nikolaus's daughter became a Dominican nun as well.

Around the age of fourteen, Johann became a Dominican novice; the ascetic life of the order attracted him. His studies began at Strasbourg but moved onto the University of Cologne where he met Eckhart and Suso. Continuing his Dominican education, Tauler returned to Strasbourg only to be forced into exile in 1339, along with his fellow Dominicans. A conflict erupted between Pope John XXII and the Emperor Louis of Bavaria. The Dominicans sided with the pope, and as such the emperor temporarily exiled the order.

---

20. In equivalent canonization a local liturgical cult is extended to the universal Church.
21. Tauler, *Following of Christ*, 136.
22. Jesuit Petrus Canius edited Tauler's sermons.

Tauler made his way to Brussels where he was a part of forming a spiritual movement known as the "Friends of God." The Friends of God grew throughout Western Germany, Switzerland, and the Low Countries. Its purpose was to cultivate a life of inner devotion and intense prayer. The society was universally popular with adherents from all socio-economic backgrounds, stations in life, and genders, with large numbers of Dominican nuns in the rank and file.

In 1343 the ill-conceived ban was lifted and the Dominicans slowly returned home. Three years later Tauler joined them. Still there was a feeling of doom in the air. Not only was the plague once again making its way through central Europe, but there remained tension between the papacy and the empire. Adding to this, Tauler believed there was a significant breakdown of morals, so he filled his sermons with calls to repentance and condemnation when in public. Most of his sermons however were not directed to the public, rather to several Dominican convents that surrounded the city. Tauler was primarily a preacher, and primarily to nuns.

Tauler died surrounded by nuns and admirers, including his sister, whose room he was in when he passed away on June 16, 1361. Following his death a friend stated that Tauler "was detained six years in purgatory for sundry faults, one of these being that on his death-bed he allowed himself to receive too much attention from his sister."[23] All things considered this was a fairly minor fault for the mystic.

Likely even before his death legends of Tauler spread. A common telling of Tauler is found in nearly every biography of him until the nineteenth century, describing a legendary character in *The Life of Tauler*. The story consists primarily of two main characters, a priest and a layman. The priest is depicted as a true master of spirituality who spends most of his life in seclusion. This is until he is sought out by a righteous layman who travels a great distance to seek spiritual truth. Eventually the master gives these truths to the layman. Much to the priest's surprise the layman points out that the master was not living up to this ideal. The master then corrects himself, going into seclusion once again. When returning from seclusion he performs a Mass and gives communion to people. Immediately a dozen communicants fall into a trance. This happens once again before the master's death. The second time forty people fall into a trance. The legend concludes that the master is Tauler. This is likely a work of inspired fiction, and not events from Tauler's life. First, Tauler was not a hermit. Second, it is an example of anti-clericalism as the layman corrects the priest, and is likely a common narrative used against the established church. There are even

---

23. Tauler, *Inner Way*, 7.

some versions of this story that are cited about Eckhart rather than Tauler; it is likely not accurate for either. It is only in the middle of the nineteenth century that this narrative was reexamined and largely viewed as false.

Tauler's legacy grew beyond a fictitious narrative about his life to include many works that are falsely attributed to him. Tauler, or more accurately, Pseudo-Tauler produced many works, including *The Following of the Poor Life of Christ*, *Exercises on the Life and Passion of Our Savior Jesus Christ*, and *Divine Institutions*, also known as *The Marrow of the Soul*. While scholars are examining Tauler's works in order to separate Tauler from Pseudo-Tauler, the distinction does not really matter for this work, since the legend and works were accepted by Protestants and Catholics, as well as the Pietists in this study. Tauler's impact was greater than Tauler himself.

Tauler was also keenly aware of the pitfalls of becoming too mystical or too impactful, having witnessed the condemnation of Eckhart. Throughout his life Tauler's desire was twofold, first to grow closer to Christ, and second to remain a good Catholic. To maintain his second objective, Tauler was never as speculative as Eckhart, and he always framed his mystical expressions in scholastic language. He also refrained from speaking about his own mystical encounters with God, referring to the theological principles rather than experience as his source of authority. This is a clear break from what the Pietists will do following the Reformation, largely because accusations of heresy would not carry the same weight.

Unfortunately for Tauler his cautious approach to mystical theology did not protect his legacy from scrutiny. Due to the popularity of Tauler amongst the Lutherans, there was a Catholic backlash against him in the sixteenth century, beginning with the Jesuits who banned his writings in 1518. The Capuchins did the same in 1590, and his works were also condemned in Spain. Even Pope Sixtus V temporarily placed Tauler's works on the Index of Prohibited Books. Eventually Tauler was reabsorbed by the Catholic Church and the bans lifted.

Two key theological messages are present in Tauler's mysticism. First is the notion of poverty and the second is concerned with the inner man. Central to his understanding of his own life is the notion that "Poverty is a likeness with God."[24] Poverty grants freedom, as the material things of this world cause attachments, which serve to isolate man from God. The key to gaining freedom is to abandon all things that are not God. It is only in this abandonment that man can find freedom and perfection in Christ. True poverty consists of abandonment of all things in this world, not only wealth.

---

24. Tauler, *Following of Christ*, 23.

This naturally brings us to Tauler's notion of the twofold nature of man. This notion is connected to Aquinas's doctrine of the *visio essentiæ Dei*, or the contemplation of the divine nature. Tauler goes further than his Dominican counterpart by holding that divine knowledge is attainable in this world, due to the indwelling of God in each man. The key to this is a nearly Manichean duality between the inner-man and the outer-man. Tauler explains that "Man is created for time and for eternity for time in his body, for eternity according to his spirit."[25] The body made of earth seeks the things of this world, and the spirit made of God seeks God. Ultimately the spirit will prevail when man is touched by God, revealing himself as a light unlike any other. This is actually the closest that we see Tauler revealing his own experience of mysticism in his works stating that "when God revealeth himself to the soul, this is without all doubt, and man cannot doubt it."[26]

After this point the inner man is the entirety of man, and the body is made subject to the soul, as it was intended on being. To do this one must look inside themselves at the divine spirit common to all, claiming "Oh! Dear children, turn your eyes inwardly, where this birth must really be born, which will cause great joy throughout Christendom."[27]

This process is also likened to the consecration of a church, the episcopacy, and the Virgin Mary. "The consecration of a church means much the same as a renewal; and this renewal ought always to be taking place in the inner man."[28] The church takes on a new spirit, which dwells in the sanctuary. This is just like the high priest carrying the vessels which hold the body and blood of Christ. The true spiritual reality is carried by the priest, just as the inner man holds God. The clearest example of this is found with the Virgin Mary who gave of herself fully and "she became one spirit with God, and she was taught by Him; for she resigned herself as a fitting instrument to His dear Will, in fervent love for His glory. She was poor in spirit."[29]

Throughout Tauler's sermons and other works the theme of giving all away to God is the attempt to strengthen the inner-man. It is this language, common since Paul used it in his letter to the Romans, and used by Thomas Aquinas, that Tauler promotes. The language of the inner-man is central to the Pietist conception of self. Tauler always couched this within terms of the church, and the authority of the church. While some Pietists follow

---

25. Tauler, *Following of Christ*, 97.
26. Tauler, *Following of Christ*, 151.
27. Tauler, *Inner Way*, 71.
28. Tauler, *Inner Way*, 99.
29. Tauler, *Inner Way*, 62.

this example, many will use the language of Tauler, specifically the notions connected to the inner man without the ecclesial restraint of the church. As such the conclusions are not ones that Tauler would be likely to support.

Thomas à Kempis 1380–1471.

Every man naturally desires knowledge; but what good is knowledge without fear of God?[30]

— *Thomas à Kempis*

While Tauler is likely the greatest of the German mystics, Thomas à Kempis and his work *The Imitation of Christ*, are likely the most used when discussing not only our Pietist authors but also Pietists in general. The *Imitation* is one of the most widely read books in the world and next to the Bible it is also the most widely translated book in Christian literature.[31] With such a popular work it is surprising that à Kempis's life has not been thoroughly treated. Like many, the exact year of his birth is unknown, he was either born in 1379 or 1380. Even his death has conflicting dates, he reposed either on July 25, or two weeks later on August 8, 1471. For a man whose impact is felt in all areas of Western Christianity, his ninety-one years of sanctity were spent largely in rote isolation and personal contemplation of the ineffable God.

Thomas was the second born son to artisan parents, John and Gertrude Haemerken in Kempen, near Düsseldorf. Thomas's brother John was fourteen years older and the two spent very little time together. Thomas was sent to school in Deventer, in Holland, when he was around thirteen, just like his older brother. While Thomas expected to see his brother at the school, John had just started a new congregation following the example of Gerhard Groote (d. 1384). Groote began a modern devotional movement in 1374. The movement, known as The Brethren and Sisters of the Common Life, was the driving force behind the Northern Renaissance. It was a mixture of lay and ordained piety which sought education as one means to grow in faith. Because of the mixture of people, the Brethren appeared to be a monastic order but lacked papal authority. According to the Council of Vienna in 1311 this was forbidden. The Brethren found a loophole and connected themselves to a monastery in Windesheim. Next to Thomas à

---

30. Thomas à Kempis, *Imitation of Christ*, 2.
31. Plantinga, "Thomas à Kempis."

Kempis, the best known graduate from these schools is Desiderius Erasmus (d. 1536).

Most descriptions of Thomas paint him as a pious but otherwise fairly unremarkable fellow. Physically he was of average height, dark complexion, with a broad forehead, and piercing eyes. Those eyes were likely the most expressive part of him, since he was otherwise silent and shy. Some describe him "as the most placid and uneventful of all men who ever wrote a book or scribbled letters."[32] Unsurprisingly most of his time was spent in books and prayer. The only time he was full of life was in his cell or when conversations turned to God. The natural place for him was with the Brethren.

Thomas à Kempis lived the rest of his life in one of the communities operated by the Brethren. These schools and monasteries received Thomas in 1399, and he made his Augustinian vows in 1407. Some accounts maintain Thomas became an Augustinian after he had a dream. The dream convicted him of his sin and revealed God's grace. Either way his priestly orders were delivered to him in 1413. He later became the sub-prior in 1425. True to form, à Kempis spent most of his time eschewing promotions and nearly every other task, choosing instead to spend his time in his monastic cell deep in thought. It was from this cell that *the Imitation of Christ* was written.

When he died, Maximilian Hendrik and others believed that Thomas à Kempis was destined for sainthood. Hendrik took great measure to preserve his relics, and began all the paperwork for beatification. Since the close of the seventeenth century no real progress has taken place to recognize Thomas à Kempis as a Saint in the Catholic Church. While we may expect that such a pious individual who wrote such an impactful work is destined for canonization, à Kempis's subdued nature and lack of self-aggrandizement resulted in controversy over the authorship of *the Imitation of Christ*.

Unlike Tauler, who had many works posthumously and inaccurately added to his resume, for centuries people have doubted that à Kempis is the author of *the Imitation of Christ*. There was some measure for speculation as the book was first issued anonymously in 1418. Today there is nearly universal agreement that à Kempis is the author of the work. Many of the earlier concerns over his theological and intellectual pedigree led people to wonder if it was not his older brother John, Gerhard Groote, or a whole host of other people who authored the brief tome. The most farfetched was the theory that it was a lost work of St. Bonaventure.

In the *Imitation*, à Kempis lays out a few meditative issues for the Christian. At the very outset is a critique of learning over piety, "Indeed it is what good is knowledge without fear holy and just, but a virtuous life

---

32. Ackerley, "Beckett and a Kempis," 81.

makes him pleasing to God."[33] This is an obvious connection for all Pietists. Other invectives, such as "A man is raised up from the earth by two wings—simplicity and purity. There must be simplicity in his intention and purity in his desires. Simplicity leads to God, purity embraces and enjoys Him,"[34] place him in line with Tauler and Angela da Foligno, who emphasized poverty, a notion found within à Kempis but nowhere near the same degree as the others.

Far more of the work is focused on other practices in piety, urging men to overcome their sinful life when he tells them to "Fight like a man. Habit is overcome by habit."[35] The new habit that should take the place of vice is the cross of Christ. He states, "Behold, in the cross is everything, and upon your dying on the cross everything depends. There is no other way to life and to true inward peace than the way of the holy cross and daily mortification."[36] à Kempis does not really view the cross as a choice though, maintaining that "No matter where you may go, you cannot escape it."[37] The choice is to carry the cross willingly, for otherwise it becomes even more burdensome.

Choosing the cross rather than fighting against it reveals God's love, which is the predominant theme of the first half of Book Three. à Kempis constantly speaks of God as the "Fountain of unceasing love,"[38] his "most beloved spouse"[39] and his "holy lover."[40] This lovefest is an example of bridal mysticism for male mystics as well as female mystics. Following this the second major theme in Book Three concerns the lowliness of man. Throughout this book à Kempis calls himself "nothing,"[41] and "dust."[42] The low status of man is used to emancipate him from pride and his desires. Like Tauler we hear "the giving up of exterior things brings interior peace, so the forsaking of self unites you to God."[43]

Unlike Tauler, à Kempis rarely uses the phrase new man. The dichotomy between the new creation and the old creation is largely absent in this work, with one noted exception, when he proclaims that the reader must "put on

33. Thomas à Kempis, *Imitation of Christ*, 1.
34. Thomas à Kempis, *Imitation of Christ*, 32.
35. Thomas à Kempis, *Imitation of Christ*, 18.
36. Thomas à Kempis, *Imitation of Christ*, 41.
37. Thomas à Kempis, *Imitation of Christ*, 41.
38. Thomas à Kempis, *Imitation of Christ*, 55.
39. Thomas à Kempis, *Imitation of Christ*, 68.
40. Thomas à Kempis, *Imitation of Christ*, 49.
41. Thomas à Kempis, *Imitation of Christ*, 47.
42. Thomas à Kempis, *Imitation of Christ*, 59.
43. Thomas à Kempis, *Imitation of Christ*, 108.

the new man. You must be changed into another man."[44] While this notion was central for Tauler, à Kempis's focus is on a different set of diametrically opposed tendencies, that of nature and grace. Later à Kempis adds a second dichotomy, the man who thinks highly of himself, as opposed to the saint.

The final book focuses on the sacrament of communion. Throughout this concluding section à Kempis marvels at the power and presence of God and the neglect found by so many Christians. The mystery of the presence of God has a real potential of becoming routine for Christians, including priests, who may forget they are communing with God. The disconnected piety is demonstrated with the difference between people traveling to honor relics of saints, "marveling at their wonderful deeds and at the building of magnificent shrines" while not noticing that "in the Sacrament of the altar You are wholly present, my God, the man Christ Jesus, whence is obtained the full realization of eternal salvation, as often as You are worthily and devoutly received."[45]

For à Kempis, communion is extremely powerful. First communion fulfills the spiritual desire for unity with God, a union that is nothing short of life itself. "Without You I cannot exist, without Your visitation I cannot live."[46] Communion is also transformative. "Holy Communion removes him from evil and confirms him in good."[47] The whole theme of the *Imitation of Christ*, is found within the Eucharistic practice, that constant communion with God reveals all that Christians are to be. He echoes this in a prayer "Let Thy will be mine, and my will ever follow Thine, and agree perfectly with it. Grant to me, above all things that can be desired, to rest in Thee, and in Thee to have my heart at peace."[48]

à Kempis, Tauler, and da Foligno represent three models of mystical piety that resonate with early Protestants in general and Pietists specifically. Partly because they were not canonized as saints their writings could be interpreted as outside the Catholic Church and the themes of individual sanctity could be elevated. Still da Foligno, Tauler, and à Kempis must be interpreted as Catholics and not as early Protestants. They strongly affirmed monastic life, the real presence in the Eucharist, and venerated the Virgin Mary. Early Protestant reformers often overlooked these essential theological positions as well as their desire to remain within the Catholic Church when they cite these mystics, decontextualizing them and borrowing portions of their theological corpus to suit their needs.

44. Thomas à Kempis, *Imitation of Christ*, 98.
45. Thomas à Kempis, *Imitation of Christ*, 117.
46. Thomas à Kempis, *Imitation of Christ*, 120.
47. Thomas à Kempis, *Imitation of Christ*, 121.
48. Potts, *Prayers of the Middle Ages*.

MODERNITY AND THE EMERGENCE OF PIETISM

> "Christianity created Western Civilization... The Modern World arose only in Christian societies."[49]
>
> — Rodney Stark

Following Martin Luther and his nailing of the 95 Theses on the door of the Wittenberg Church in 1517, the medieval period begins to fade.[50] While a convenient moment to mark the break in the epochs of history, more than the Protestant Reformation was taking place to separate the Medieval from the Modern. The early modern period was one of great fluctuations. Luther and his confrontation with the sale of indulgences was just one change. The sixteenth, seventeenth, and eighteenth centuries saw economic changes, mass urbanization, changing roles of government, new definitions of appropriate violence, shifting views towards the emancipation of women, and Jews throughout Europe.

The discussions about religion in general and Christianity specifically in the modern period are one of two extremes. Either Christianity is at a great loss, unable to cope with the changing nature of the world, or Christianity is the great catalyst spurring on the behemoth that is the modern project. Truth can be found in each of these extreme positions. Christianity in the early modern period, just like religion in all periods of history, effected great changes and social advancements. Religions also found themselves at a loss as to how to react to a shifting world. Change is constant and religions are forced to change within this larger world. This is true even if the change is to resist the world.

The early modern period of history shifts how we are to view Christianity and its relation to Europe. This shift affords us an opportunity to see the manner in which people construct meaning in this epoch. With the fracturing of Western Christianity following the Reformations, different people offer different polemics against the modern world and their confessional rivals. One can never speak of Protestantism as a single entity, like one could at least in part do of the Roman Catholic Church and Eastern Orthodoxy.[51] Because of the multitude of Protestantisms, each must

---

49. Stark, *Victory of Reason*, 233.

50. This is the date often used for Germany. Others include 1400 in Italy and 1485 in England.

51. Regrettably, many terms for Christian branches, denominations, and movements share the same labels. Specifically here the term Orthodoxy and Orthodox can mean two separate groups who share little in what they believe the term "Orthodoxy" implies. Keeping in mind that the central focus of this paper is Pietism and primarily its

display why they are true. They must also provide evidence why the others, be they a different sort of Protestant, Catholic, or even to a lesser degree Eastern Orthodox are in error on some level. Of course polemics against opposing theological points of view are not unique to modernity, nor to Protestants. Many of these exact critiques existed long before Luther and Zwingli. We have plenty of examples of criticisms and condemnations upon Waldesians and Cathars, let alone many soliloquies expounding the veracity of one particular scholastic claim or the other. What Protestantism coupled with modernity does is provide us a fast paced, even reactionary response to theological claims of truth and the ways that practical theological concerns are to be lived out in those who believed they were selected by God.

This brings us to another crucial point. Protestantism, like other expressions of Christianity, and indeed like all the Abrahamic faiths, shares a common world view vis-à-vis man's relation to God. In addition to common stories of creation and sin, Abrahamic faiths also maintain a necessary dualism. This dualism is the byproduct of covenantal relationships; there are those who are in and those who are out. While the treatment of those in the covenant and those outside of the covenant varies from religion to religion, as well as within each religion, this basic framework exists. It is essential that the covenant excludes, even while it may be inclusive, for this defines the adherents and dictates how they are to live with others, both with those who share the covenant and those to whom it does not apply. To borrow and modify a term from Pierre Bourdieu, covenantal relationships establish a habitus, in this case a habitus of exclusion. Bourdieu defines a habitus as "Systems of durable, transposable dispositions, structured structures predisposed to function as structuring structures, that is, as principles which generate and organize practices and representations that can be objectively adapted to their outcomes without presupposing a conscious aiming at ends or an express mastery of the operations necessary in order to attain them. Objectively 'regulated' and 'regular' without being in any way the product of obedience to rules, they can be collectively orchestrated without being the product of the organizing action of a conductor."[52]

---

relation to the Protestant world; in an effort to minimize potential confusion as to what group I am identifying as "Orthodox" or "Orthodoxy"—unless otherwise prefaced with specific labels, like "Eastern," "Greek," "Russian," etc.—references to Orthodoxy are specifically addressing what has become known as Protestant Orthodoxy, Protestant Scholasticism, Rational Protestantism, etc. and not to the Eastern Orthodox Christians.

On a separate note, it may be interesting and ultimately beneficial to see the overlapping beliefs between Eastern Orthodoxy on the one side and Pietism and Protestant Orthodoxy on the other; however, that lies beyond the scope of the present work.

52. Bourdieu, *Outline of a Theory*, 53.

The habitus of exclusion is codified with creeds. The nature of a creed is defining those to whom the creed applies. In doing so, creeds only partially illustrate the characteristics and beliefs the group possesses, but more importantly they define what the group is not. As J.Z. Smith put it "the most basic sense of the 'other' is generated by the opposition in/out."[53] In many ways creeds function in a greater sense to illustrate what a community does not believe than what they in fact believe. It traces the border of belief and practice, rather than illustrating the life of a member of the community. The expected practices occur as normal and unexpected, or at least not worth mentioning, until a rival group believes that things should be done otherwise. Definition is through subtraction, thus a habitus of exclusion is established with creeds.

A habitus of exclusion and definition through subtraction are not unique to creeds or religions but are found in all facets of society. William Scott Green states, "In creating its others, a society confuses some part of its neighbor with its neighbor and a piece of itself with itself, and construes each in terms of the other."[54] Randal Styers, in his work *Making Magic: Religion, Magic, and Science in the Modern World*, argues that moderns identify themselves in negative terms, namely, arguing that they are not what non-moderns or pre-moderns are. Modernity, unlike religions, is an empty signifier to be filled only in opposition, having nothing intrinsic. This defining self in negative terms through others is borrowed from Gustavo Benavides, who argued that the "condition of modernity presupposes an act of self-conscious distancing from a past or a situation regarded as naïve."[55] Styers takes what Benavides is arguing about modernity and applies it in his discussion of magic.

Closely related to Styers is the work of Zakiya Hanafi. Hanafi argues in her work *The Monster in the Machine: Magic, Medicine, and the Marvelous in the Time of the Scientific Revolution*, that modernity has defined itself in opposition not to magic but to the monstrous. Hanafi defines a monster not as any singular object, rather "it is a category that becomes constituted in different ways according to different cultural and historical contexts."[56] As such the monster is defined by the larger society and it can be applied to individuals, groups, and institutions. The term monster is not a category that is defined in itself, but from the outside. "For in each case, a theory of difference, when applied to the proximate 'other,' is but another way

---

53. Smith, *Relating Religion*, 230.
54. Smith, *Relating Religion*, 232.
55. Styers, *Making Magic*, 4.
56. Hanafi, *Monster in the Machine*, 15.

of phrasing a theory of 'self.'"[57] Both Hanafi and Styers address the demonization of others to suit the social, religious, and political aims of the larger group. In this way modernity mimics the normative practice of religion. Modernity in many ways is itself a new religion, with new civil creeds, councils, and clerics.

With the actions and expressions of Christianity being co-opted by the modern project, Christian groups needed to reinforce their identities with new statements of beliefs. For most groups this is not a difficult task, as a synod or council can be called wherein modernity can be condemned or extoled. The new creeds and statements of faith will now include or exclude modernity, in part or in whole, but the definition by subtraction is still the normative exercise. With the established habitus of exclusion, modernity can be faced from a top down level and those adherents will be expected to fall in line with the new dogma.

Scholars such as Dale T. Irvin contend that traditions always remake themselves; they are never stagnant. Even liturgical and creedal religions still remake themselves in how they view themselves, their tradition and the surrounding culture. Irvin states "I would go so far as to assert that the recreation of Christian tradition is not an option, but an imperative of Christian faith."[58] Furthermore he contends that this is not just a byproduct of the pace of change over the last few hundred years, rather "there are reasons internal to Christian traditions of faith that drive them toward rejuvenation and recreation."[59] Irvin believes that the message of personal renewal that is central to the Christian message encourages various Christian traditions to renew themselves whenever stagnation begins to be set in. Combining this with Styers and Hanafi, the primary modes that various Christian denominations and movements define themselves through, explicitly those during the era of modernity, are negation and exclusionary practices.

Modes of exclusion are necessary for any group to maintain a sense of identity. Even radically tolerant groups exclude some ideas or persons, usually on the basis of their rejection of the new dogmas. Group identity is not simply about acceptance of one idea but the acceptance of that one idea to the exclusion of another. In most cases the group will believe that the abrogated notions lack some of the coherence, charm, utility or ease of the supported ideas. How individuals and groups choose ideologies, statements, and beliefs varies depending on the relation that group has to the whole, its members, and the challenges it currently faces.

57. Smith, *Relating Religion*, 246.
58. Irvin, *Christian Histories*, 9.
59. Irvin, *Christian Histories*, 9.

Anthony Wallace calls this act mazeway reformulation. The mazeway is rather similar to Bourdieu's notion of the habitus, in that it is something taken for granted. According to Wallace, the process of reformulation takes place when the current society fails to satisfy its members. While this causes stress, the desire is that a new system will replace it and will better address the needs of the community. The standard way this is done is through a revitalization movement. "A revitalization movement is defined as a deliberate, organized, conscious effort by members of a society to construct a more satisfying culture."[60]

The easiest way that most organizations and religious confessions define official dogma is through declarative statements from the groups clearly identified authorities. Business and political organizations usually have spelled out delineating titles which carry with them clearly understood authority and responsivities. Many, if not most religious organizations, have distinct titles and an understood ordination process that also gives these men and women hierarchical roles. Wallace identifies these authorities as either the prophet, or in more cases as the priest. The trouble emerges when groups lack clear hierarchies or if the hierarchies' declarations lack authority amongst their constituents. Often the elites are elite only in title or status and their decrees are defied, rejected, or simply ignored by those to whom they direct or represent. In these cases, while the CEO, president, or priest has authority, they do not really hold authority and the hierarchy may only exist as some sort of Frazierian survival, waiting for its time to disappear or be reformed into something new. In either instance if the hierarchy is absent or simply lacks authority, clearly identifying the tenets of the group becomes rather difficult, and often is only understood from an etic or historical perspective.

This is the case when addressing Pietism. While Eastern Orthodoxy, Roman Catholicism, and most Protestant confessions can choose to promote an authoritative statement from on high, Pietism does not have the ability to do this. Pietism is distinct from other forms of Protestantism because it is by its very nature "experiential." While excluding others from the elect, it does so not with creeds, confessions, and synods, but with experiences. These experiences naturally exclude the acceptable experiences of previous generations and are replaced with newer experiences and modes of practices that are contrary to the established order. This is not to say that an emphasis on experience is lacking in Orthodox or Catholic circles, but the emphasis is not to the exclusion of the episcopacy.

---

60. Wallace, *Revitalizations and Mazeways*, 28.

This extreme emphasis on experiences leads those like Mark Noll to a false conclusion when he says, "At its extreme, the Pietist emphasis on religious life gave very little attention to self-conscious Christian thought. To be consumed by feeling was to have no time for thinking through the relationship between God and His creation."[61] Clearly this description fails to take into account the existence of prominent Pietistic figures from the beginning of the Reformation. Paul Tillich is a bit kinder than Noll in his treatment of Pietism when he states that "Pietism was dependent on the Orthodoxy which it wanted to transform into subjectivism."[62] Tillich, like Noll, still maintains that the core of the Pietistic impulse was towards the subjective rather than the established *doxa*, but illustrates the interconnectedness of Pietism and the classical systems of Orthodoxy. While subjective, Pietism is not a rejection of the rational world, only a rejection of the system that focuses on self-evident objective truth in light of what many Protestant leaders view as mysteries inherent in the created world. Tillich points out that even Martin Luther fought against the notion that the "categories of reason should transform the substance of faith. Reason is not able to save but must be saved itself."[63] The instinct of the Pietist is to answer the world of reason with an experience steeped in experiential faith.

What those critics of Pietism like Noll can emphasize is the question of authority, which remains in Pietist circles. Namely if experiences not synods define the right Christian life, what experiences are valid? And which ones are not? These must be defined through individuals. It is here that theology plays a central role for Pietists. Many early Pietists found themselves within the same Lutheran, Reform, and Anglican communities. While rejecting the synod's statements as too cold and impersonal, they had to rely upon reason to justify their experiences. As such, a new literature arises specifically for the edification and justification of the Pietistic position. Instead of synods, what become authoritative are journals, sermons, and books promulgated amongst their fellow Pietists. Scholars like Peter C. Erb state "Pietism must be counted among the two or three most important developments in Protestant spirituality."[64] In many cases the rejection of the establishment spurs on a support of lay religion, giving a voice to the unconventional and underrepresented within a community.

These writings of Pietists are an example of European Christian ecstatic religion. To borrow from I. M. Lewis, "Possession is a culturally normative

---

61. Collins Winn et al., *Pietist Impulse in Christianity*, xii.
62. Tillich, *Complete History of Christian Thought*, 276.
63. Tillich, *Complete History of Christian Thought*, 278.
64. Collins Winn et al., *Pietist Impulse in Christianity*, xiii.

experience."⁶⁵ As classic possession is not permitted, experiential religion fills this void. Pietism affords individuals and minority groups the ability to air grievances against the larger group. The new shamans of Pietism are those authors and theologians. In order to better understand Pietism as a whole, we need to understand who these key leaders are and what ideas they advance.

With that said, Pietism is never a single thing, rather in the smallest definition Pietism is simply experiential Protestant Christianity. Many of these leaders would not agree with one another, and the manner in which devotees may experience God varies. With this overly broad definition we must always remember that Pietism at no time is monolithic. Again it will serve us best to revisit my definition of Pietism as *a quasi-mystical experiential revivalist movement, found within Lutheran, Reform and Anglican Protestantism of every age, in which the faithful Christian seeks to understand and rework their world, both inside and outside of themselves along lines of personally meaningful relationship between themselves as individuals and God, while maintaining a general antipathy or outright hostility to the greater Christian culture and religious formalism which dictates that culture's norms and practices.* This definition applies to a greater or lesser degree depending on the community, person, location, and era that we hope to address.

Pietism's conflict with Protestant Orthodoxy and the Modern World.

"The dominance of religion was taken for granted. Gradually every dominant relationship was pronounced a religious relationship."⁶⁶

— *Karl Marx*

Following the Reformation, Christian thought in Western Europe moved in three different and often contrary directions, one of which is the subject of this work. The three directions were Protestant Orthodoxy or Protestant scholasticism, rationalism, and Pietism. Until fairly recently, Pietism was the often neglected of these three strains of modernity, and the neglect is the reason for this work.

Protestant Orthodoxy or Protestant scholasticism has its own origins following the Reformation. Different forms of Orthodoxy exist among the different Protestant branches. Lutheranism develops differently than

65. Lewis, *Ecstatic Religion*, 65.
66. Marx, "German Ideology," 148.

Anglicanism, which develops different than Calvinism and other Reform. Briefly, Protestant Orthodoxy emerged when Protestants sought to place supremacy of the Bible over the value of tradition found within the Catholic Church. Protestantism became a religion, or rather several religions, of a book, rather than the Bible being the book of a tradition. With this shift in authority a new system was created to make sense of the religious world. It was in these discussions where Protestant Orthodoxy was created. Possibly the first and clearest division of Protestant Orthodoxy was developed within the Lutheran circles.

The Pietists were also not alone in their challenge to the Protestant Orthodoxy. The orthodox establishment encountered challenges on two different fronts, from both the Pietists and the Enlightenment. Pietism was just one mechanism of dealing with the challenges of modernity. The supreme faith in science and reason also challenged the status of Protestant Orthodoxy. Eventually rationalism, with is basis in philosophy and logic, proclaims that it won the day for modernity. There is reason to challenge this proclamation, but the normative view is to accept this as a truism.

Rationalism was a byproduct of the Reformation process as much as the other two strands. Following the Reformation, rationalism was as diffuse as any of the other movements. Many times it worked within the Christian context, such as cases of Christian deists, and the Archbishop of Canterbury, John Tilloston (1630–1694), who posited religion was simply the system of rational propositions that were tested by human reason. Georg Wilhelm Friedrich Hegel (1770–1831) and the philosophical framework he created can also be found within this strand. Hegel maintained simultaneous faith in Christianity and reason and created a system that held both in concert, a system that often lay outside the frame work of Protestant Orthodoxy and any Pietistic impulses. In other cases rationalism was strictly opposed to religion in general and Christianity specifically. Some key examples are found in the anti-Christian Deists. Many of the Enlightenment authors, such as Voltaire (1694–1778), typify this wing of rationalism.

It may be interesting to note that as often as not, the Pietists and Enlightenment philosophers would side together against the same Orthodox system. In many cases, such as Immanuel Kant and Johann Christoph Woellner, a single individual occupied both camps. Nearly just as often these two also opposed each other. Too often have scholars approached the early modern period from the perspective of the Enlightenment or from the confessionalization process, and not enough attention has been focused on the interplay between these three major strands in the history of ideas.

A simpler definition of a Pietist may help to best understand the interplay between Pietism, rationalism, and scholasticism. *A Pietist would* be a Protestant who emphasized experience of the divine over rationalism and orthodoxy. The central focus of a Pietist is this experience. The emphasis on experience produced theological or rational errors that otherwise could be tempered by a strong emphasis on church tradition. The Reformation eliminated the power of church tradition for the Protestant world, and with this new wave of iconoclasm a distinct form of religious expression emerged. Pietism differs from the early mystical expressions of Christianity in Western Europe not because of its priority of experiential religion, but because the Pietist does not have their experience tempered or shaped by a strong tradition that seeks to curtail aberrant theological or ecclesial forms.

Confessionalization is still an important discussion as to how Pietism differs widely between the three main Magisterial Denominations. Lutheran Pietism emerged as an opponent to Lutheran Orthodoxy. Reform Pietism emerged because of the theology developed by a Calvinist Orthodoxy. Anglican Pietism emerged due to a lack of Anglican Orthodoxy and an overly powerful rationalism that infiltrated England following the theological spasms that were the Tudor Reformations.

Lutheran Conflict Pietism vs. Orthodoxy

> *"Orthodoxy, Straight, or rather straightened, opinion, which aims, without ever entirely succeeding, at restoring the primal state of innocence of doxa, exists only in the objective relationship which opposes it to heterodoxy."*[67]
>
> — *Pierre Bourdieu*

To best understand Lutheran Pietism, it would benefit us to highlight some of the key differences between Lutheran Orthodoxy and Pietism. There appears to be an obvious tension between the two groups. The tension is created by both theological and practical points of conflict. For Lutheran Orthodoxy, the discussion of acceptable Lutheran beliefs emerged even before Martin Luther's death in 1546. The tension of Lutheran Orthodoxy produced and continued through many documents. The first of these was formulated in 1530, the *Augsburg Confession*, and later that same year *the Apology for the Augsburg Confession* would follow. These documents, as well as the *Smalcald Articles* (1539), were the source of controversy and a development of different strands of interpretation.

---

67. Bourdieu, *Outline of a Theory*, 169.

Lutheran Orthodoxy developed to answer five early questions. The first question was more practical than theological. It asked if certain Catholic practices could be accepted as *adiaphora*.[68] The second controversy, known as the Majoristic Controversy[69] centered on the idea that good works were required for salvation. The third controversy asked whether or not man cooperates in his conversion; this is known as the Synergistic Controversy. The fourth, known as the Antinomian Controversy, stressed God's grace over the Law. Taken to an extreme, Antinomians maintain that there is no law, therefore no sin for the true Christian. The final controversial issue proposed that a union could be found connecting Luther's theology with the theology of John Calvin, specifically dealing with Christ's nature and his presence in the Eucharist.

While there are many different schools of thought on these issues, the two dominant interpretations were those following Philip Melanchthon, often known as Philipists, and the Gnesio-Lutherans. With the exception of the Antinomian position, Melanchthon supported these ideas, while the Gnesio-Lutherans opposed them. Antinomianism was rejected by both the Philipists and the Gnesio-Lutherans, and only upheld, denounced, and upheld again by Johann Agricola. These controversies served to create a specific dialogue. This dialogue resulted in two interconnected developments. As a byproduct of the theological discussions, a new theological methodology resulted, along with an insistence of legalist doctrinal statements. This methodology is also known as Protestant Scholasticism. These statements bring us to their highest form within Lutheranism, the construction and adoption of the Formula of Concord in 1580. Both the methodology and the Formula of Concord defined Lutheran Orthodoxy.

The Formula of Concord and Lutheran Orthodoxy sided with Melanchthon's views on Adiaphora,[70] and most of his views on Synergism and Calvin's theology. Similarly the Gnesio-Lutherans had success in their limits on some Calvinist inroads while also rejecting the Majorist position.

---

68. Things neither commanded nor forbidden by God.

69. Named after George Major.

70. The *Solid Declaration of the Formula of Concord*: Section X. *Ecclesiastic Practices* states: "As regards genuine adiaphora, or matters of indifference, we believe, teach, and confess that such ceremonies, in and of themselves, are no worship of God, nor any part of it, but must be properly distinguished from such as are.... Therefore we believe, teach, and confess that the congregation of God of every place and every time has, according to its circumstances, the good right, power, and authority [in matters truly adiaphora] to change, to diminish, and to increase them, without thoughtlessness and offense, in an orderly and becoming way, as at any time it may be regarded most profitable, most beneficial, and best for [preserving] good order, [maintaining] Christian discipline, and the edification of the Church" (Kolb and Wengert, *Book of Concord*, 637).

Antinomianism was flatly rejected. Calvinism underwent similar challenges with similar results at the beginning of the seventeenth century, resulting in Calvinist Orthodoxy and the Synod of Dort (1618–1619).

Early in the seventeenth century, Lutheran Orthodoxy had possibly its greatest champion, Johan Gerhard (1583–1637). While not the earliest Lutheran systematic theologian, Gerhard is certainly one of the most thorough Lutheran Scholastics. His *Loci*, written in 1622, is over four thousand pages, and examines the place of scripture and eternal life and nearly every point in between. Under Gerhard, Lutheran theology developed not only against Roman Catholics, but against the Rationalists, Reform, and other strands of Protestant thought. This included the Pietists. Like nearly all Protestant Scholastics, the focus of the work places the Bible as the supreme authority, with God as the principle cause. Following Gerhard, the Bible, and not the church, is the sole authority for Lutherans. The Bible is also the only efficacious medium for salvation. The Bible is true, perfect, and sufficient for Christians. Gerhard does admit that scripture is clear to all, but really only to mature Christians who undergo a degree of training and are open to scripture. These claims are maintained, modified, and echoed in the twentieth century by neo-orthodox and fundamentalists, while both view the reasons for this from a different perspective.

Gerhard contended that "God determined that revelation should be committed to writing in order to preserve it in a pure state through all future time, establish concord in the church, provide a summary of the faith for secular authorities, and distinguish heretics from true believers."[71] There is a similar claim about the role of the church by Roman Catholics and Eastern Orthodox. The Bible replaces tradition and apostolic succession as the legitimate means of authority.

Gerhard and other Lutheran scholastics' conclusions are so cemented by the close of the seventeenth century that Protestant tradition accompanies the Bible as the source of authority. Pietists and the Orthodox began to engage in greater controversies at this same time surrounding the idea of how a Christian society is to operate. The majority of these controversies were practical rather than theological. Essentially Pietism was a reform movement that sought not to reform the structure of society but its members. The piety of individuals challenged the status quo, the clash concerned visions more than specific theological or practical differences. It is a clash between doxa and heterodoxa.

The Lutheran Pietists rarely rejected the theological outcomes of their Orthodox counterparts. The thrust of the Pietist challenge to

---

71. Johnson, *Evolution of Christianity*, 144.

Lutheran Orthodoxy was against the system rather than the conclusions. The emphasis of the Lutheran Scholastics on dogma dictating divine intervention contrasted the Pietist fidelity to experiencing God. The synods conclusions were still upheld. The Pietists which deviated furthest from this Lutheran Orthodoxy were the ones who were only in part connected to the Lutheran Church to begin with. Predictably the Moravians, who were only partly Lutheran, and Methodists who were Anglican, drifted much further away from the conclusions of the orthodox Lutherans than the Pietists from the Halle School. Pietists emphasized the practice of piety over the systematic interpretation of abstract theological concerns, but those from Halle especially do not flatly reject the developed Lutheran systematic theology.

Reform/Calvinist Pietism—Because of Scholasticism.

"In all history, we do not find a single religion without a Church."[72]

— Emile Durkheim

While the Lutheran Pietistic tradition emerged in response to the development of Lutheran Orthodoxy, it may be said that Calvinist Orthodoxy created their version of Pietism. Calvinist/Reform piety develops not in opposition to the Scholastic tradition but in response to it, and the theological necessity created by Calvinist doxa.

The Calvinists, like the Lutherans before them, establish their Orthodoxy through Synods. Calvinist theology took longer to develop than Lutheran theology, and Reform theology differs considerably from the Lutheran theology. The highpoint of Reform debate occurs at the Synod of Dort in in 1618. The theological settlement focused on five key theological propositions. Underlying the five points of Calvinism are two central theological propositions, the first concerned with God, the second with mankind. For the Calvinist, God is primarily the sovereign of the universe. Man is completely dependent upon the will of God and is currently in a fallen state. Issues of salvation and damnation are related to these two starting points for the Calvinist. It is interesting to note that much of the Reform language used at Dort came from William Perkins, an Anglican Pietist, who we will address in the next chapter.

Man's fallen state is understood through the doctrine of Total Depravity. Total Depravity has its roots in an extreme Augustinian understanding that

---

72. Durkheim, *Elementary Forms*, 59.

due to Original Sin man is completely and totally depraved. Man in his fallen state is at enmity with God. The condition of man is not just that he lacks a connection with God but willfully chooses to go against God's wishes for man. As such man deserves eternal separation from God. This separation is known as hell. From the Calvinist perspective hell is always justified because of man's sin, and without God's grace all would rightfully end up in hell.

Luckily for the Calvinist, Christ died to save some from their fate. This group is commonly known as the Elect. The rest of humanity is commonly called the Reprobate. The Elect are a chosen remnant taken out of the whole. Not all Christians are elect, and Calvin himself believed that most of Geneva during his leadership consisted of the Reprobate. While Catholic, Lutherans, and Eastern Orthodox may point to verses like John 3:16[73] as an example of Christ's sacrificial atonement for all, Calvinists reject this idea. For Calvinists, one theological doctrine must be held without exception, the idea that God is sovereign. For God's sovereignty to be actual, God must know all and be able to control all. This directly applies to the notion of the limited atonement. The reason is simple, if God truly knows all, why would Christ die and atone for the sins of the Reprobate, who by their very nature will reject Christ's sacrifice. For the Calvinist, God in all his sovereignty cannot do that. The logical outcome is that Christ's atonement on the cross does not extend to the Reprobate, only the Elect.

The doctrine of predestination is a logical consequence of the doctrine of limited atonement. For God to know who the Elect are and Reprobate are, God simply decides ahead of time. Christ died solely for the Elect, and God predestined the Elect. An in-house Calvinist debate occurs over the doctrine of "Double Predestination." According to double predestination, God also predestined the Reprobate to hell, just as God predestined the elect for heaven. In either case the doctrine of predestination continues to grow and change throughout the centuries for those of the Reformed Calvinist traditions.

The difficulty for the Calvinist is their inability to know if they are the Elect or the Reprobate. This uncertainty leads some, like Max Weber, to propose his interpretation of Calvinism. Calvinism is the first example of worldly asceticism that Weber gives in his *Protestant Ethic*, as Weber contends that Calvinism emerged in the most developed countries and had the most rational treatment of theology. Weber likewise proposes that a central tenet to Calvinism is the sole interest in God. Weber maintains that for the Calvinist "God does not exist for men, but men for the sake of God.

---

73. "For God so loved the world that he gave his one and only Son, that whoever believes in him shall not perish but have eternal life" (John 3:16).

All creation, including of course the fact, as it undoubtedly was for Calvin, that only a small proportion of men are chosen for eternal grace, can have any meaning only as means to the glory and majesty of God."[74]

As a result Weber points out a dilemma for the Calvinist. Man must remain simultaneously humble before God, yet preserve the notion that they are chosen. Of course the lack of certainty of one's own status before the Almighty creates an uneasy feeling. This lack of certainty for one's own salvation is only amplified in the salvation of their neighbor, spouse, or children. Central to Weber's critique of Calvinism is that it produces an intense sense of inner loneliness, as devotional life is reduced to the individual rather than the corporate body known as a church.

While often criticized, Weber's view of dread found at the heart of devout Calvinists has merit. The numerous Calvinist tracts written on the same subject can attest to that. Equally revealing is Weber's view of Pietism. Pietism increased "the need of the Reformed 'saints' to prove themselves with a view to the life hereafter, the directing of religious need to an inward emotional *feeling* in the present."[75] Reform Pietists develop the supremacy of the emotional component of religion as a balm for the pain and isolation inherent in the Calvinist notions of predestination. Assurance is found, not in theological tests, but in a personal accounting of God's grace in the lives of the seemingly redeemed individuals.

Paul Tillich supports this idea as well. For Tillich it is not a wholesale rejection of the Protestant Orthodox theological system that should identify one as a Pietist. Specifically Tillich points out the divergent beliefs on the theology of the unregenerate or "*theologict irregenetorium*." This dogma concerns the notion of being born again. The prevailing orthodoxy maintains a belief that theology is a rational science, therefore all issues pertaining to theology can be understood. As such, it would be rational to write a theology addressing whether one was reborn or not. According to Tillich, Pietism's response to this dogma is to say "No, that's impossible; you must be reborn with respect to everything in which you participate, in all that you talk about; you can be a theologian only if you have the experience of regeneration."[76] Yet for the orthodox Lutheran there is no assurance of regeneration, as an emotional experience may not be real rebirth. Rather the process of regeneration is one of accepting guidance from the Holy Spirit, the "moment" of rebirth is not a single moment, rather a long conscious acceptance of the will of God. The tales of conversion and rebirth are central

---

74. Weber, *Protestant Ethic*.
75. Weber, *Protestant Ethic*, 94.
76. Tillich, *Perspectives*, 16.

to Pietists. Many of the Pietist theologians we are addressing in the work have this conversion experience which assures them of their regeneration, but others do not. For Tillich a key difference between the orthodox and the Pietist is how theology is interpreted and shaped by experience.

Interestingly, due to the strict devotion of Calvinists and their working for salvation, as understood by Weber and Tillich, some Lutheran critics of Pietism believed that Pietism is "nothing more than an attempted 'Calvinizing' of the Lutheran Church by the introduction of a spirit of monkish piety."[77] Then again many of these same Lutherans believed that Melanchthon was doing the same thing. Furthermore this particular Lutheran critique fails to see the extension of Pietism into Calvinist Churches as well. Many examples could be given, such as Jean de Taffin,[78] William Tellinck and his brothers,[79] and of course Jadocus von Lodensteyn,[80] but due to the scope of this work, and because William Perkins argues vehemently from a Calvinist perspective in England, it is best to limit our discussion of them.

We also have an extensive autobiographical tradition from the Reform Dutch Pietists as well as other Reformed Pietists. Fred Van Lieburg, in his work *Living for God, Eighteenth-Century Dutch Pietist Autobiography*, illustrates the role conversion experiences had upon the Pietists in the Low Countries. Van Lieburg demonstrates the interconnection of Pietistic thought as the use of autobiographies was taken from English Puritans and demonstrated how experience in general, and experience of conversion specifically, separated the Dutch Pietist from their Calvinist neighbors. The key difference became the mode in which the "Precisionists" live out their experiential theology. Often this resulted in isolation from the larger community.

Unlike the Lutheran Pietists, who often rejected the notion of theological formation of Protestant scholasticism, many Reform Pietists

---

77. Nagler, *Pietism and Methodism*, 13.

78. Jean de Taffin (1529–1602), reform advocate of piety in Antwerp, Metz, Heidelberg, and Amsterdam. He maintained that man's true end is a state of bliss found in the resurrection. To have this one must know they are a child of God by looking at the outward and inward signs.

79. The Dutch brothers were Amesius and Eewout. William (1579–1629) maintained that faith was not simply assent but must also include reform of one's own personal life. He contributed to the doctrine of the two states, natural man and spiritual man. Self-Denial is central to overcoming the natural man. Tellinck was also one of the first Protestants to emphasis mission work

80. van Lodensteyn (1620–1677), a Dutch hymnographer and preacher. He held conventicles for mature Christian students. Most of his work revolves around the idea of repentance, and like Tellink, he, too, emphasized missions and the doctrine of two states.

were Pietists as an attempt to provide certainty of their status as the Elect. As we read in the autobiographies of these Pietists, the notion of a conversion experience was central to their claim of being chosen. This assertion is further supported by the pious lives they live now that they are the Elect. Appeasing the existential angst becomes the catalyst for Reform Pietism. Reform Pietists are not opposed to the formation of doctrine to the same extent as their Lutheran counterpart; they simply view it as a waste of time, given the urgency necessitated by the doctrine of predestination.

Anglican Pietism: Despite Orthodoxy and in Opposition to Rationalism.

> "We should not forget that Puritanism embraced a world of opposites."[81]
>
> — Max Weber

The formation of Anglican Pietism differs from the Lutheran and Reform. The key difference between the English model and what is found on the continent is the central place of theological formation. While the Lutheran and Reform Pietists spent little time emphasizing doctrine, this appears to be one of the key contributions of Pietists in England. There are two major strands of English Pietists. The first are commonly known as Puritans, and the second emerges from Wesley's synthesis of Puritanism with Zinzendorf's brand of Pietism. We will address Wesley in greater detail in chapter four. English Pietists of both types are products of the time and historical machinations in England.

Before we can proceed further with English Pietism, an issue must be addressed. A debate among scholars exists as to the place of English Pietists. Much of the debate is a byproduct of the ambiguous and contentious definitions of Pietism in general. Like so many ideological and practical movements, the lines of who should be included and excluded are difficult to discern. As such, there is a contingent who protest the inclusion of Puritans as a subset of the Pietist movement happening on the continent.

Historically there are two main objections to including Puritans as the English version of Pietism. The first is an outgrowth of the older understanding of Pietism, the view put forth by nineteenth-century theologian Albrecht Ritschl. Ritschl maintains a more negative and formulaic view of Pietism. For these influential theologians, Pietism was too mystical,

---

81. Weber, *Protestant Ethic*, 114.

Ancestry of Pietism

subjective, emotional, and individualistic. Furthermore, for Ritschl, there is a clear beginning of Pietism. Pietism emerged in Frankfurt during the late seventeenth century. Central to this older view of Pietism is Philipp Jakob Spener. The narrowest definitions of Pietism exclude any movements that were not products of Spener's *collegia pietatis*. Since Puritanism existed well before Spener, Puritanism is therefore a separate movement.

The second objection to Pietism including Puritans is confessional or theological, and is a consequence of the first objection. If the definition of Pietism is extremely narrow and only includes the inheritors of Spener, then Pietism should be a specifically Lutheran concern. The notion that Pietism is restricted to Lutheranism is not only outdated but lacks historical evidence. Zinzendorf was Lutheran, but infused Pietism with Protestant refugees, becoming the Moravian Church, which at best is nominally Lutheran and in actuality is a separate denomination. Furthermore Wesley's formative theological training came under a Moravian in Georgia and London, and Methodists are clearly inheritors of Spener, but are also in no way Lutheran. Wesley borrowed much of his theological outlook from Puritans such as William Perkins. We also have the plethora of Reformed Dutch Pietists, which very few scholars are willing to exclude from Pietism. As such the objection to including Puritanism from Pietism simply because it is not Lutheran is nonsensical.

Essential to this project, and reason, is the understanding that Pietism is a larger Protestant wide phenomena. Nearly every claim used in the definitions of Pietism are the same claims we see in definitions of Puritanism. J. I. Packer claims, "spiritual revival was central to what the Puritans professed to be seeking."[82] This spiritual renewal is best characterized as an emphasis on experiential Christianity, as maintained by historians Richard F. Lovelace, Leland Ryken, and Charles Hambrick-Stowe.

Lovelace maintains "that throughout most of its history English Puritanism can best be understood by examining its predominating stress on Christian experience."[83] Ryken claims "The practical bent of the Puritans led them to emphasize the experiential nature of the Christian faith."[84] Hambrick-Stowe defines the Puritans as "a devotional movement, rooted in religious experience."[85] For these scholars and Geoffrey Nuttall, Puritanism is "a movement towards immediacy in relation to God."[86] This is identical

---

82. Packer, *Quest for Godliness*, 36.
83. Lovelace, *American Pietism of Cotton Mather*, 36.
84. Ryken, *Worldly Saints*, 120.
85. Hambrick-Stowe, *Practice of Piety*, vii.
86. Nuttall, *Holy Spirit in Puritan Faith*, 134.

to the definitions of experiential medieval mystics and Pietists in general. Stoeffler tells us "the fact is that essential differences between continental Pietism and what we have called Pietistic Puritanism cannot be established because they are non-existent."[87]

John Spurr maintains that the essence of Puritanism is found in the individual's conviction of their own salvation. For Spurr this includes not only notions of election but also the formation of a new church, one based upon how Puritans envision the church of the New Testament, and the formation of a new society around that church. Kelly M. Kapic and Randall C. Gleason also point out that there is not one thing that we can call Puritans. The Puritans encompassed many theological differences including extreme and moderate Calvinists, as well as Armenians. Also numbered among the Puritans were those devoted to the Church of England, as well as Separatists, Baptists, Presbyterians, and Independents.[88] Rather than organizational or even theological, Puritanism, like Pietism, is identified as a piety movement that emphasizes individual salvation through experience rather than scholastic understanding or rationalism.

Since we have significant justification to count the Puritans as Pietists, their origin and confrontation with the Anglican Church should be addressed. The Puritans emerged from the multiple reformations that England underwent following their break with Rome under Henry VIII. Henry's Reformation was not theological but practical. Following the scholarship of Eamon Duffy, it is a challenge to hold that the English Reformation under Henry was one that the people inherently wanted. Duffy points out that "the Henrician religious revolution had been preceded by a vigorous campaign against heresy, in both its familiar Lollard and its newer Lutheran forms."[89] Duffy contends that "In the liturgy and in the sacramental celebrations which were its central moments, medieval people found the key to the meaning and purpose of their lives."[90] Unlike the disconnect that existed in Germany between the people and their priests, the status quo of the sacred was something the English supported. As a result Henry did very little to change the way church was experienced for the masses of people.

Only under Edward did England really become Protestant and not simply schismatic. Following Mary and Elizabeth's reigns, England

---

87. Stoeffler, *Rise of Evangelical Pietism*, 29.

88. Extreme Calvinists: John Owen and Thomas Goodwin; Moderate Calvinists: Richard Baxter and John Goodwin; Moderate Church of England: Richard Sibbes; Separatists: William Bradford; Baptists: John Bunyan; Presbyterians: John Howe and Thomas Watson; Independents: Thomas Goodwin, John Cotton, and John Owen.

89. Duffy, *Stripping of the Altars*, 379.

90. Duffy, *Stripping of the Altars*, 11.

vacillated once again from Catholic to nominal Protestant, especially considering the radical shift that occurred under Edward's reign. During and following Elizabeth's reform of the church, theological debate was largely minimized, especially when considering what was taking place on the Continent. England failed to provide state support for a coherent theological leader like a Luther, Zwingli, Bucer, or Calvin.[91] The Puritans believed that England failed to truly reform itself, and called for yet another reformation to complete the process begun with Henry. English Christianity was Protestant, but emphasized commonality and conformity.

This is where the Puritans found their point of departure. For those English experiential Protestants, England was lukewarm, neither hot nor cold. England did not devoutly follow Rome and all it took from Canterbury was a tepid and confused Christianity. Puritans needed not only to express their piety in experiential terms but also in theological terms that separated them from what they perceived to be nominal Protestant Christians that surrounded them in England. The central critique of the Puritans was against the overly rational and subdued attempts of the established church. The Church of England was ruled by Christian Rationalists and not the scholastic theologians that dominated Germany, the Low Countries and Scandinavia. The void in both piety and systematic theology was taken up by the Puritans as the most efficient way to combat the rationalist establishment clergy.

Two tenets are found within Puritan theology. First is the supremacy of the Bible as the source of authority. Unlike the Lutheran counterpart, England still maintained a modified hierarchy borrowed from Rome; therefore tradition still held a place of value for the Anglican Church. The Puritans echo the rejection of this hierarchical system and chose to adopt the theological language necessary for the Lutheran and Reform Churches. Puritans also borrow heavily upon the Calvinist doctrines connected to predestination. For the Anglican, predestination gives purpose to life and structures it accordingly. What separates the Puritan is how predestination is understood, not merely as a theological truth, but also an experiential truth. The centrality of experience shapes the theology to a point where a difference of degree may indeed be a difference in kind.

What may be an interesting commonality for all three of our forms of early Pietism is the common foe they faced with their literature. In reading Perkins, Arndt, Spener and other foundational Pietists, we find two simultaneous critiques. The first, as we may expect, is directed against their

---

91. John Knox may provide some of the theological foundations for England but was primarily in Scotland.

fellow Protestants who they view as lacking faith, piety, and an experience of God. The second is a critique of Rome. For these early Pietists, the break with Rome was still fresh and there was a fear that the bridges they burned in order to separate from Rome might be rebuilt. There was a fear that the waters of the Tiber could still be crossed. In many cases their critiques against Rome were simultaneously a veiled critique of their perceptions of non-Pietist Protestant communities. Often Roman practices were exaggerated and mischaracterized, not only because of a lack of familiarity but also because of a desire to spur on greater reformation.

Non-Confessional Differences in Pietism.

"Institutionalization is not, however, an irreversible process, despite the fact that institutions, once formed, have a tendency to persist."[92]

— *Peter L. Berger & Thomas Luckmann*

With such different causes for the rise of Pietism, there are also many different types of Pietists, irrespective of confessional ties. It is clear that not every Pietist would hold the same theological or practical differences. Andrew Landale Drummond defined four types of Pietists, each with a point of conflict with their orthodox counterparts. What is central to all of these types of Pietists was their belief that the church needed further reform. The first group believed that the righteous minority would maintain the church and try to grow their numbers within the larger church. The second group believed that the established church was too far gone, but remained due to social pressures, often meeting for additional studies and pietistic confraternities. The third group separated themselves from the official churches altogether. The final group were the extremes, whom Drummond defines as mystics and heretics.

Other scholars like Dale Brown maintain that regardless of which extremity we find within Pietist camps, there exists a central theological tenet that cuts through the social and ideological tensions. Brown identifies the Pietist theology as a *"love theology."*[93] While not rejecting the notion of the wrath of God, the Pietists stress the love of God and their response. In doing so, theologically the Pietists lean more towards universal restoration, Spiritualism, emphasizing a mystical inner world, rejection of creeds,

---

92. Berger and Luckmann, *Social Construction of Reality*, 81.
93. Brown, *Understanding Pietism*, 21.

Ancestry of Pietism

communalism, celibacy, and an emphasis on the millennial kingdom. In each of these cases the subjective experience of the individual trumps the rationalism of the whole or established orthodoxy.

John Dillenberger and Claude Welch view the conflict between the Pietists and their orthodox counterparts as combining practical and theological differences. Central to both types of concerns is the role of experiences. The role of experiences, along with the supremacy of the Bible, is the key conflict between orthodox Calvinists and the Puritans in England. Most Calvinists and Anglicans would agree that God is sovereign and contained in the sovereignty of God is the role of the Bible as authoritative and that salvation is for the Elect. What separates the Puritans is how they interpret these theological notions. The Puritan, far more than the Calvinist, rejects the notion of multiple sources of authority, including ecclesial hierarchy and tradition. Oddly enough, Dillenberger and Welch illustrate that this Biblicism lends itself to an insistence that they "were returning to the church in its original state."[94] This claim simultaneously embraces the value of tradition while rejecting all tradition that has followed from the point where they believe something went wrong. Potentially it is this conflict that would lead Wesley in England and the Pietists on the continent to maintain a conservative status quo while greatly influencing the social order.[95]

With such a wide swath of types of Pietists, it is important to revisit the reasons why mystically inclined Catholics or Orthodox are not Pietists. After all, we see a similar movement in Catholic France with Jansenism. This is a fair question, and it would be too broad to simply maintain that Pietism is a Protestant phenomenon, since we see many similarities with Catholic mystics and Hesychaism in the Eastern Orthodox. There remains a clear difference between what is found within the Eastern Orthodox and the Roman Catholic Churches and what is found within Protestantism. The difference is the *ecclesia* and the role of the church in interpreting and fostering this movement.

In many ways the difference is directional and confrontational. For the Eastern Orthodox and Roman Catholics, the church is the authority and can sanction, verify, and promote certain forms of piety, people, and practices. This authority is largely lost within Protestantism. While Lutheran, Reform, and Anglican traditions have an ecclesial hierarchy, the emphasis on *Sola Scriptura* eradicated the claims of authority for these ecclesial bodies. As such, Pietism, including Puritanism, emphasizes the Bible as the authority

---

94. Dillenburger and Welch, *Protestant Christianity*, 107.
95. Dillenburger and Welch, *Protestant Christianity*, 131.

rather than the church as the authority. There exists within all three strands of Christianity the impulse toward experience. Protestantism diverges from the Roman Catholic and Eastern Orthodox because the Protestants abandoned the church as a check on this experience. While sharing a history, due to theological concerns, the history is appealed to only as inspiration rather than supremacy.

The movement is confrontational as well because of this same shift in the fount of authority. While both the Bible and tradition can be interpreted in a number of ways, tradition for the Orthodox and Catholics is interpreted by the churches hierarchies. Inherent to this mode of interpretation, change in theology or practice is generally slow and often reactionary. The Bible, while largely static, is used to support the *ecclesia*. For Protestants, the Bible is used to challenge the *ecclesia*. Tradition is subjected to interpretation of the Bible, and the source for interpretation is found in the individual rather than the church as a corporate body. While new traditional understandings of the Bible are formed and formulated, many of these new modes of interpretation are only in their infancy at the times of the synods of Westminster and Dort and the Augsburg Confession.

In many ways the essential difference between Protestant piety and Catholic and Orthodox piety is the place of the church in the individual's salvation. Catholics have maintained for centuries that "there is no salvation outside of the church,"[96] a phrase likely first used by Cyprian of Carthage in the third century. The Orthodox have a similar phrase, that "we are saved together but damned alone."[97] Both phrases have at their heart the same thing, that salvation is a corporate process including the church as a whole and its member therein. Individually and outside of the church there is no salvation because you are alone and outside of the body of Christ. For many Protestants, especially Calvinists, salvation becomes an individual affair. Personal piety, as well as being elect, is the means of salvation. One may never be sure of their own salvation and they are equally unsure of the salvation of anyone else. While Orthodox and Catholic piety are similar in many respects to Protestant Pietism, this fundamental idea of salvation as it relates to the church and the individual creates a movement that is categorically different.

With so many types of Pietism, a representative sample is necessary to truly understand both the context and development of Pietism. Six key representatives are addressed in these chapters, William Perkins, Johann Arndt, Philip Jakob Spener, August Hermann Francke, Nicholas Ludwig

---

96. Oddie, *Pope Francis*.
97. Dreher, "*Purgatorio, Canto XIX.*"

von Zinzendorf, and John Wesley. Each of the six representative men, for in this case we are looking at men, developed or advanced their own notions of piety and Protestant devotion that is best understood as Pietist.

These six men contribute to my definition of Pietism with the traits of experiential revivalism, antipathy towards Christian culture, reworking the world, mysticism, and a commitment to personal relationship with God as the expression of the Christian life. While all of these traits are common to one degree or another with all Pietists, these individuals express some of these singular traits to a greater degree than others. Over the next three chapters the foundational, institutional, and denominational expressions of Pietism develop through the life and work of William Perkins, Johann Arndt, Philip Jakob Spener, August Hermann Francke, Count Nicholas Ludwig von Zinzendorf, and John Wesley.

II.

Foundational Pietism
Perkins, Arndt, and Spener

> *"The reformer is not usually welcome to the representatives of the status quo, and the early Pietists meant to be reformers."*[1]
>
> —*F. Ernst Stoeffler*

EARLY PIETISTS VIEWED THEMSELVES as a necessary corrective. Protestantism in all its mainline confessional forms was eager to prove itself the valid expression of Christianity. The result was an explosion in theology with little room left for mysticism. Any appeal to mystical encounters with Christ as the source of authority smacked of the Radical Reformation. Still many who remained within the newly formed magisterial confessions sought to temper reason and scholasticism with practical experiences of the divine, building upon the Medieval Catholic mystics rather than debating the finer points of theology. Among the choir of voices three Pietist theologians emerged from the pack in the sixteenth and seventeenth century, William Perkins, Johann Arndt, and Philip Jakob Spener. Their expressions of Protestantism lay the foundations for later expressions of Pietism in its institutional forms.

---

1. Stoeffler, *Rise of Evangelical Pietism*, 3.

WILLIAM PERKINS (1588-1602)—PURITANS: THE ENGLISH PIETISTS

"Faith is that alone instrument created in the heart by the holy ghost, whereby a sinner lays hold of Christ his righteousness, and applied the same unto himself."[2]

— William Perkins

The life and work of William Perkins is inexorably tied to Puritanism during the reign of Queen Elizabeth. Perkins was born the first year of her reign and died a year before Elizabeth. Scholars described him as "the principal architect of Elizabethan Puritanism," "the Puritan theologian of Tudor times," "the most important Puritan writer," "the prince of Puritan theologians," and "the father of Puritanism." In a very short forty-four years Perkins shaped English piety in ways that no one else could.

Perkins was born in 1558 in Marston Jabbett in the parish of Bulkington, Warwickshire. His parents Thomas and Hanna had some financial resources available to them, enough that William enrolled as a pensioner of Christ's College, Cambridge at the age of nineteen in 1577. Pensioners paid for common expenses of the college which required considerable financial contributions by the Perkins family. Little else is known of Perkins's family background or his youth. We can assume through the choice of school that William Perkins grew up in a family that was pious and Protestant, but this is just supposition.

Four years after beginning his studies Perkins received his BA, and his master's degree three years after that in 1584. A promising student, it was said of him that, "Mr. Perkins had a surprising talent for reading books. He pursued them so speedily, that he appeared to read nothing; yet so accurately, that he seemed to read all."[3]

Perkins's time at Cambridge was not without its difficulties. Early biographies point out that he wrote all his works with his left hand, being lame of the right. In addition to this physical deformity Perkins also took advantage of his freedom from parental oversight to indulge in immorality. Very early Perkins supplemented his studies with a desire to understand "natural magic," astrology, and witchcraft. He also took to strong drink, public drunkenness, and profane speech. Additionally there is the possibility that Perkins fathered a child out of wedlock during this period. There is some reason to challenge these claims. First it is rather common

---

2. Perkins, *Reformed Catholic*, 62.
3. Brook, *Lives of the Puritans*, 2:130.

for Pietist biographies to exaggerate the depravity of the pre-converted, in order to illustrate the power of the conversion experience. It is likely that some of these claims are simply exaggerations, but have some basis in fact. Furthermore Perkins had many detractors in England during and after his life and some of these claims could be made by critics to deter his followers.

Whether or not the story is true, it is clear that Perkins had a religious awakening sometime between 1581 and 1584. The turning point occurred when he heard a woman say to her child, "hold your tongue, or I will give you to drunken Perkins yonder." This idle threat made to a child served as a wakeup call, and the impetus for Perkins's conversion. Upon receiving his master's degree in 1584, Perkins was ordained and immediately began preaching.

The first stop in his career was the local jail. It was here at the Cambridge jail that reports of his eloquence and power as a preacher emerged. It was said that Perkins could pronounce the word 'damn' with such an emphasis as it left a doleful echo in the ears of those present for a good while after. His preaching must have impressed, as the next year in 1585 Perkins became the rector of St. Andrew's Church in Cambridge, a post he would hold until his death.

The church was located right across from Christ's College where Perkins retained one of a dozen fellowships upon completion of his Masters. Perkins was certainly the college's most distinguished fellow. For the next decade he split his responsibilities teaching at the University and preaching at the church. These two tasks were interrelated and Perkins was a draw to both institutions. Perkins prized pupil, William Ames (1576–1633), evaluated his preaching and teaching stating, "he instructed them soundly in the truth, stirred them up effectually to seek after godliness, made them fit for the kingdom of God."[4] It is really in his preaching where Perkins had his greatest impact. Perkins elevated the role of the preacher in England during this time. For many parishes in England preaching was neglected. Perkins recognized this failing and took it upon himself both as a preacher and a teacher to prioritize preaching in England.

It was also as a preacher that Perkins found himself under suspicion. In his January 13, 1587 sermon he denounced many common practices found in the Church of England such as kneeling to receive communion, and facing the cross during this time. Most of these critiques allied Perkins with the more extreme elements of the church and this necessitated an immediate response. He, along with others, was apprehended, and carried before the star-chamber. Once before the tribunal Perkins backtracked many of his

---

4. Beeke and Yuille, *William Perkins*, 64.

statements, and maintained that he was a loyal son of the church. To prove this point Perkins offered some "clarifications" on his previous statements. In these Perkins pointed out that he was not opposed to kneeling as he implied in the sermon. Perkins added that he was opposed to many other practices of the church at this time, including the practice where priests self-administered communion. Perkins was ultimately released since he was not a separatist, though he opposed Elizabeth's desire for a uniform church.

Perkins lost his fellowship at Christ's College eight years later. This was not due to any controversy, rather because he chose to marry, and the rigors of a fellow excluded the possibility of marriage. The widow Timothye Cradocke of Grantchester was of more value for Perkins than his position at the school. The two wed on July 2, 1595. Over the next seven years Timothye bore William seven children, only four of which survived infancy.

William Perkins was never a healthy man. In addition to his malformed right hand he also suffered from kidney stones. This developed into renal colic by 1602. This form of colic is generally described as rather painful, and often persistent. While upon his death bed Perkins was accompanied by a friend who was praying for the mitigation of his pains, Perkins then cried out "hold, hold! Do not pray so; but pray the Lord to give me faith and patience, and then let him lay on me what he pleases."[5] Perkins died on October 22, 1602, at the age of 44. His funeral was widely attended, and the expenses paid for by St. Andrews. John Montague preached a sermon titled "Moses my servant is dead."

In addition to his four surviving children and his wife, Perkins left behind a large production of books. Nearly fifty works are attributed to Perkins, many of which are commentaries on books of the Bible. Three works stand out above the rest, each pointing to one of his primary concerns. The first work is entitled *A Reformed Catholic;* not surprisingly this work is directed against Catholics. The second work is *A Golden Chain*. In this work Perkins clarifies his Calvinist theology against other forms of Protestantism and Catholicism. Finally in the *Art of Prophesying*, Perkins expounds on the role of the preacher and the topics of sermons.

Shortly before his fortieth birthday, Perkins penned a critique against the Catholic Church. This critique, published in 1597, is titled *A Reformed Catholic or, A declaration shewing how near we may come to the present Church of Rome in sundry points of religion: and wherein we must forever depart from them with an advertisement to all favorers of the Roman religion, shewing that the said religion is against the Catholic principles and grounds of the catechism*. Having already developed most of his theology, Perkins was

---

5. Brook, *Lives of the Puritans*, 2:133.

confronted by what he believed as too much influence that Roman Catholic beliefs still held in England. Duffy sees within Perkins the challenges of the Reformations in England.

> William Perkins thought that most of the common people were papist at heart, given to saying that 'it was a good world, when the old religion was, because all things were cheap,' that 'a man eats his maker in the Sacrament,' that they might sear by Our Lad 'because she is gone out of the country,' that they believed in Christ 'ever since they could remember.' Yet he also reported the common view that 'it is saver to doe in religion as most doe.' In that paradox lies the key to understanding the Reformation in the English parishes.[6]

Perkins desired to point out the areas where the English Calvinist differs from Rome, believing that Rome is corrupted and Perkins and those who follow the Reformation are the true Catholics. Perkins hoped that by illustrating these differences Rome would correct itself. In actuality this is more a polemic than a pastoral letter. This is made clear when he says of Rome "they are the ministers of Christ, but THEY SERVE ANTICHRIST. Again, the beast spoken of in the Apocalypse, to which a mouth is given to speak blasphemies, and to make war with the Saints of God, is now gotten into Peter's chair, as a lion prepared to his prey."[7]

Specifically Perkins addressed a dozen or so issues where he maintains Rome erred, including free will, original sin, issues concerning salvation, traditions, sacraments, and the place of the saints. In each of these Perkins illustrates places of agreement, as well as disagreement. Concerning the doctrine of Original Sin, Perkins upholds the doctrine but opposes the efficacy of the sacrament of baptism in removing many of the consequences of original sin. As such Perkins believes that "The Roman Catholic Church had developed an exaggerated concept of the role of man's will in salvation."[8] In the issues concerning salvation, we see the difficulty Perkins has in reconciling his beliefs with Rome.

The issue of faith and its relation to salvation causes great difficulty for Perkins. He concedes that "both Papists and Protestants agree, that a sinner is justified by faith."[9] But Perkins does not want to concede that the Papist has a saving faith. Holding that the faith for the Roman only provides

---

6. Duffy, *Stripping of the Altars*, 591.
7. Beeke and Yuille, *William Perkins*, 40.
8. Beeke and Yuille, *William Perkins*, 40.
9. Perkins, *Reformed Catholic*, 78.

a notion of hope in salvation, and not a real faith in their own salvation.[10] Perkins maintains that the Protestant has saving faith, with the caveat that no one can truly know if they are the Elect. As a result, it appears that the Calvinist has an equal degree of hope in their faith, as does the Papist. Yet Perkins is not willing to concede this point, essentially arguing that the Catholic is justified by their doctrine, but this doctrine is wrong, primarily because it is Catholic. The Protestant, assuming they are the right kind of Protestant, is justified by their doctrine being correct, namely because it is not Catholic. It is here that the polemic falls apart.

Moving onto traditions, Perkins defines these as doctrines derived from things other than the Bible. Surprisingly he concedes that the Bible is a product of tradition, at least in its early forms. The difference is that scriptural tradition is directly delivered by God, unlike other traditions, which must be subordinated. Largely Perkins disdains apostolic and ecclesiastical traditions, believing they are not profitable for salvation. Perkins singles two traditions out for his disapproval, the intercession of saints and sacraments as means of salvation. Perkins simply renounces the efficacy of intercession of saints; little reason is given, save the fact it is held by Catholics. Perkins then challenges the physical nature of sacraments. Perkins contends that the sacraments are voluntary instruments, just as the minister who dispenses them. Ultimately the sacraments cannot be signs of God's grace because salvation is unknown. If someone is not the Elect then the sacrament merits them nothing.

Reflexively Perkins believes that Rome is simply wrong, not through any profound reasoning other than they are not Calvinists. The different theological system held by Rome, while sharing many things in common, is negated because of its origin, because that origin is tainted with traditions rejected by Protestants in general.

In 1591 Perkins wrote what many, including Stoeffler, believe was his major work, *A Golden Chain*. In this work Perkins outlines the basic Calvinist beliefs concerning salvation. Indeed the chain is the theological assumptions of Puritan Calvinists at the time. The chain consists of four or five links, depending on how one counts them. First is either predestination or man's calling, the two are in fact one and the same. From here the three remaining steps are justification, sanctification, and glorification. Essential to this entire discussion is the doctrine of double predestination. The work begins with Perkins's definition of theology being the principle science. In addition to being the principle science, theology is defined as "the science of

---

10. Perkins, *Reformed Catholic*, 39.

living blessedly forever."[11] The source of this theology is found only within the Calvinist interpretation of scripture and not in any traditions that predate the Reformation.

Only the tradition of Calvin's theology is upheld, including the supreme theological notion of God's sovereignty. Echoing Calvin, Perkins clearly states "God controls all things for the good of His people. God is sovereign, therefore, His control is absolute. God is immutable; therefore, His will is certain. God is mighty; therefore, His power is limitless. God is most wise; therefore, His plan is perfect. God is incomprehensible; therefore, His providence is inscrutable."[12]

Before man can be called, Perkins lays out what man is being called out of. While initially man was created in a state of innocence, this was lost. Innocence has two parts, first is wisdom and second is will. Both were perfect until the fall, where sin robs man of the perfect knowledge of God and corrupts the will, making man an enemy of God. Fallen man, and not humanity in its entirety, must be called by God. This calling is the doctrine of predestination, but what and who are predestined is not universally agreed upon. Perkins posits there are four categories of belief concerning predestination. The first of the options are held by Pelagians. According to Perkins, the Pelagian, both old and new, believe that man chooses to be with God or not. It is the individual man or woman who chooses to be predestined or rejects God. Free will, and a completely free will, is the essential belief of the Pelagians, and God only foresees the choices of men.

The Lutheran view is the second option. Perkins likens the Lutheran belief to the Pelagian, both are dependent on free will and God's foreknowledge determining who will be saved and who is not. The difference is for the Lutheran view man's will is not as free as it is for the Pelagian, and sin has a greater weight in preventing man. As such God chooses some, as sinful man would reject God's grace. An omniscient God knows who would accept grace if sin was not total and chooses those to be saved.

The third category Perkins identifies are Catholics, or more precisely semi-Pelagian Papists. Perkins maintains that Catholics believe that some men can see God's grace and choose to act meritoriously. Sin is not as encompassing as for the Lutheran but restricts more than the Pelagian. Obviously Perkins reject these three views. It may be of note that some Lutherans and Catholics would also reject Perkins's depiction of their respective views as well.

---

11. Perkins, *Golden Chain*, 1.
12. Beeke and Yuille, *William Perkins*, 92.

Perkins holds a fourth view which he bases on a sovereign God wholly predetermining who is saved. Unlike the other three views which emphasize free will, Perkins, like Calvin, minimizes man's involvement, instead supporting a belief that God simply chooses. Since man is in a state of sin, the logical conclusion for Perkins and Calvin is that man deserves nothing but damnation. God in his mercy chooses some to save. God is free to choose who is saved and who is damned, and man has no choice in the matter and no reason to object.

While an Anglican, Perkins speaks to both the English and Reform aspects of Pietism; indeed for him the two are one and the same. Perkins prefigures and lays the groundwork for the Calvinists at the Synod of Dort years later, maintaining a doctrine known as double predestination. This notion is that God not only chooses who is saved but also who is damned, who is the Reprobate. "Predestination hath two parts: Election and Reprobation . . . Election, is Gods decree, whereby of his own free-will, he hath ordained certain men to salvation, to the praise of the glory of his grace."[13] The Reprobate equally serve the same function, giving glory to God but the manner in which they glorify God is by being justifiably eternally damned. This is also the justification for not only creation and the atonement, but also for the fall. The fall provides the justification and rationale for condemning the mass of humanity to hell. God is free to then do whatever God wants to do, which is provide the means of bringing God's self the most glory.

Opposed to this doctrine at the time is the Dutch Calvinist Jacobus Arminius. Arminius, in response to Perkins's work, maintained a notion of single predestination. God chose only the Elect but did not will the Reprobate. Arminius labeled Perkins as one of those who did "not fear to add to the Scriptures whatever they think proper, and are accustomed to attribute as much as possible to their own conceptions which they style natural ideas."[14] As far as who will win this debate, it really depends on where one looks. By the eighteenth-century England will largely hold Arminius's position, and the Reformed Dutch will hold Perkins's.

It is unquestioned for both Perkins and Arminius that man begins as sinful and in need of regeneration. This is the purpose of the law. The law exposes sin, then the law expounds upon the flesh the effects of sin. Finally the law explains the concept of justice by announcing "eternal damnation for the least disobedience, without offering any hope of pardon."[15] Of course

13. Perkins, *Golden Chain*, 33.
14. Beeke and Yuille, *William Perkins*, 50.
15. Perkins, *Golden Chain*, 148.

not all men remain unregenerate; some are chosen and for those the law is appeased by grace. "The covenant of grace, is that whereby God freely promising Christ, his benefits, exacts again of man, that he would by faith receive Christ, and repent of his sins."[16] Neither the Elect nor the Reprobate have any choice in the matter, but the law and gospel are the same, one to illustrate damnation and the other to provide the means of salvation.

This brings us to the next link of the golden chain, namely justification. For those lucky enough to be the Elect, they are made elect through the obedience of Christ and Christ's obedience to suffer death on the cross. The law and the gospel provide the avenue for faith and the accompanying repentance. Repentance is a work of grace, arising of a godly sorrow, whereby a man turns from all his sins to God. One must remember for Perkins this is not a work that merits salvation. Rather faith is simply the means of justification, and justification consists of both the remission of sins and the imputation of Christ's righteousness. The sins are no longer counted, as Christ's death appeases God's wrath. The regenerate are also counted as righteous, but not of their own righteousness, rather they "are accounted just in the sight of God through Christ's righteousness."[17] Once again justification and faith have no meaning apart from Christ. Faith is "a principal grace of God whereby man is engrafted into Christ and thereby becomes one with Christ and Christ one with him."[18]

Once man is justified, the process of sanctification begins. Sanctification has two parts, the first is mortification, where the power of sin is abated, and the second is vivification, where holiness in the elect is augmented and enlarged. Both of these parts result with the elect choosing and desiring what is holy rather than what is sinful. Becoming holy is the process of sanctification. In addition to the work of the spirit within man, Perkins believed the answer was found in the Beatitudes. The Beatitudes become instructions for holy life.

One may expect to find the sacraments as the means of sanctification, but Perkins rejects this notion. The two remaining sacraments of baptism and Eucharist, for Perkins, are not the avenues for communing with God as the Catholic and Eastern Orthodox believe. Rather sacraments differ depending on the pre-determined status of an individual. Essentially the sacrament is only a sacrament for the Elect and it is not for the Reprobate. For the Elect "A Sacrament is that, whereby Christ and his saving graces, are by certain external rites, signified, exhibited, and sealed to a Christian

---

16. Perkins, *Golden Chain*, 149.
17. Perkins, *Golden Chain*, 179.
18. Beeke and Yuille, *William Perkins*, 106.

man."[19] For the Reprobate receive only the sign, but not what the sign signifies, therefore they do not really receive a sacrament.

Perkins treatment of sign and signifier differs in many ways from conventional thinking. For example, Susanne Langer contends that "to each sign there corresponds one definite item which is its object, the thing signified."[20] Perkins holds that the sign signifies something different than what the individual may believe it actually signifies. This is not simply the case of a sign being interpreted, rather signs become symbols instead. Following Langer "the fundamental difference between signs and symbols is the difference of association, and consequently of their use by the third party to the meaning function, the subject; signs announce their object to him, whereas symbols lead him to conceive their objects."[21] While a sign is acted upon, the symbol is an instrument in thought. A sacrament is a sign for the Elect as it directly corresponds to the signifier, but for the Reprobate the same sacrament is only a symbol, a conception, and an incorrect one at that.

More important for Perkins is the added distinction of sacrament and sacrifice. Accordingly a sacrament is an act wherein God bestows grace, and a sacrifice is the faith and obedience of the Elect. The Reprobate may choose to sacrifice for God but they may never truly receive a sacrament.

This brings us to the fourth and final link in the golden chain of salvation, specifically, glorification. Upon this step the Elect is glorified, and spend eternity with God. "Those whom God hath predestinated by his absolute predestination, which cannot be lost, shall infallibly die in grace: but they which are predestinate, by that predestination which being according to present justice, may be lost by some mortal sin which follows, are not infallibly saved, but oftentimes such are condemned, and lose their crown glory."[22] The Elect, upon death and final judgment are proved to be elect and will share in this glory. They will live forever in a state of blessedness. Blessedness is defined as the condition whereby the elect enjoy fellowship with God. It is here that saints, that is the Elect, will fully be transformed into "the image of the Son of God."[23]

Perkins theology concerning salvation is in line with the theological developments of Calvinism. In fact many of his arguments are used to condemn Arminius at the Synod of Dort. Perkins theology keenly illustrates

---

19. Perkins, *Golden Chain*, 151.
20. Langer, "Logic of Signs and Symbols," 134.
21. Langer, "Logic of Signs and Symbols," 36.
22. Perkins, *Golden Chain*, 214.
23. Perkins, *Golden Chain*, 207.

the difference between the Lutheran Pietists and the Anglican Pietists, specifically in their use of theology in the early days. The Lutherans Pietists rejected the theological system that was set up by the Lutheran Scholastics, and the Anglican Pietists, not having an adequately pious theological system in place were foundational in creating one, which not only emphasizes the Scholastic tendencies in the Reform tradition, but also promoted a mechanism for pious living.

The pious living emerges largely not out of the theological advancements but from the use of the pulpit. From here we should address Perkins's writing concerning prophesying, that is preaching. "*Prophesying* was the Elizabethan term for penetrating preaching, preaching that expressed correct doctrine but also convicted of sin and gloried in Gods sovereign grace."[24] It is this revival of dynamic preaching that Stoeffler identifies as one of the hallmarks of Pietism. Preaching was also the thrust of Perkins's mission. Following Perkins death in 1602, many of his works were collected and published. In 1607 Perkins's treatment of preaching was published under the title *The Art of Prophesying*. The work is described as a Puritan classic by many. With the Bible as the supreme authority, how one is to interpret it and preach is essential to the Puritan way of life.

Perkins proposes that prophecy consists of two parts. The first is obviously preaching itself. The second is public prayer. In many ways the second is assumed under the first, and the majority of the work concerns not prayer but preaching. Preaching itself consists of two parts as well. The first is the subject of the preaching, the second is the style. Surprisingly, for a work entitled *The Art of Prophesying*, the majority of the work treats the subject rather than the style of preaching. Preparation comes before preaching and takes precedence in the work.

Obviously the subject of preaching is the Bible. In many ways Perkins echoes Calvin's concept of the Bible as a sacrament, in that scripture is an effective grace. The "sacramental Word" holds a stronger connection to the Catholic notion of sacrament than do the two remaining actual Protestant sacraments. As earlier discussed, Perkins believes that the sacraments of baptism and the Eucharist, may actually not be sacraments if the recipient is the Reprobate. Scripture on the other hand is described as "its perfection, or purity, or its eternity."[25] It remains so for all who hear it.

This naturally leads the reader to question which books count as scripture. The authority to determine what books are counted in the Christian canon is not the church, since the church is diminished. Perkins

---

24. Perkins, *Art of Prophesying*, 39.
25. Perkins, *Art of Prophesying*, 9.

hold that "The church can bear witness to the canon of Scripture, but it cannot inwardly persuade us of its authority."[26] Rather the Bible itself is the source of the authority for revealing which books are included and which are excluded. An odd imperative since the Bible is not a single work with a provided table of contents.

Regardless of the formation of the Biblical canon, Perkins maintains "The Scripture itself testifies to itself with the kind of testimony which is more certain than all human oaths."[27] The thrust of this argument is to provide two functional truths for Perkins. First, Puritans do not need the judgment of Rome to prescribe the canon. Second if one is the Elect, they, through hearing the Bible will intrinsically know which books should comprise the Biblical canon, since "The elect, having the Spirit of God, first of all discern the voice of Christ speaking in the Scriptures. Furthermore, they approve the voice which they discern."[28]

This is important for Perkins as he needs a way to modify the existing Roman canon and bring it closer to the canon supported by Luther and Calvin. Accordingly Perkins discounts the Deutero-canon on the basis of four assumptions, many of which are false or simply ill informed. Perkins believes that the Apocrypha was not written by prophets, not written in Hebrew, that the New Testament fails to appeal to these books, and that they are contrary to the rest of the Bible. While these critiques are not historically or exegetically accurate, they do echo the sentiments of Luther, Calvin, and many of the other Reformers.

Perkins actively excludes over a dozen books from the Bible, but surprisingly he does not automatically exclude all appeals to church tradition and the church Fathers in the use of interpretation. In sermon preparation, Perkins encouraged his readers to draw upon the church Fathers as well as the Reformers if they could assist with their task. The fathers and tradition serve to safeguard against some heresies. When facing a resurgence of previously condemned beliefs, Perkins finds it acceptable and even effective to utilize Patristic writings and the Councils, stating "We do not need to look for any novel way of rejecting and refuting these heresies; the ancient ones found in the Councils and the Fathers are well-tested and still reliable."[29] Still Perkins discards any appeal to these as authority if he believes they contradict his interpretation of the Bible, the sacraments, and church tradition. For example using Justin Martyr's First Apology chapter 66 to

---

26. Perkins, *Art of Prophesying*, 18.
27. Perkins, *Art of Prophesying*, 18.
28. Perkins, *Art of Prophesying*, 18.
29. Perkins, *Art of Prophesying*, 23.

argue for the real presence of Christ in the Eucharist, with no distinction for the Elect or Reprobate; or the preceding chapters on the efficacy of baptism and the Eucharist would hold no weight as Perkins's own interpretation of scripture precludes this historical understanding of the sacraments.

Perkins rejects the Catholic mode of interpretation. According to Perkins "the Church of Rome believes that passages of Scripture have four senses: the literal, the allegorical, the topological and the anagogical."[30] This is viewed as faulty and overly complex. Rather Perkins creates a new system of interpretation based upon the reading of a text. Verses are either plain or analogies. Similar statements are still found within modern Evangelicals who claim a "Strict Biblical literalism"[31] similar to John Nelson Darby's appeal in the late nineteenth century. Darby, Dwight L. Moody, and others claim to "literally" interpret the Bible, inheriting the language from Perkins.

The question still remains, what is one to do with a passage that is cryptic? How should you read an analogy? Perkins spends quite a bit of time on this process since the natural sense of the statement is hidden. Rather than appealing to historical knowledge, the church, or tradition to answer these questions, it is left to logic and reason. The problem is that logic and reason can be, and often are, skewed by one's previous ideological conceptions. For example Perkins goes out of his way to promote Calvin's notion of the Spiritual Presence of Christ in the Eucharist and discount the Lutheran, Roman Catholic, and Eastern Orthodox beliefs in the Real Presence.

In this example we see the failing of this sort of system of thought. Perkins uses his "logic" to disregard a clear statement like "This is my Body." Rather than clear, this statement becomes a philosophical puzzle to be solved. In order to solve this puzzle Perkins takes other statements that are more obscure and prioritizes them. While he may appeal to tradition earlier, this is only as a sort of proof texting, rather than viewing anything else as an authority as we saw with the example of Justin Martyr. The authority is Calvin and Perkins's own interpretation rather than the Bible itself. As Perkins himself admits, the text provides room for interpretation. The rest of the first half of the work is really setting out a new tradition in interpretation. New doctrines are introduced with a new set of supporting evidence, in many ways echoing the Lutheran Scholastics and what the Calvinists produce at Dort shortly after Perkins's death.

The last third of the work focuses on the style one should preach with rather than the source of the sermon. Perkins's style of preaching was

---

30. Perkins, *Art of Prophesying*, 25.
31. Balmer, *Mine Eyes Have Seen the Glory*, 34.

rather simple by comparison to Calvin's legal treatment of the Bible and the Protestant Scholastics on the continent. Thomas Fuller said of Perkins, "His sermons were not so plain but that the piously learned did admire them, nor so learned that the plain did understand them."[32] Style is important. In addition to being knowledgeable yet approachable, Perkins tells his readers they must be humble yet powerful.

Humility is the first step to delivering a good sermon. For Perkins this humility largely consists of letting the text speak rather than overly complicating what he believes should be clear to the audience. Also unlike the scholastics on the continent, the sermon is not the opportunity to expound on the preachers theological knowledge. The preacher should not speak in Greek, Latin, or specialized jargon that is over the head of the average hearer of the words delivered. For Perkins, "The Preaching of the Word is the testimony of God and the profession of the knowledge of Christ, not human skill."[33]

Second, the sermon must deliver the power that Perkins believes scripture is. The preacher is encouraged to gesture with both the voice and the body to drive home the point. The voice must be loud enough for all to hear and vehement in tone.[34] In addition to the gestures and tone, the minister must also not reveal their own infirmities. For Perkins, the minister still represents the whole church, therefore if they are sick or weak, it implies weakness for congregation. Ordinary people, according to Perkins, "do not distinguish between the ministry and the minister."[35]

Throughout the sermon the preacher is to remember the distinction between the law and the gospel and apply it appropriately. In order to do this, the minister must know their audience. Audiences consist of six types of people,[36] not only believers and nonbelievers, but those who are simply

---

32. Stoeffler, *Rise of Evangelical Pietism*, 51.

33. Perkins, *Art of Prophesying*, 68.

34. "The voice ought to be loud enough for all to hear (Isa 58:1; John 7:37; Acts 2:14). In the exposition of the doctrine in a sermon we ought to be more moderate, but in the exhortation more fervent and vehement. There should be a gravity about the gestures of the body which will in their own way grace the messenger of God. It is appropriate therefore, that the preacher keep the trunk of his body erect and still, while the other parts like the arm, the hand, the face and eyes may express and (as it were) speak the spiritual affections of his heart. Also speaks of the personal holiness of the minister, and grace they should possess" (Perkins, *Art of Prophesying*, 72).

35. Perkins, *Art of Prophesying*, 70.

36. Perkins, *Art of Prophesying*, 54–60.
1 Those who are unbelievers and are both ignorant and unreachable.
2 Those who are teachable, but ignorant.
3 There are those who have knowledge, but have never been humbled.

ignorant and those who need to be humbled. As Perkins explained in the *Golden Chain*, humility is an essential step, the sinner's will must be broken. Once the will is broken, God then causes faith little by little to spring and grow in the heart. The means of this is through the sermon. It is with the effective hearing of the Bible that faith is introduced and the knowledgeable come to saving knowledge. In addition to providing saving knowledge to the Elect, the minister must also provide an application from the sermon. The application can either be mental or practical. A practical application is always preferred.

Perkins offers one final point to the preacher. Knowing that the sermons are large and have many parts, it may tax the memory to remember all the points they wish to deliver. Many may choose the use of common memory aids, but Perkins urges the preachers to refrain from doing so. First he believes that the use of aids are likely to make the mind dull. In addition to this Perkins believes that the use of these aids may also allow for demonic influence, both in the mechanism and also in the reliance upon the aid rather than the Holy Spirit. Perkins concludes with the use of public prayer, as this is the second use of prophesying.

The Christian requires additional education. If the sermon is the only means of cultivating the Elect, they may fall short of a proper understanding of the Christian life and God. To this end Perkins produced a brief catechism in 1591, called *The Foundation of Christian Religion Gathered into Six Principles*. The purpose of the work is to instruct the ignorant on the basics of Christianity. The beginning of the catechism looks similar to Lutheran or Catholic Catechisms, including rehearsing of the Ten Commandments, the Lord's Prayer, and the Creed. The first three and last principles are wholly in line with others, including a belief in only one God, upholding Original Sin, believing that Christ's death on the Cross provided a substitutionary atonement granting salvation, and confirming the resurrection of the death.

The intervening two principles are unique to a Calvinist perspective. They focus on the mechanism of salvation. Having a contrite heart is the first step, but this can only occur if one is elect. Hearing the gospel is also essential, but the sacraments aid in salvation as well. Unlike the other churches which hold the sacraments as the sole or primary mechanism of salvation, hearing the Bible is prioritized above the sacraments. Furthermore

---

4 Those who have already been humbled.
5 Those who already believe.
6 Those who have fallen back. Some may have partly departed from the state of grace, either in faith or in life-style.

there are only two sacraments, and as mentioned earlier they are only of benefit if one is elect.[37]

One may naturally assume that Perkins, as the Puritan theologian of Tudor times, promoted an ascetic lifestyle, but this is not the case. Perkins believed that sound doctrine and a pious life were essential for salvation, but a pious life did not require asceticism. Food, drink, sleep, dress, and even music were acceptable, as long as they were in appropriate moderation. Sports were also acceptable, but only if they were not played on the Sabbath.

The issue of sports and the Sabbath became a central issue under James I. So much so, that in 1618, James issued a Declaration on Sports, permitting many types of sports, in direct contradiction to many Puritans who opposed all game play. Perkins impact upon Puritanism extended to how the Sabbath is viewed. Perkins's treatment of the Sabbath obviously was in line with Calvin's, and became known as Sabbatarianism.

According to Sabbatarianism, strict observance of the Sabbath is required. No ordinary work may occur. Perkins believed the Sabbath was established not at Sinai but in Eden. As God rested on the seventh day, so too man is to rest. This rest is a holy rest which would exclude all labor, and be spent worshiping God.[38] What is not an acceptable use of the day is idle leisure or playing games.

Aside from the Sabbath, work was to be done. All work was not for the individual, but for the collective good of the nation and community of saints. Like Luther's notion of the *Beruf*, all labor is tied to a calling. Man is not only called to serve God, but also called to work. Weber famously treated this issue in the *Protestant Ethic and the Spirit of Capitalism*. "The only way of living acceptably to God was not to surpass worldly morality in monastic asceticism, but solely through the fulfilment of the obligations imposed upon the individual by his position in the world. That was his calling."[39] When one does their labor well, they are laboring not for a wage, but for God.

The final issue often connected to Puritan morality is the issue of sex. It is taken as a truism in the modern usage of the term Puritan to believe that sex is something inherently evil. This is not the case from a historical perspective and very much not the case for Perkins. William Perkins was married and had children. He even gave up his post as a fellow in order to enter into marriage, illustrating just how highly he held the estate of marriage. "As for the marital bed, Perkins demonstrated little antipathy

---

37. Perkins, *Foundation of Christian Religion*, 44.
38. Beeke and Yuille, *William Perkins*, 96.
39. Weber, *Protestant Ethic*, 29.

toward the body." He viewed sex between husbands and wives as "due benevolence."[40] While encouraging couples to not burn with passion, they were encouraged to enjoy the sexual company of one another. There was further stratification of the married life. Perkins viewed his wife, and wives in general, as homemakers and advisors to their husbands, contrary than the modern notions of feminism. Still the view is not terribly retrograde for the sixteenth century from the "prince of Puritan theologians."[41]

Perkins impact during his life is rather great. Often identified as the Father of the Puritans, his life and work focused on the individual's experience of piety. Stoeffler believes that for Perkins "Piety was applied theology, theology was the intellectual foundation of piety. The basic concern was piety."[42] Still this piety was not reduced to feeling, rather it remained an issue of faith. Perkins's own faith produced waves throughout England. At the height of his fame, his works outsold Calvin's. In order to promote distribution after his death, John Legate gathered Perkins's works into three volumes in 1608–1609. These three volumes were subsequently translated into Latin, French, Dutch Italian, German, Irish, Welsh, and Spanish. The works became an essential mainstay for England. In 1611, the East India Company required that all English agents who worked for them receive three collective works, first Richard Hakluyt's *Principal Navigations of the English Nation*, then John Foxe's *Book of Martyrs*, and finally William Perkins's *Works*.

In addition to his works, Perkins greatest effect upon Puritanism was in his disciple William Ames.[43] Ames first encountered Puritanism in England's Suffolk County. Suffolk County was indebted to Perkins Puritanism more than any other. Ames attributes his own conversion to hearing the "rousing preaching of Master William Perkins, father of experimental Puritan theology."[44] As time went on, Ames became a student of Perkins and the two became close friends. Ames echoed Perkins message with an even louder voice in America, where he is "Quoted more often in the New World than either Luther or Calvin, Ames was read in Latin by undergraduates at Harvard and Yale as part of their basic instruction in divinity."[45]

---

40. Beeke and Yuille, *William Perkins*, 87.
41. Kapic and Gleason, *Devoted Life*, 19.
42. Stoeffler, *Rise of Evangelical Pietism*, 54.
43. William Ames or Amesius (1576–1633).
44. Beeke and van Vliet, " Marrow of Theology," 54.
45. Ames, *Marrow of Theology*, back cover.

The impact in America was essential as the fate of Puritanism in England was a powder keg. The keg exploded during the English Civil War of the 1640s. Oliver Cromwell set up a new haven for the Puritans but this haven could not last beyond his death. Once Cromwell died the English grew tired of Puritans and what they brought. The Civil War was a worse conflict than any in England since the Norman Conquest six hundred years earlier. With the explosion of the powder keg, all that was left was ruin in England. The blame for the Civil War was attributed to the Puritans, and with good reason. The solution was to restore the king to the throne, but following his decapitation Charles I was not able to reassume the throne. This honor was passed to his son Charles II. With the Restoration, the fires of religious enthusiasm quickly died down. The rampant "religious individualism" that characterized the earlier period as well as any form of religious enthusiasm became suspect. Perkins and his works lost favor and became obscured to the point that few of his works were reprinted in either of the Puritan reprint revivals of the nineteenth or twentieth centuries. Few Puritans remained in England, but the language and theology remained influential.

Puritanism as interpreted and perpetuated by Perkins survived but largely only outside of England. Puritans take their theological vision of the world and move it to the colonies England is establishing in North America. Central to the Puritan regime is the Massachusetts Bay Colony. Ever since the early waves of Puritan persecution at the hands of William Laud in the 1630s, Puritans sought a new home. Some chose to immigrate to the Netherlands, but many more chose the New World, with the desire to rid themselves of the apostasy of Anglicanism and set up a true Calvinist society. This new Calvinist society began in Plymouth as a new Geneva on a larger scale.

The Plymouth colony survived, but by 1692 the colony was changed from a theocracy to a secular form of government, and the Puritans ceased to be a major political force. Ames and Perkins's works remained an important feature of any library. The typical Plymouth Colony library had a Bible, Henry Ainsworth's translation of the Psalms, and the works of William Perkins. Ames's works were read at Harvard and Yale, ensuring some degree of theological fealty to early Puritan ideals.

Puritanism in America and England continued its descent in the eighteenth century, but Perkins impact upon Anglican and Calvinist theology remained. His *Golden Chain*, and the crucial links of predestination, justification, sanctification, and glorification remain the basic framework for Protestant doctrines of the atonement. Following the Armenian position concerning predestination, Wesley and Palmer further challenge Perkins theological conclusions, and Schleiermacher and many theological Liberals will interpret the doctrine as the predestination of humanity rather than individuals, but still the chain remains. Perkins emphasis on preaching, including an emphasis on style, also has lasting repercussions for preachers in England, America, and continental Europe. Furthermore, Perkins illustrates beyond a shadow of a doubt that Pietism is not simply a Lutheran phenomenon, as he was a Calvinist Anglican who dismissed many notions of Lutheran Orthodoxy and tried to make room for genuine experience of the Divine in England following the Reformation.

JOHANN ARNDT (1555-1621)
—EXPERIENTIALIST REVIVALIST

"What Profit is it to be honored by all the world, if we are despised by God?"[46]

— Johann Arndt

Johann Arndt's role in Pietism is crucial while pointing out the difficulty with most definitions of Pietism. Depending on when scholars date the beginning of Pietism, Arndt is either the father of Pietism, the Grand-Father of Pietism, or evidence that Pietism is an expression of experiential Christianity as a thread that has always existed in Christianity in general and in Protestantism specifically. R. Friedman contends, "Arndt can be regarded as the real 'father of Pietism,' who transformed the doctrine of the Word, as Luther understood it, into an ethical doctrine, and thereby changed the experience of justification into one of sanctification." Stoeffler contends that "The father of Lutheran Pietism is not Spener but John Arndt."[47]

Regardless of how one wishes to date Pietism, Arndt undoubtedly gave shape to the Lutheran expression, and must be included as foundational. This shift to an ethical doctrine for Lutheranism led Albert Schweitzer to call Arndt the "prophet of interior Protestantism."[48] The popularity of Arndt merits discussion concerning his influence of Pietism. His devotional works were the basis for Spener and many Pietists who followed. As a model, prophet, forerunner, or father of a movement, Arndt's work demonstrates the Pietistic ethos that lasted for centuries. Spener, Francke, and others base their understanding of Christianity on Arndt's *True Christianity*, and the experience of Christ therein.

Comparatively little is known of Arndt given his impact as the bestselling devotional author of the seventeenth century. Unlike other Pietists and notable clergy Arndt kept no journal or other record of his life, and upon his death no inventory of his library or letters were collected. Of the sources we have of his life most are fabrications attempting to make a saint or sinner out of the man. Johann Arndt was born on December 17, 1555 the son of Jakob Arndt, a village pastor in Edderitz bei Köthen who was ordained two years before Johann was born, and Anna Söchtings. Jakob and Anna had three children of which Johann was the oldest. 1555 is an auspicious year; the Peace of Augsburg was signed granting legal status to

---

46. Arndt, *Garden of Paradise*, 215.
47. Stoeffler, *Rise of Evangelical Pietism*, 203.
48. Arndt, *True Christianity*, 1.

the Lutheran confession held by the Arndt family. Johann grew up with an established legal though contentious Lutheranism. Lutheranism was still in the throes of establishing its Orthodoxy during his formative years. This tension is evidenced in in Arndt's life and works.

Johann's early life is shrouded from view. The Arndts moved at some point from Edderitz bei Köthen to Ballendstedt, with Jakob accepting a congregation there. The move was mixed for the family, as Jakob was horned by his congregation but also died within a decade of his appointment in 1565. No information exists for Johann until he began his education at the University at Helmstadt at age nineteen. The University was recently formed by the Lutheran Duke who wanted to combat the creep of Calvinism into his duchy. Martin Chemnitz and David Chytraeus, who helped form the Book of Concord, assisted in the establishment of the school, ensuring Lutheran fidelity. Following the completion of his degree in philosophy Johann decided to continue his studies at Helmstedt. He chose to study medicine but this pursuit was ill fated, as his own health began to suffer. Johann came to the realization that being an aspiring doctor could not overcome his own illness. Before the year's end his attentions began to focus on the next life. Undoubtedly his philosophy degree, which included some theology, and his memories of his pastor father pushed Johann towards his ultimate future as a church leader. Some stories of Arndt's decision to pursue theology seem reminiscent of Luther. Luther's first life changing moment was grounded in a prayer to Saint Anna in the thunderstorm, where he pleaded with her that if his life was saved he would join a monastery. Arndt's illness resulted in his vowing that if he recovered he would dedicate his life to theology. While not the same as Luther taking up the Augustinian habit, the story provides a good Lutheran tale, similar to Luther but with an acceptable Protestant emphasis. Instead of seeking out a saint as Luther did, Arndt addresses his prayers to God directly. Similarly, instead of becoming a monk, Arndt studies theology.

In any case Arndt's pursuit of medicine ended as quickly as it began and he shifts his attention toward theology. Leaving Helmstedt, he commenced his studies of theology at Wittenberg the following year. Wittenberg was at this time, and remained for centuries, the center of Lutheran scholasticism. While at Wittenberg, Arndt was engulfed in the crypto-Calvinist controversies of the day. Melanchthon and the crypto-Calvinists swayed Arndt until he left Wittenberg to study in Strasburg, where Johannes Papus suppressed Calvinist theology in favor of a more "orthodox" Lutheran perspective.

In 1582 Arndt's life began to take shape in two complementary and contrasting directions. Johann wed Anna Wagner and had a marriage most described as happy, even though they remained childless. That same year or early in the next Johann was ordained to the deaconate. Arndt's ministerial life grew both in its scope, becoming a pastor in Badeborn in 1583, and in controversies.

The next twenty years were contentious. Arndt's chief adversary was his Calvinist Duke Johann Georg of Anhalt (d. 1618). The Duke possessed an unrealistic goal, desiring the Lutheran Churches to conform to Calvinist prescriptions. The two key areas of conflict were the use of images in worship and the practice of exorcism before baptism. The Duke's standard was not one most Lutheran ministers would accept, though it was clear that for political expediency it was necessary. Arndt's steadfast refusal resulted in his dispossession in 1590. It was also at this time that Arndt published his first theological tract, *Ikonographia*. In this work he argues against the Iconoclasm that gripped the Protestant world, blaming Calvin and Theodore Beza as the propitiators of this harmful doctrine. This direct attack against Calvin and his refusal to abandon the practice of exorcism did not sit well with the Duke and Arndt was barred from the pulpit and forced to quickly move on from Anhalt. The Duke quickly replaced Arndt and other Lutheran pastors with Calvinist clergy. Arndt believed that he was forever in exile from his home because of his stand against the Duke, wringing "I am an exile, as I was driven out of Anhalt by the Calvinists."[49]

Not to be outdone, Arndt founded an asylum in Quedlinburg that same year. Though not facing the ire of the Duke, the townspeople of Quedlinburg were at best ambivalent to Arndt. Many of the townsfolk liked his long Lutheran sermons; he even had some of his old parishioners travel three hours from Anhalt to hear him speak. But for the less devout the long sermons were taxing. Furthermore, Arndt differed from a number of his fellow Lutheran clergy by opposing compulsory attendance. This actually alienated the laity as the belief that attendance aided or assured salvation was common. Arndt, from the beginning of his decade tenure at Quedlinburg, desired true piety from his congregation and not simple attendance. Arndt also sought to reform the education system in Quendlinburg, publishing *De Antiqua Philosophia*. The message of *De Antiqua* mirrors his criticism of church attendance. Arndt desired practical application rather than simple theoretical knowledge. He always sought experiential piety and not simply theological assent. In the end it was not confessional allegiances, but his forceful preaching and poor politicking that caused him so much trouble in Quendlinburg.

---

49. van Voorhis, *Johann Arndt*, 86.

If it were only for a call of increased experiential piety Arndt's time in Quendlinburg may have continued unabated until he chose to move on or retire. Unfortunately, the plague swept through the region in 1598 and three thousand or so citizens of Quendlinburg died. Arndt chose to rely too heavily upon his younger clergy to assist with the sick, both in their medical and spiritual needs. While he began a relationship with the young Johann Gerhard at this time, most of the city began to favor other pastors, and his payment was often delayed. While there was probably little that could have been done with such a high death toll, the constant call to repentance did not sit well with the survivors, or at least that is what Arndt reported to the Abbess Anna von Stollberg.

In 1599, Arndt was transferred to St. Martin's Church at Brunswick, also known as Braunchshweig. The following year he was involved in another political storm. Braunchshweig was not an imperial city but was allied to the local Duke Heinrich Julius. The Duke sought to control the city and a crisis ensued. Arndt favored the more conservative patricians, those who ruled the city up until the crisis, but their voice was not echoed by the growing merchant class. Unfortunately for Arndt the merchant class was much larger in his congregation and his choice to side with the old guard only seeded hostility and resentment. More controversy arose in 1605, but this time from his fellow Lutheran clergy. The source of the dispute was the first book *Wahres Christentum,* or *True Christianity.* The publication of *True Christianity* signaled the final confrontation Arndt faced. After already alienating the Dukes, merchants, and now the clergy, Arndt's ultimate success with *True Christianity* was unforeseen at best. By 1605 the *Book of Concord* was twenty-five years old and Lutheran Orthodoxy was established. The problem with *True Christianity* was that it no longer fit within the mold of Lutheranism. The work was not Calvinist, Catholic, or Anabaptist; it was mystical and not purely theological. The focus was the practice of Christian life, not the established theological debates that Lutheran Scholastics wanted to address. This challenge to the traditional Lutheran Orthodoxy served to relax the rigid Lutheran orthodoxy, and to introduce a devotional element that was sorely missing.

The question among scholars though is how to define the nature of *True Christianity* and Arndt for the last fifteen years of his life. Was he a mystic or experientialist? Some believe that the purpose behind the fifth book was to promote the idea of mystical union with Christ, and as such Arndt should be numbered with Jakob Boehme and Valentin Weigel as

Lutheran mystics. The connection between Arndt and mysticism following his death is unmistakable. Many of his followers, including Friedrich Dame (d. 1635), and Paulus Egardus (d. 1643), wrote mystical tracts *Of the Old and the New Man*, and *Exposition of the Book of Job*, mirroring the themes of Arndt's *True Christianity*. Indeed it is clear to see the influence that Thomas à Kempis, Johannes Tauler, Angela da Foligno, and Valentine Weigel have in the work, but the question of whether this was the aim of Arndt, or just the source material he was borrowing from remains unanswered.

Against the clear mystical language of Stoeffler contends that "The central theme of Arndt was not that of union. For that reason he ought not to be referred to as a mystic. It was that of a new life, an emphasis which is of the very essence of Pietism."[50] Arndt urges an individual revival, a transformation to a new life in Christ. The old life is abandoned and surrendered to Christ and the individual Christian is made new in Christ. This language is directly from Tauler, a mystic. Instead of the mystics call for a mystical union with Christ, Arndt wants a practical reform. The difference is not great except for the accessibility for the average Christian. Arndt does not want to argue that only the mystics are true Christians. If this was the case, then Protestantism in general and Lutheranism specifically is doomed to fail. Most of the Catholic mystics were monastics and without a monastic community the promotion of mysticism within the Lutheran Church as the only real form of Christianity serves only to point out the deficiencies of the Reformation. The slight difference of language separates the experience of God found in the pre-Reformation mystics from the monastic community. Arndt still calls for a new life with Christ, but not union with Christ as modeled by the communities of monks and nuns. This distinction is important for Arndt in the sixteenth century and is increasingly less important for later Pietists.

Arndt defines the true Christian as the one who experiences God, not one who merges themselves with God. The first step in this experience of God is not the notion of election as Perkins advocated, rather it is found in Christ's atonement. The focus of *True Christianity* is on the atonement and its impact on the heart of the believer. Arndt believes that true Christianity involves a non-monastic union with Christ that reaches a true transformation and can only take place after the heart is open to God. It is easy to conflate transformation with mystical union as they do share many traits in common. In many ways the work promotes a monasticism for the individual. There exist all the spiritual benefits of the monastic cell without the cell, monastic community, or monastic rules. This is why we see the

---

50. Stoeffler, *Rise of Evangelical Pietism*, 209.

proliferation of *True Christianity* to such a wide audience. Arndt saw twenty editions of the work before his death and a total of six books expanding the concepts laid out in the first book. The appeal to a light mysticism brought Arndt under heavy criticism. Books five and six were specifically written in order to defend himself in front of his fellow Lutheran clergy. In none of these works does he simply abandon himself to the idea that his experiences are those of a mystic, rather they reflect a newness of life that is far more open and common to every Christian.

There were some clergy who supported Arndt and *True Christianity*, though they are outweighed by the detractors. Polycarp Leyser argued that "The book is good, only when the reader is good."[51] Others, such as Paulus Wolf, opposed the work because it appeared to support a Calvinist understanding on predestination. Once Arndt clearly stated his support for the Lutheran view this objection faded. Writing Petrus Piscator in January 1607, Arndt further cemented his allegiance to Lutheranism, maintaining that he relied upon the Formula of Concord for this understanding of original sin and its effects in this age. He also insisted that the work was clearly Lutheran and opposed to the Papists and Synergists. The frequent use of Catholic mystics, while concerning, was overlooked since Luther cited many of these same mystics as well. The charge of synergism was the greatest difficulty to overcome for most Orthodox Lutherans. Even Gerhard, who was encouraged to study theology by Arndt, challenged him on this matter. Arndt maintained that over twenty places in *True Christianity* show his opposition to this theological position.

With the success of *True Christianity*, Arndt published a prayer book to help the believer experience divine grace, called *Paradiesgartlein aller christlichen Tugenden, The Garden Paradise: Or, Holy Prayers And Exercise: Whereby The Christian Graces And Virtues May Be Planted And Improved In Man, Pursuing The Design Of The Famous Treaties Of True Christianity.* In *The Garden Paradise*, Arndt offers prayers on dozens of issues such as thanksgiving, Christian Graces, the suffering of Christ, self-denial, friendship, and contempt of the world. These all serve as meditative guides, not to enter into a mystical union with God, but as an expression of a new creature of God.

Beginning as early as 1616 Arndt's health began to suffer. His sickness led him to write his last will and testament. Recovering slightly, he once again complained about sickness in 1619. Arndt finally succumbed and reposed on May 11, 1621, telling his wife that he had seen the glory of the Lord

---

51. van Voorhis, *Johann Arndt*, 8.

and "I have now overcome."⁵² His impact upon Lutheranism grew following his death as Lutherans sought further devotional works to encourage them through that time. His works *Wahres Christentum, True Christianity* and *Paradiesgartlein aller christlichen Tugenden, The Garden Paradise*, fit the needs of the time, Arndt dying just three years into the Thirty Years War. These two works, far more than his career as a Lutheran pastor, tell us what Arndt and later Pietists believe "True Christianity" is and what practices it follows. To best understand the theological legacy of Arndt, I will address the central themes and characteristics in his transformational work.

Arndt's series of six books of *True Christianity* began with book one, *Liber Scripturae*, the book of Scripture. This book opens with a seemingly simple question to his Lutheran audience in the seventeenth century. Following the settlement of Lutheran scholasticism Lutherans should be able to answer the question "what is the image of God in man?" More precisely Arndt is asking, "What is man and his relation to God?" Arndt quickly answers the question, stating that the image of God in man "is in the conformity of the human soul, understanding, spirit, mind, will and all internal and external bodily and spiritual powers with God and the Holy Trinity and with all divine qualities, virtues, wills, and characteristics."⁵³ An answer that faced little opposition. Throughout the rest of the work, Arndt unpacks notions of conformity of the human soul and he does so within an established Lutheran theological paradigm, law and gospel. Like Martin Luther, Arndt's beginning assumption is that man is in need of a savior and this is the point of the work. While the opening question is answered within the scholastic framework, the remainder of the work goes far beyond the typical Lutheran Scholastic's interpretation of God and Man.

In Martin Luther's *Heidelberg Disputation*, the basic frame work for his theology is constructed. The very first thesis Luther makes is the law of God. Throughout the work, Luther's theology focuses on a dialectic between the Law, which is futile to save, and the Gospel of Christ, which is full of grace. Lutheran scholars such as Timothy Lull contend that the law and the gospel are the two key poles of understanding Luther's conception of the Christian Life.⁵⁴ Arndt's theology follows a similar pattern when he contends that "If Christ and his holy blood are to be our medicine we must first be ill."⁵⁵ A sickness is present in man, that sickness is sin.

52. van Voorhis, *Johann Arndt*, 9.

53. Arndt, *True Christianity*, 29.

54. Dr. Timothy Lull was president of the Pacific Lutheran Theological Seminary (ELCA) in Berkeley, California. He gave countless lectures on this topic while I was his student, before his death in 2003.

55. Arndt, *True Christianity*, 55.

For Arndt this sin is the starting point of all. "Indeed, the man who lives in such sins lives in Adam, and in the old-birth, indeed, in the Devil himself."[56] Man begins in sin, which is enmity toward Christ. The entire Christian life is therefore defined as "a spiritual battle against original sin and the rooting out of this by the Holy Spirit."[57] It is for this reason that Christ died, and it is here, like Luther, that the gospel is preached.

For Luther and most Protestant Reformers, the law is futile to save on its own; its only real purpose is to illustrate the need for God's grace as found in the preaching and hearing of the gospel. As such, the gospel is the key to the Christian life. The heart of the gospel is not only Christ's sacrifice but also what this sacrifice does. First, and most straightforward, is the process of justification. Man, who is inherently sinful, finds himself justified before God. Justification is based upon Christ's death on the cross; this is the atonement for humanities sins. Unlike the Calvinist view held by Perkins, Arndt remains firmly Lutheran and believes that the atonement is a general atonement. Salvation may not be universal, but the atonement is not limited, as Perkins and Calvin maintain. The Christian's justification is based solely upon Christ's atonement and not due to the Christians actions. Man's only possible reaction to Christ's sacrifice is to worship Christ. "True worship must proceed from the ground of the heart out of faith, love, and humility."[58] This worship does not justify man, nor does it save, but it does make one holy.

For Arndt, as with many Lutheran Christo-Calvinists, Calvinists, Reform theologians, and possibly Luther, the key to the gospel is the surrender of self towards the process of sanctification. As Arndt put it, "man does not act according to his self-will, but his will is God's will; man has no self-love, but God is his love; no self-honor, but God is to be his honor; no wealth but God is his wealth and possession without any love of creature and the world."[59] The process of sanctification is an ongoing personal revival wherein everything is based upon "the rebirth and renewal of man."[60]

This renewal results in man being different than before, not only in their standing with God, but also the Christian is a fundamentally new creature.[61] This new creature is one who is justified and undergoing

---

56. Arndt, *True Christianity*, 68.
57. Arndt, *True Christianity*, 188.
58. Arndt, *True Christianity*, 132.
59. Arndt, *True Christianity*, 31.
60. Arndt, *True Christianity*, 49.
61. "Note that Christ is thus in you the way to life; in him you are a new creature" (2 Cor 5:17).

sanctification, where the old sinful self is forcibly evicted from one's life and replaced with a creature capable of worshiping God. Arndt describes the struggle by saying "In each true Christian are two men, an inner man and an outer man. These two live together but they oppose one another. The life of the one is the death of the other. If the external man lives and rules, the internal man dies. If the internal man lives the external man must die."[62] This language is clearly a reference to Tauler. Central to Tauler's mysticism was the conflict between the old and new man. Tauler "Points to a renewal of the outer and inner man, and shows how man must deny himself and die to all to which he cleaves and is attached by nature; and how God will then make His dwelling-place in him."[63] Arndt echoes this tenet. The old man must die in order for the new man to live.

The true Christian, as described in *True Christianity*, is one whose life is made new through faith. For Arndt, as for most Pietists, theology and doctrine are worth very little in themselves and their only value is in service to the new life of faith. Arndt sets up an ecclesiological tension between what the Protestant Scholastics were fighting for and his vision of Christianity. The tension is between a theological understanding of justification and sanctification and the experientialist model wherein faith is found in "a joyous, happy, and living trust, by which I discover in myself, in a strong and consoling way, God's power, how he holds me and bears me, and how I live, move and have my being in him."[64] Faith is about living rather than knowing. Here Arndt agrees with à Kempis, who argues "True peace of heart, then, is found in resisting passions, not in satisfying them."[65] Faith which creates the new man is an ongoing battle against the old through constant attention to the life of faith.

This life finds its joy in Christ, not in this world and not in the things of this world. As man is made new his pleasures are only found in personal renewal and growing closer to God and farther from his old sick and sinful nature. Arndt maintains that "this repentance and conversion is the denial of oneself."[66] This denial includes the mortification of the flesh[67] in addition to the rejection of the world. In the emphasis towards personal renewal, Arndt draws heavily upon Thomas à Kempis. This renewal is a constant choosing of the cross over all the benefits of this world. With à Kempis primarily on

---

62. Arndt, *True Christianity*, 87.
63. Tauler, *Inner Way*, 199.
64. Arndt, *True Christianity*, 111. Arndt uses Acts 17:28 here.
65. à Kempis, *Imitation of Christ*, 6.
66. Arndt, *True Christianity*, 42.
67. Arndt, *True Christianity*, 41.

his mind in Book One, Arndt borrows from other mystics as well. One can easily read Angela da Foligno and Johannes Tauler's views of poverty and renouncing the world as the source of joy in this chapter as well.

In Book Two of *True Christianity*, Arndt continues his focus on the transformation that accompanies sanctification. Many chapters of the second book of *True Christianity*, are adapted from Angela da Foligno. It is easy to see the notion of penance borrowed from Foligno, when Arndt preserves the idea that the true Christian must constantly judge themselves "according to the heart, be certain that it is internal and not a mere external appearance."[68] The Christian life is too easy to put on without any real changes to either the heart or life of the Christian. Like Foligno, Arndt witnesses a constant procession of piety. Steps are repeated and greater intimacy with God is the benefit.

Within Book Two, Tauler's influence is still manifest. The death of the old man and life of the new is found not only in renouncing this world, as is key for Foligno, but also with the growing new life of the Christian. As such, Arndt emphasizes the fruits of the spirit that must then accompany the Christian life. In so doing he synthesizes the mysticism of both Foligno and Tauler.

The answer of how to best judge yourself is found in Book Three. Once again Arndt bases this chapter upon Tauler. In this book, Arndt explains that the true Christian must find the kingdom of God within themselves rather than from the outside world, including the theological proofs that are championed by the various Protestant Orthodoxies. Very clearly Arndt contends that "Perfection is not, as some think, a high, great, spiritual, heavenly joy and meditation, but it is a denial of one's own will, love, honor, a knowledge of one's nothingness a continual completion of the will of God, a burning love for neighbor, a heart-held compassion, and, in a word, a love that desires, think's, and seeks nothing other than God alone insofar as this is possible in the weakness of this life. In this is true Christian virtue, true freedom and peace in the conquering of the flesh and fleshly affections."[69]

Arndt' discussion of perfection draws heavily upon Tauler once again. When Tauler speaks of perfection, he states "A perfect will is an abandonment of all that is not God. If a man hath not done this in works, he must do it in will if he will be perfect."[70] In addition to drawing from Tauler, it is clear that Arndt leans heavily on à Kempis as well. à Kempis points out that "he who desires perfection must be very diligent . . . Our outward and inward

---

68. Arndt, *True Christianity*, 203.
69. Arndt, *True Christianity*, 224.
70. Tauler, *Following of Christ*, 136.

lives alike must be closely watched and well ordered, for both are important to perfection."[71] All three would also agree that "Every perfection in this life has some imperfection mixed with it."[72] None of these men will go so far as to argue for Christian Perfectionism that we will find with Wesley. For Tauler, à Kempis, and Arndt, perfection is a process that remains incomplete and momentary at best. Perfection is the act of repentance, not a permanent state of the Christian. Repentance is its own reward, for as à Kempis states, "neither fear nor sorrow shall come upon you at the hour of death."[73]

In the remaining books Arndt seeks to strike a balance between himself and his fellow Lutheran clergy by illustrating the place of the church in the Christian life. Likely many of Arndt's critics noticed the liberal usage of medieval Catholics and were accusing him of either being too mystical or too Catholic, and in no way a good Lutheran. Arndt primarily seeks to appease his critics by validating the sacraments, especially baptism. Baptism is the vow of the Christian to become a true Christian. This vow is then maintained and encouraged through the sacrament of the Eucharist. The Eucharist bears witness to the baptism. Arndt clearly values the efficacy of sacraments much more than Perkins and Calvinists do. Still, for Arndt the Christian life is found not only in the two remaining sacraments of the church, but in the individual's meditation, prayer, and contemplation. This never appeased the scholastic minded Lutheran clergy. Arndt always found scholasticism to be a tool of division and conflict. As evidenced in Arndt's letter to Duke August on January 29, 1621 "streitsüchtigen theologie daraus fast wieder eine theologica scholastica ist,"[74] Quarrelsome theology is almost always scholastic theology.

In *The Garden of Paradise*, also known simply as Johann Arndt's Book of Prayers, Arndt presents what the meditation and prayers of the Christian should be. There exists the same theological message as in *True Christianity*, but now directed towards God from the Christian, rather than from Arndt to his readers. Arndt models what he expects the Christian prayer life to be, with the common theme of repentance, a vehement rejection of the life in this world and a plea to God to renew himself. "Holy, heavenly, merciful Father, I lament and confess before thee, that by nature I am altogether carnal, unholy, ungodly, having suffered myself to be guided and governed

---

71. à Kempis, *Imitation of Christ*, 15.
72. à Kempis, *Imitation of Christ*, 3.
73. à Kempis, *Imitation of Christ*, 25.
74. van Voorhis, *Johann Arndt*, 180.

by my Flesh and Blood, and by the impulse of the evil Spirit, rather than by thy holy, pure, and gracious Spirit."[75]

Arndt is consistent throughout both works in demonstrating his belief that Christianity is far more than a theological understanding, but is found in an experiential life of self-denial and renewal. While Arndt tries to remain within the ecclesial bounds of the Lutheran Church, his message often rejects not only the prevailing trends within Lutheranism, but the role of the church as the sanctifying body. While Lutheranism rejected the Roman Catholic claim that salvation was found within the church and the sacraments administered by her, Arndt and most Pietists following him continue the departure from the view that salvation is a corporate act. The critics of Pietism are correct when they assert that Pietism creates an individualized Christianity. As M. Schmidt and Christos Yannaras in his article "The Freedom of Morality" state, the result of Arndt's theological message is an individual and individualistic piety. "It is individual piety and the subjective process of 'appropriating salvation' made absolute and autonomous, and it transfers the possibility of man's salvation to the realm of individual moral endeavor."[76] While Arndt tries to maintain salvation as something found within the church, the sacraments become secondary to salvation, and the members of the church are decreasingly the body of Christ and increasingly individuals working on their own personal renewal, rather than a choir of voices worshiping the same God. As mentioned earlier, Arndt's pseudo-rejection of mysticism while simultaneously maintaining the experience of the same mystics is an attempt to individualize the monastic experience of God for the Lutheran.

Arndt's intensified individualist Christianity spread throughout the Protestant world as a constant counterbalance to the scholastic system. In most cases, readers of *True Christianity* remained within their Protestant confessions. Remaining Lutheran, Anglican, or Reform may have potentially served as a check against the individualist impulse that accompanies Pietism. Nevertheless, for the next century or so, the attention of Arndt's followers on the Continent was exclusively focused on experiencing personal revivals rather than a revival of the church or culture at large. This does not take away from Arndt's legacy as the impetus for experiential Christianity transforming Protestant Christianity for subsequent generations.

Arndt begins the Pietistic practice of advocating for an experiential revival. Anthony Wallace points out that revivals tend towards three forms of identification, traditional, foreign, or utopian, or a combination thereof.

---

75. Arndt, *Garden of Paradise*, 33.
76. Yannaras, "Pietism as an Ecclesiological Heresy," 119–36.

In very clear ways Arndt advocates for a traditional and utopian revival. Knowing that advocating for a traditional revival lends itself towards Catholic monasticism, Arndt tempers this with notions of utopianism. In doing so he validates the pattern for future Pietists to seek medieval mystics as a source of authority while holding out hope for a mystical utopian revival. For Wesley this is fundamental to their developing doctrines of Christian perfection. Furthermore, Arndt's transformation of the doctrine of the Word into a lived ethical doctrine allows other Pietists to intensify their doctrine of sanctification and apply an outsider ethic to theology. Foligno, à Kempis, and to a great degree Tauler are also thoroughly incorporated within Pietism following Arndt. The return to a pure anti-Catholic Christian past does not need to extend much before the days of the Medici Popes for Arndt and other Pietists. Ardnt's *True Christianity* also serves as the theological playbook for Lutheran Pietism from his death through the middle of the eighteenth century.

The legacy of *True Christianity* is the lasting legacy of Arndt. Instead of fading away a pastor who alienated all strata of society, his monumental work grew to dominate not only discussion of Christianity in Germany but throughout all of Europe. Wittenburg, under Abraham Calov and Johann Quenstedt, began teaching from *True Christianity* by the second half of the seventeenth century. By 1740 sixty-five other works were published either defending or criticizing *True Christianity*. Furthermore, within a century of his death, *True Christianity* had over 140 editions, and was translated into over a dozen languages including expected languages such as English, French, Dutch, Swedish, Danish, and less expected ones such as Hebrew and Old Church Slavonic. Between 1660 and 1821 *True Christianity* was second only to the Bible in estate inventories of Europe, having one quarter of the number, but twice as many copies as the third most popular work, à Kempis's *The Imitation of Christ*. Apocryphal stories also emerged surrounding the tome, including its miraculous ability to survive a fire and a story of a Jesuit library in Madrid giving out a copy of the work as an example of the best devotional book, albeit with the cover altered and the work renamed. *True Christianity* is not only an example of Lutheran Piety in the Early Modern Period but also a phenomenon which dominated devotional work for a century after Arndt's death.

PHILIP SPENER (1635-1705) — ANTIPATHY TOWARDS CHRISTIAN CULTURE

> "Theology is a practical discipline and does not consist only of knowledge, study alone is not enough."[77]
>
> — Philip Jakob Spener

The next stone laid upon the edifice of Pietism and the prime inheritor of Arndt's revivalist message was Phillip Jakob Spener. Spener broadened the scope of Lutheran Pietism beyond the individual in his attempt to stand against the wave of modernity. As William Cardwell Prout argues, "The publication of Spener's *Pia Desideria* in 1675 with its attack on the contemporary Lutheran Church and a reform platform, was the official launching of a new religious movement."[78]

Like Perkins and Arndt, Spener, as well as the direct inheritors of his teachings and practice, Herman August Francke and Count Nicholas von Zinzendorf, are products of their time. Spener was born in the town of Rappolstein in the Upper Alsace,[79] not far from Strasbourg, on January 13, 1635, in the middle of the Thirty Years War. The war was only in its infancy when Arndt died. By Spener's birth it had raged in the German cities and countryside for seventeen years. While the war could have ended the year Spener was born, Catholic France decided to join the Protestant side of the war against their co-religionists, the Hapsburgs. The French intervention moved the conflict from one between Protestant countries in Northern Europe, such as Denmark and Sweden, to one where Catholics faced each other on both sides of the front. The net result was a devastated Holy Roman Empire, and a war that lasted another thirteen years. Eventually the war ended with the treaty of Westphalia in 1648. Anywhere between 30 and 50 percent of the population of the Holy Roman Empire died. The war weakened the Empire; not only was its population decimated, but there was also economic collapse and a fractured political system. The Thirty Years War became the lens through which Germans viewed their future. The existential dread that accompanied the modern period that Giddens addresses can clearly be found during the post war period. The primal fears of death and loss, economic and political changes, as well as increased secularism, contributed to this ontological insecurity.

---

77. Spener, *Pia Desideria*, 112.
78. Prout, "Spener," 48.
79. At this time, Alsace was a part of the Holy Roman Empire and not France.

With such great losses, there were many changes to the socio-economic structure of the Holy Roman Empire, and Europe as a whole. One unforeseen change was the decrease in price of grain throughout the seventeenth century as England and Prussia developed agrarian mercantilism. The basic cost of goods moved away from local farming communities, and increasingly became a global commodity. The war also reworked longstanding power structures. The old nobility made way to new absolutist rulers. The clergy was also affected by these changes. The Catholic clergy became increasingly remote. While they maintained a degree of wealth, as their estates ensured a livelihood, this varied by location. The Protestant clergy was more immediate to their parishioners, but faced similar economic challenges, as did their congregation. In either case, the clergy lost power as the princes sought to eliminate "the dead hand of the church" from everyday life. In many ways science, distinct from any form of theology, came into its own, leading to the Enlightenment. These changes echo the fragmentation and dispersal of society that concerns Giddens's treatment of modernity. Both in economics and secularization, the traditional society was evaporating.

This period was one of increasing secularization as faith in the scholastic preachers waned. While the religious reformers of the sixteenth century placed their trust in their princely authorities, this resulted in the Thirty Years War. With the war over, these governments became increasingly secular. Despite the fact that the princes desired religious uniformity in their realm and mandated that their subjects attend church, this was rarely done out of a notion of religious conviction.

Spener, like all Germans, was forced to react to this thrust of modernism. Spener was better equipped to deal with these challenges than most. His education illustrates his position in society as well as his passions. Spener's early education was as a student by the court preacher at Rappolstein, Joachim Stall. Under Stall, Spener received a classic and pious education, learning Greek, Latin, history, and philosophical science. In 1651 Spener entered the University of Strasburg, where his uncle was a Professor of Jurisprudence. At this time Spener earned an income by tutoring two princes from the Palatinate. At eighteen he received his Master's in Philosophy after a disputation with Thomas Hobbes. After two years of traveling in Basin,

Bern, and Geneva, Spener returned to Strasbourg for his doctoral studies. By 1664 Spener received his Doctorate in Theology, on the same day as his marriage to Susanna Erhardt, a young widow. Throughout this time Spener was intimately familiar with the rationalistic secularizing tendencies of his day, yet he refrained from impious actions such as drinking, dancing, or fencing matches that his fellow students engaged in.

Spener's early life may be representative of Richard Antoun's notion of fundamentalism, namely, Antoun's claim that all fundamentalists place "God and his sacred scriptures, as well as the struggle for good and evil, at the center of both individual and group concern."[80] While a part of the secularizing world in colleges, Spener refrained from the everyday social actions of his classmates. Even more so, he did not engage in theological studies on Sundays. Echoing the Sabbatarianism found in Perkins's England, Sundays were a day of devotion. Spener read the sacred scriptures as devotion and not an object of study. Spener also engaged in the secular world with prominent thinkers of the day, like Hobbes. Spener's life was guided through a removal from the profane practices of everyday life.

The University of Strasbourg sought to keep Spener as a faculty member, but he refrained from this honor. Instead he became the chief pastor in Frankfurt in 1666. This move to Frankfurt placed Spener as the foremost religious leader of the chief city of Protestant Germany. As the "spiritual counselor of all Germany,"[81] he sought to enforce legislation that resulted in a more religious society. Unlike the purely inward focus of Arndt, Spener attempted to physically reform the society by such actions as eliminating trade on Sundays and curbing ostentatious attire. These actions were not unheard of, but they met with poor results. Following Marshall Sahlins, Spener had a difficult time reconciling his structure and this event. Spener's society was structured in such a way that the religious leader enforced the dictates of everyday life. In his religious education, Spener saw how Martin Luther shaped the civil life of Wittenberg, along with the religious life. The chief pastor dictating everyday life was reinforced by his travels to Geneva following his Master's degree. While society may be profane, it was the duty of the pastor to bring the sacred. Spener was forced to shift from a leader of civic life to a protest against the displacement of religion.

Over the next three years, Spener's view of religion shifted from a top down model to one that increasingly focused on the laity. This focus on the laity becomes increasingly important for Pietism in general. Spener's shift towards the laity began through a conflict with the city governance. Gottfried

---

80. Antoun, *Understanding Fundamentalism*, 16.
81. Spener, *Philip Jacob Spener*, 12.

Foundational Pietism

Wilhelm Leibniz, the prominent philosopher of the day, encouraged his friend Spener to rebuild his shattered structure, by confronting the city and himself. Spener never lost his faith in God, but he did lose his faith in his fellow Lutherans. The Lutheran culture that dominated Frankfurt was not the sort of pious Christianity that Spener could support, and they did not support him. The University of Wittenberg accused him of two hundred errors and heresies. These critiques did not dissuade Spener from forming religious communities. In a sermon given in 1669, Spener urges his congregation to speak to one another about divine mysteries, and to instruct their weaker brethren. He continues,

> It is certain, in any case, that we preachers cannot instruct the people from our pulpits as much as is needful unless other persons in the congregation, by who God's grace have a superior knowledge of Christianity, take the pains, by virtue of their universal Christian priesthood, to work with and under us to correct and reform as much in their neighbors as they are able according to the measure of their gifts and their simplicity.[82]

The universal Christian priesthood addressed here is echoed in another work written in 1677, titled *The Spiritual Priesthood*. In this work it is "the right"[83] of all believers to be priests, both men and women. Every believer is anointed by the Holy Spirit and the priesthood purchased by Christ. The sermon, delivered in 1669, created a new version of experiential Christianity, one indebted to Arndt and others, but something recognizable as new. While Gananath Obeyesekere focused on the erratic and ecstatic passions of new religious movements in Hinduism, Spener also utilized myth models that "are popular refractions of doctrinal myths."[84] In Frankfurt, the sermon, rather than spirit possession is the medium for religious performance. Spener's message echoes Luther's notion of the priesthood of all believers. Additionally, this universal Christian priesthood is a socially acceptable medium for protest. The key takeaway from the sermon is the new institution Spener created, the *collegia pietatis*, a lay group that focused on holy living. Spener and this group lacked power to reform the whole of society, but they used the pulpit and the *collegia* as a means of demonstrating the failures of the larger Christian society. The *collegia* echoes I. M. Lewis's view of *sar*[85] possession, wherein possession

82. Spener, *Philip Jacob Spener*, 13.
83. Payne, *Pietists*, 50.
84. Obeysekere, *Medusa's Hair*, 100.
85. *Sar* possession is a spirit possession that largely impacts disaffected women in Eastern Africa.

serves "as a means both of airing their grievances obliquely, and of gaining some satisfaction."[86] Spener, who has now found himself reacting from a prominent position that lacks power in the increasingly secularized Empire, is able to use his sermon as a way of creating a movement that rivals the political power of the city.

The *collegia* also becomes the normative expression of Pietist communities. While most Pietists were content to stay within their churches, they wanted more out of their time, and the *collegia* gave them the experience of the divine and a holy community to be a part of. It is for this reason that those scholars who have a very narrow view of Pietism maintain that the *collegia* is the essential aspect of Pietism and that the emergence of this institutional practice is the foundation to which future Pietism is laid upon. As we have already seen, the *collegia* is only an expression of a pious desire to live out a true Christianity.

Some recent scholarship places the creation of the *collegia* not on Spener, but as an outgrowth of his congregation, specifically a young lawyer in Spener's parish, named Johann Jakob Schutz. Schutz's dramatic conversion in Spener's congregation produced the first Lutheran Pietist conventicle in Frankfurt in August 1670.[87] If this is the case, then the relationship between Spener and the laity is even closer than previously thought. Spener likely encouraged and adopted a practice from Schutz as a model of piety. We also have other examples of smaller meetings taking place earlier than the *collegia*, which only serves as a reminder that this event should not mark the beginning of Pietism as a whole, but rather serve as an example of how Spener implemented his view of a pious life. It may also be interesting to note that the use of the *collegia* to demarcate the beginning of Pietism only came into prominence with Heinrich Schmid's *Geschichte des Pietismus*, published in 1863 and largely used to exclude Arndt from what Schmid viewed as the errors of Pietism.

It is during this time in Frankfurt that Spener writes his monumental work *Pia Desideria*, or *Pious Wishes*. Written in 1675 as a preface to a new publication of John Arndt's *True Christianity*, the work was soon published by itself. *Pia Desideria* emphasized the religious and moral duties over the dogmatic intellectualism of the day. The work was written in reaction to secularization of thought and Spener's attempt to reform the corrupt conditions that Spener found in the church. The work is divided up into three sections. The first section deals with the corrupt conditions of the

---

86. Lewis, *Ecstatic Religion*, 77.
87. Shantz, *Introduction to German Pietism*, 3.

church, the second addresses the possibility to better the church, and the third gives proposals to correct these conditions.

In the first section of *Pia Desideria*, Spener concentrates on the corrupt nature of the church. In this attack on the church, Spener addresses the defects in each of the three estates, the civil authorities, the clergy, and the common people. Beginning with the political estates, Spener argues that they should "remember that God gave them their scepters and staffs in order that they use their power to advance the kingdom of God!"[88] Rather than promoting the church, the civil authorities are hindering the work that is done. They are depicted as abusing the power God has given them, and "whenever some ministers of the church, moved by God, propose to do something that is good, they arbitrarily obstruct it."[89] This is no doubt a reference to Spener's failed policies at reforming civil life in Frankfurt.

Following the defects in the civil estate, the clergy are themselves brought under attack. Spener freely admits, that "we preachers in the ecclesiastical estate cannot deny that our estate is also thoroughly corrupt."[90] The main defect is in the political nature of the ecclesiastical estate, namely the desire for promotions. Spener views himself as immune to this critique. To his credit, he did turn down some opportunities for advancement throughout his life. According to Spener, the clergy should be models for the laity, and they should avoid carnal pleasures. The clergy should follow what he called the first practical principle of Christianity, specifically denial of self. Spener argues that the main problem is that they are stuck in the "old birth" and do not live according to the "new birth." Spener clearly is a student of Arndt's *True Christianity*, and echoing Tauler's mysticism.

The third estate is naturally in a dire position, as their rulers failed to lead them in godliness. Spener insists that "it is evident on every hand that none of the precepts of Christ is openly observed."[91] The masses did not have a proper understanding as to what it meant to be Lutheran. The sacraments of baptism and the Eucharist were abused, or used to justify sinful behavior. Spener believes that vices were treated as virtues, and chief among these was drunkenness. The common people believe that this is no true sin, or at least not one worth mentioning. In addition to drunkenness, Spener turns his attention to the general practice of lawsuits. While the third estate should be allowed use of the civil government, lawsuits are used in order to oppress and impoverish their neighbors. Rather Spener urges that all things need to

---

88. Spener, *Philip Jacob Spener*, 43.
89. Spener, *Philip Jacob Spener*, 44.
90. Spener, *Philip Jacob Spener*, 44.
91. Spener, *Philip Jacob Spener*, 57.

be viewed as owned by God. All property should be used for the service of God and neighbor. Looking toward the early church where all things were held in common, Spener urges his fellow Germans to do the same. While approaching a hallowed past, Spener is using this to condemn the entire society, not to set apart a select few. Spener uses this early church as a mythic example that is to be modeled on and pursued by the entire community.

The defects of the church include a subsection on offenses that result from these defects. In this section Spener argues that the church should not only reform itself for itself, but also for the sake of the Jews and all sorts of heretics, including Roman Catholics, commonly referred to as papists. Spener urges people to model their lives on Christ, as those who are not a part of the church will judge him on their actions. Additionally Spener sets up a distinction between the Catholics and the Lutheran Church, in a very similar manner that Perkins did with the Anglican Church and Rome. While the Catholics are called papists, Lutherans are called Evangelicals. Even though there are many abuses by the Evangelicals, they are not to be likened to the papists; they are the true Babel. This is the only point in the work were Spener makes a distinction between true Christians and false ones. The work is strongly focused on the fraudulent Christian culture that needs massive reformation, and Spener's antipathy towards that corrupted Christianity. Following the confessionalization that took place throughout the sixteenth century and the Thirty Years War, it is only natural that a degree of animosity persists between Protestants and Catholics. While not evaluating the distinctions between Protestants and Catholics, the Catholics are made into an evil other. This is a part of every structure of society for Spener at this time. Building on Bourdieu's notion of habitus,[92] Spener follows 'regular' assumption without being the product of obedience to rules. Since Frankfurt was Protestant, it was natural to view Rome as unchristian, possessing all the defects of Protestant society.

In the second part, Spener continues by arguing that a better church is promised to them. Spener believes that this promise is found in scripture, and that this better church will see the Jews converted, weakened spiritual power of the papacy, and a general reform of the church. Throughout this section of the work Spener also exhibits characteristics of the existential

---

92. Habitus is defined as "systems of durable, transposable dispositions, structured structures predisposed to function as structuring structures, that is, as principles which generate and organize practices and representations that can be objectively adapted to their outcomes without presupposing a conscious aiming at ends or an express mastery of the operations necessary in order to attain them. Objectively 'regulated' and 'regular' without being in any way the product of obedience to rules, they can be collectively orchestrated without being the product of the organizing action of a conductor" (Bourdieu, *Logic of Practice*, 53).

dread that Giddens describes is characteristic of modern society. For Giddens this existential angst arises because of a lack of religious authority that promotes notions of uncertainty. Yet Spener experiences this angst over a future he believes is certain, and he possesses a multiplicity of authorities. In addition to scripture, Spener borrows rather liberally from early church fathers such as Origen, Justin, and Tertullian. The dread he experiences is that in his age Christians are not examining themselves, and not living a life worthy of the calling to which they received. Spener must search daily for his faults and move away from the "hot-and-cold condition" of the church.

In the final section of the work, Spener proposes ways in which to correct the conditions of the church. The first is through more use of scripture. The lack of scripture causes the problems in society, thus "*all scripture, without exception, should be known by the congregation if we are all to receive the necessary benefit.*"[93] It may be an interesting side note that when Spener asserts that "all scripture without exception" should be used, he is undoubtedly referring to a Protestant Canon held by Luther and other Reformers, excluding the English that eliminated the half dozen or so Deuterocanonical books as well as other chapters from Old Testament Prophets. This shows the complicated nature of a simple statement that would be taken for granted by Spener's audience.

Echoing his earlier claims that scripture holds the answers to the questions about the future, scripture also provides the path back to holiness. The Bible is to move beyond the church, but find itself in home life. The laity, who are knowledgeable of the scripture, are to "present their pious opinions on the proposed subject to the judgment of the rest."[94] Here Spener urges a more active laity in the ecclesial life. The educated laity should hold additional assemblies or services and preach for the rest of the community. This call for an increased use of the laity echoes his previous works on the spiritual priesthood.

This spiritual priesthood is the second solution that Spener proposes to fix the ailment of the church. The clergy is not the only body that is anointed; rather every Christian has a duty to one another. It is a "presumptuous monopoly of the clergy,"[95] as well as the prohibition of Bible reading that has impoverished the church. The renewal of both of these will enrich the church, as well as limit the power and authority of the papacy.

Knowledge of scripture and the renewal of the spiritual priesthood will necessarily lead to the third solution the Spener puts forth for the church.

---

93. Spener, *Philip Jacob Spener*, 88.
94. Spener, *Philip Jacob Spener*, 89.
95. Spener, *Philip Jacob Spener*, 93.

The people must realize and accustom themselves to live their beliefs out in the world. Christianity is more than an intellectual exercise for Spener, but a lived religious community. Related to this is the fourth solution. Christians must be aware of how they conduct themselves in religious controversies with unbelievers and heretics. Christians are to pray for their unconverted neighbors and seek not to offend them, showing them rather that they are examples of Christ, while professing Christ's teaching. Love is supposed to guide these encounters. Interestingly enough, at this point Spener also leaves open the door for a union with the variety of Christian confessions.

The final two means for reforming the church lie in the role of the clergy. First, the clergy must be better educated. The role of schools and universities must be integral to the notion of religious calling. Second the role of preaching must grow more earnest. Sermons should not be dry theological addresses; rather they should focus on practical issues that will edify the congregation. In many ways Spener is taking what he learned from Arndt's *True Christianity* and using the power of the pulpit and lectionary to instill an inner revival in his audience.

In addition to the emergence of the *collegia pietatis* and the publication of *Pia Desideria*, Spener's publication of *On Hindrances to Theological Studies*, in 1680, marks the third break with the institutional Lutheran Church. In this work Spener points out the fallacy of modern theological training. Pride is encouraged and more time is spent upon learning Latin than Greek or Hebrew. This assault against Latin was a not so veiled attack against scholasticism. As evidenced in *Pia Desideria*, Spener believed that the clergy should preach sermons that were immediately beneficial to his congregation and not speculative theological addresses. Hebrew and Greek should be learned, as they could provide a truer understanding of the scriptures; Latin was only good for reading scholastic works. Spener sets up a dichotomy between learning about God and learning human disciplines. Under the academic system that Spener is challenging, "the goal of study largely remains a temporal goal."[96] While Spener was not opposed to study, scholastic and dogmatic theology was of little use. What concerned Spener was a revival of living, not fruitless learning.

While reforming the church in another fashion, this time away from dogmatic theology, Spener maintains that "I could not permit myself the folly of appearing as a reformer of the church; I realize my own weakness and that I have not the wisdom or the power."[97] Spener maintains a habitus of Reformation. He believes that he is called to purify, not innovate the church;

---

96. Payne, *Pietists*, 67.
97. Payne, *Pietists*, 39.

in many ways he is echoing Luther. To this end Spener places himself along the lines of other pietistic theologians like Johann Arndt, Lewis Bayly, John Gerhard, John Dury, and Jean de Labadie.

Interestingly, while Spener attempts to echo Luther, many of his critics maintain that he was closer to Calvin and the Reform tradition. This is largely due to Spener's view of justification. Spener maintains that the same God who justifies also sanctifies. Essentially maintaining the belief that God enables holiness for the believer, this led Spener to push for more emphasis on the need for sanctification, not solely the Lutheran dogma of "Justification by faith." While not a radical divergent from Lutheran theology, this illustrated the impact that Reform teachers had upon Spener. For many Lutheran Scholastics, this looked too close to Calvin. This connection between justification and sanctification was also Schmidt's main critique of Pietism. As this work shows, this critique is a fair one, as Pietists emphasized increasing holiness as the true mark of one who is justified, either through a double predestination as found with Calvinists or only fulfilling their *Beruf* or calling in a Lutheran sense.

This assault on scholasticism and dogmatics should not lead one to believe that Spener was opposed to reason or practical science. On November 14, 1680, a different sort of phenomena grabbed the attention of Spener and the rest of Germany. A comet was discovered by Gottfried Kirch and remained visible for four months. This mystical, or at least unusual natural wonder, evoked many scientists and theologians to write about the meaning of this comet. Blake Lee Spahr analyzed these writings on the comet and found three general categories of thought. The majority of views were superstitious in nature. They believed the comet to be a warning about God's punishment for evil behavior. There were others who wrote in a more scientific manner, believing that the comet operated by laws of nature, though the timing was a sign from God about disasters to come. Finally there was the smallest group of writers, who were skeptical as to supernatural implications of the comet.

Spener wrote a letter to poet-historian Sigmund von Birken on February 15, 1681 concerning this comet. While criticizing the universities for unfruitful study of Latin and scholasticism, Spener has a very scientific approach to viewing this comet. The comet was created along with the universe, and while it reflects God's glory, it is not a dire prediction of things to come. The comet operates according to natural laws and is not a source of revelation.

While in Frankfurt, we should not overlook the value women played in Spener's *collegia pietatis*. We can see the internalization and structural organization of Spener's system in the lives of numerous women. Women, after all, made up the rank and file of the Pietist networks preceding and following Spener. While women held no official office and had no formal theological education, women still played prominent roles in the foundational phase of Pietism. Three women stand out, as they pushed the boundaries of leadership and personal piety, namely Anna Elisabeth Kissner, Johanna Eleonora von Merlau, and Maria Juliana Baur von Eyseneck.

Anna Elisabeth Kissner was a pious and intelligent woman. Anna and her husband had a conventicle in their house for their servants. After Anna's husband died, only six years into their marriage, Anna was left with two children, one boy and one girl. Remaining unmarried for the next 52 years, Anna continued to model piety as a leader of more than just her household. In 1677 Anna was accused of preaching at a women's meeting. Spener defended her in a letter, stating she "was incapable of anything foolish or improper."[98] The church still pursued an investigation of Kissner and her family both in 1677 and 1686. Some of these investigations may be due to the connection Kissner had with Spener.

Kissner on multiple occasions passed funds from Spener to those refugees in need in both Frankfurt and the neighboring cities. She also contributed to Spener's writings. In the appendix to Spener's *Nature and Grace*, published in 1687, Anna assembled many of the relevant passages from Thomas à Kempis and Johannes Tauler.

Johanna Eleonora von Merlau and Maria Juliana Baur von Eyseneck worked together to implement Spener's educational program for girls. They purchased the Saalhof Estate in 1675 and opened a school for girls. Originally the school was rather small, with only twelve girls attending, but two years later the school grew to include academic discussions for theology students. While women were marginalized in Spener's *colleiga*, at the girl's school at the Saalhof Estate women were full participants.

This early version of the salon attracted many theological voices, including William Penn, who visited twice in the summer of 1677. From these meetings they convinced Penn to buy land and settle Pennsylvania for himself and other persecuted believers. Von Merlau and von Eyseneck were set to go with him until their plans fell apart. Their contribution to the founding of Pennsylvania and openness to theological divergence illustrates both the impact Pietist women had during the lifetime of Spener, and the way Pietism opened a door for women that were previously closed to them within the Lutheran system.

In 1686 Spener was called to serve in Dresden by the Elector of Saxony, John George III (d. 1691). While involved in controversy in Frankfurt,

---

98. Shantz, *Introduction to German Pietism*, 183.

Foundational Pietism

controversies only continued to grow around him when he moved to Dresden. In Dresden, he challenged the institutional church through his work entitled "The Freedom of Believers from the Views of Men in Matters of Faith." Spener wanted to ensure freedom from the Hamburg Ministerium, which sought religious uniformity, and directed their attentions toward Spener. Spener maintained his freedom to preach, but this only led to another misstep.

In February 1689, Spener modestly admonished the Elector concerning his lifestyle. While the Elector initially was shocked and touched by this appeal, this turned to offence. Spener's opponents excited the Elector against Spener. After this the Elector never again attended any sermons delivered by Spener, and at communion was served by another preacher. This near disastrous interchange between Spener and John George III was only slightly pacified by the princess, Anna Sophie of Denmark, the wife of the Elector, who cherished Spener's teaching. The princess and her two young sons were great admirers of Spener. She attempted to circumvent the growing problem between her husband and Spener by providing a different position in Dresden, but Spener rejected this. Additionally, during this time Berlin took an interest in Spener, but he discarded this opportunity, believing that he was not called there, rather he remained in Dresden. The rift between the Elector and Spener resulted in John George III dismissing Spener in the summer of 1691, writing the dismissal letter in his own hand. This dismissal included a provision that Spener would receive a pension for life, and it would revert to his wife if he died before she did. Spener was dismissed from his position and that September the Elector died. Spener maintained contact with the princess and her two children.

It was not long before Spener took up an appointment in Berlin under Brandenburg-Prussia's Elector Frederick III (d. 1713), where he became a preacher in the Church of St. Nicholas. From this church Spener led the Pietists and confronted many controversies that Pietism engendered. In addition to the continued controversies that surrounded Pietism, it was during this final period in Spener's life that four major events occurred. The first three events were nothing new for Spener; they only emphasized and furthered his teaching. The first dealt with the very nature of his appointment in Berlin. The Elector Frederick III was a Reform Christian, and not Lutheran. Frederick III permitted the Lutherans to worship freely, as long as they did not slander the Reform Church. As a result of this atmosphere of love and tolerance, Spener attempted to unify these two different denominations while in Berlin. Spener's time in Switzerland, as well as his longstanding friendship with Leibniz, gave him hope in the possibility of this union. The final section of *Pia Desideria* even allowed room for this to occur. It was not until this last part of his life that Spener was truly willing to throw off the assaults that he was not Lutheran enough. Ultimately all those who hoped for union would have to wait for another hundred years before seeing even a modicum of success.

The second event was the publication of *The Necessary and Useful Reading of the Holy Scriptures*, in 1694. It was this work that reiterated Spener's view of the Bible. Reading it was not intended to provide academic knowledge, rather it was a form of heartfelt prayer. According to Spener, the Bible is a book that makes others foolish, as it alone contains eternal life. The Bible contains the elements of eternal life but does not come forth without practicing what it contains.[99]

1694 saw another key event in Spener's life, the founding of the University at Halle. This was done in large part by his follower and theological heir, August Hermann Francke. Spener met the other man who is often viewed as Spener's heir during his time in Berlin. This was Count Nicholas Ludwig von Zinzendorf, both of which will be addressed in the next chapter. The fourth key event during this time period was the young Count's baptism. Zinzendorf's parents were involved with the Pietism that Spener was calling for. Spener was one of the godfathers of the young boy.

In June 1704, Spener preached his last sermon in St. Nicholas's Church. After this he went on to preach to his friend the Electress of Saxony. The subject of this sermon was on the difference between the death of the believer and the unbeliever. He then returned home to Berlin and made further preparations for his death. "As his weakness increased he was filled with ecstatic joy that he knew to be the approach of his final release."[100] On his seventieth birthday, January 13, 1705, he prayed for the forgiveness of his sins. Spener died February 5, 1705, but not until after he forbade his burial in black. He and his coffin were to be white. Spener exclaimed "I have sufficiently lamented the condition of the church; now that I am about to enter the church triumphant, I wish to be buried in a white coffin as a sign that I am dying in the hope of a better church on earth."[101]

Spener's life and work demonstrate much of the angst that Giddens supplies to modernity. While beginning his theological journey with Arndt's *True Christianity*, Spener would extend the antipathy that Arndt had for the "old man" to the broader Christian culture that existed in Germany. Spener would take the Pietist impulse and form the *collegia*, the practical means of replicating Pietism for the next century. Spener should be viewed as creating

---

99. In this respect, Spener could be viewed as a forerunner of neo-orthodoxy.
100. Payne, *Pietists*, 89.
101. Spener, *Philip Jacob Spener*, 24.

a modern revitalization movement that provided an alternative method to cope with the angst that modernity has brought forth.

Spener lays the foundation for institutional Pietism and the development of the University of Halle. From here Pietism begins to dominate the Prussian society. Spener's lasting legacy, the introduction of the *collegia*, advances the cause of lay involvement in churches, taking Luther's notion of the priesthood of all believers seriously. Spener's work in promoting women Pietists as well as men extends this priesthood for all believers to women in tangible ways. Often called the father of Pietism, Spener stood in an already existing line of Pietists and medieval mystics, but laid a secure foundation for institutional and denominational expressions of experiential Protestantism. He also serves as an example for twentieth-century fundamentalists, as many of the events and positions in his life foreshadow the fundamentalist response to modernity in the twentieth century.

WHY PIETISM CANNOT STAY JUST AN IDEOLOGICAL MOVEMENT

> *"Sorcerers were the first poisoners, the first surgeons."*[102]
>
> — *Marcel Mauss*

Scholars not only disagree as to the definition of Pietism, but also how long it lasts. For many, such as Johannes Wallmann, Pietism lasts little past the era of Perkins, Arndt, and Spener. With Francke, who we will address in the next chapter, Pietism becomes entrenched and intertwined with the larger cultures of Protestant nations, forever changing its character from a purely ideological movement to one that seeks to replicate itself through institutionalized forms. A movement changing, however, does not equal its conclusion. Since Pietism is primarily an intellectual spiritual movement, we should expect to see the introduction of the idea, adaptation with entrenchment, and adaptation because of the entrenchment. That is the point of this work. So far we have addressed the initial introduction of the Pietist impulse. In the next chapter we will address how it adapts into the institutional forms of Halle Pietism, Moravianism, and in chapter four, Methodism. As of the death of Spener in 1705, the institutionalization of Pietism is well under way.

England at this point already had its experiment with nationalizing Pietism during the Civil war and rejected it with the Restoration and even further with the Glorious Revolution. Perkins laid a foundation of Pietism that survives, but the foundation erodes. Unlike the legacies of Arndt and Spener, his survives, but in a marginalized capacity, primarily surviving in the modes of preaching used at the pulpit rather than the experienced life of the churchmen in the pew.

The greater success for Pietism is in Germany, the Netherlands, and North America. In Germany, the Prussian Monarchy founds the University of Halle with the help of Spener and Francke. This begins the process of formally training Pietist theologians that will transform Prussia. With the University at Halle, Pietism begins striking back against the Lutheran Orthodox. Paul Tillich sees the heart of the earlier Pietists within any conflict between biblical theology and systematic theology.

Helmut Walser Smith views the growth of Pietism as inexorably linked with the construction of the modern world. "This sense of freedom, as Leonard Krieger famously argued, was not based on an invisible hand bringing together the actions of men pursuing their own interests; rather,

---

102. Mauss, *General Theory of Magic*, 94.

it was based on self-reflection—on the notion, Pietist in origin, that when men look into themselves they discover not self-love but the moral law, and that this moral law is a fact of reason and condition of freedom."[103]

Outside of Halle, Pietism continued to exert influence of the lives of Reformed Pietists in the Netherlands and in North America. A common practice among the Dutch Pietists focused on personal conversion experiences and sharing those experiences through autobiographical stories of personal conversion and lived piety. In America, Pietism is found within English, German, and Dutch settlements, many of which began as Pietist colonies, but through interaction with other settlements lost much of their initial character.

As Wallace points out, the prophet's message is accepted and then institutionalized. From here the priests must minister the message, and create a system around the prophet's message. The same occurs for the Pietist. The only way to succeed is to grow and be willing to change, even if the change is the very thing that the revitalization movement is opposed to. Pietism is more than just a nativist revitalization movement; it is also a utopian one. For the utopia to arrive, success must be guaranteed. The challenge is how a movement predicated on being outsiders accepts success.

The reason why Pietists institutionalize in the eighteenth century is eschatological. Throughout all three strains of Pietism and the messages found within *The Golden Chain, True Christianity,* and *Pious Wishes,* there exists a constant cosmic battle between God and the devil, between the spirit and the flesh, the Elect and the Reprobate, the real Christians from the false ones. These themes are not wholly unique to these Pietists, but neither is their need for success. Most Pietists not only prioritize the experiential over the rational or scholastic approaches to God, but hold those other views in contempt. If the Rationalist or Scholastic succeeds as the expression of Christianity, then not only does Pietism fail, but God does as well. The only way to ensure God's success is to remove these forces from authority and create a new Pietist authority over the others. While many Pietists may not wish to become the new authority and may even oppose these institutions, the eschatological need to do so is a siren song sung too loud. Pietism of the sixteenth and seventeenth century will crash upon the rocks of the establishment in the eighteenth century.

---

103. Smith, *Continuities of German History,* 61.

III.

Institutional Pietism
Francke and Zinzendorf

> "The most basic sense of the 'other' is generated by the opposition in/out."[1]
>
> — J. Z. Smith

FOLLOWING THE FOUNDATION LAID by Perkins, Arndt, and Spener, the edifice of Pietism grew into institutionalized forms through August Hermann Francke, Count Nicholas Ludwig von Zinzendorf, and John Wesley. The institutionalization of Pietism creates opportunities for experiential Protestantism, but also confronts the need of Pietists to remain outsiders. While the previous chapter largely focused on the theological ideas inherent to Perkins, Arndt, and Spener, with limited time focused on their lives, this chapter pays closer attention to not only the lives and theology of Francke and Zinzendorf, but also the institutions created by them. Wesley will be addressed in the next chapter.

---

1. Smith, *Relating Religion*, 230.

NO LONGER JUST A CHURCH WITHIN A CHURCH

> "That whatever it may be on its FARTHER side, the 'more' with which in religious experience we feel ourselves connected is on its HITHER side the subconscious continuation of our conscious life."[2]
>
> —William James

The description of Pietism as a "church within a church," is true, but it becomes less and less true as the movement develops. This is especially the case where Pietists become the ruling majority. Following the success of Spener, Pietism now has a foothold in the institutional life of Brandenburg-Prussia. Pietism moves from a church within a church to a church in and of itself. More accurately, Pietism becomes several churches independent of each other and the larger confessions they sprout from by the end of the eighteenth century. There are historical, sociological, and theological reasons why this occurred.

The first, and possibly the clearest reason, was theological. The foundational Pietists held that Christians must work out their salvation. Greater intimacy with God required greater work, and this work is transformative. For the Christian it is the process of sanctification, becoming more holy. For a church this is largely the same thing; the churches needed to become more holy. As a result of this push and pull between those who want a more devout church and those satisfied with the status quo, as well as those who prioritize different aspects of the church life, congregations ultimately split apart. The scholastically minded members of the church and the Pietists values were divergent. The orthodox esteemed fidelity to the confessional tradition and orthodox teachings. The Pietists cherished experiential and emotional Christianity. Each side maintained the others pursuit was folly. One side must submit or separate.

This separation, while theologically driven, is also rather practical. From the Pietist perspective, remaining within the established churches limited their expression and further marginalized their ideology. The only way to transform society is by first transforming the self. If scholastic sin is entangling you, fleeing is the appropriate response.

This also makes sense from a sociological perspective. If we look at Wallace's notion of revitalization movements, we expect the prophet to give way to the priest, who then orders followers. Pietism is largely a network of different prophets and priests at different times, but in order for the message

---

2. James, "Varieties of Religious Experience," 457–58.

to be successful, Wallace and logic tell us that there are two main challenges to these movements. The first challenge is believability, and the second is overcoming resistance. The key for Wallace is not in the believability of the message, rather in the amount of resistance. The Pietistic message faced serious institutional resistance. Left unchecked, these institutions would exert their strength and further marginalize and eliminate the Pietist message, leaving only Protestant orthodoxy, and rationalism. Therefore, it is only reasonable to find a way to overcome the resistance to survive. Creating new churches, movement, and denominations is an outgrowth of the challenges inherent in the established Protestant church structures.

The question may be why did this not happen before? After all, Pietism existed in one form or another since Luther. The answer is twofold. First, despite the followings of Perkins, Arndt, and other Pietists, until the Prussian monarch commissioned Spener to start a school, the opportunity was severely lacking. Second, the seventeenth century is the point where these lines are clearly drawn and institutions could truly separate and form new institutions. The events of the seventeenth century, the increase in secularization following the Thirty Years War, and the mixture of theology with Protestant philosophy, allowed for a demystification that dominated earlier forms of Protestantism. As of the eighteenth-century Protestant scholasticism and rationalism asserted their voices once again, claiming they could talk clearly about God. Once this happened, Pietists, rationalists, and scholastics could clearly label the different theological traits within a surviving Protestant world. The first Pietist to truly understand the new opportunity available to the Pietists was August Hermann Francke.

AUGUST HERMANN FRANCKE (1663-1727)- REWORKING THE WORLD

"Let self-denial then be earnestly recommended."[3]

— August Hermann Francke

Augustus Hermann Francke[4] is the clear inheritor of Spener's Pietist movement. Yet to reduce Francke to simply the leader of the movement after Spener's passing is both troublesome and misleading. The view that Francke simply took what Spener started and continued it promotes the idea that Pietism began with Spener as opposed to a movement of experiential Protestantism that existed before and outside of Spener. As much as Francke is an heir of Spener, he is also an innovator and participant in his own right. To understand Lutheran Pietism, Francke must be addressed for the work he did to advance not only notions of an experiential Christianity, but also his development of the modern Prussian state.

Augustus Herman Francke was born in Lübeck in Northern Germany on March 23, 1660. His childhood was filled with piety and loss. The loss included the death of his father when he was only seven years old. To make sense of the loss, Francke grew close to his mother and sisters. The strongest connection he formed was with the younger of his older sisters. She was still three years older than Augustus, but the bond the two had was strong. According to his memoirs, much of his early childhood was spent in prayer with his sister and reading Johann Arndt's *True Christianity*. Francke describes his love he held for his sister until she died while he was still at an early age, presumably several years before he began his time at the gymnasium at thirteen.

Following his sister's passing, the young Francke's devotion to God seemingly died as well. From what he recorded in his autobiography and his memoirs, he was a very conflicted young man. Francke lost much of his love of God. Replacing this lost love of God was a new love of learning. This learning was still learning about God. The majority of his studies were foreign languages, specifically the languages of the Bible. Francke's education led to his eventual ordination. Though Francke's educational pursuits focused on God, he was not pious. Franke recollected that "Theology was to me a mere science, in which only my memory and judgement were concerned. I did not make it practical."[5]

---

3. Francke, "Letter To A Friend," 125.
4. Sometimes his name is recorded as Augustus and other times as August.
5. Francke, *Memoirs of Augustus Hermann Francke*, 19.

Throughout his teens and early twenties, Francke procured scholarships and fellowships to several universities throughout Germany. This began with a stay at the University of Erfurt at the age of sixteen, then a move to Kiel at the direction of his uncle. Following Kiel, he moved onto Hamburg and Leipzig. During his educational treks through Germany, he supplemented his income by tutoring other students in Hebrew and Oriental languages. Francke's skilled tutoring did not go unnoticed. By 1684 his mastery of languages secured him a job as a professor in Wittenberg.

While in Wittenberg, Francke and another private teacher formed a "Society for the Study of the Bible." There are two interesting things about the society. First is the similarity this has to the *collegia* that Spener set up following his sermon in 1669. The mirroring of what many contend as the key feature of early Pietism, illustrates how prolific the idea became in such a short time, and how Spener tapped into a much larger impulse in Christianity. Within fifteen years the idea of practical Bible studies took root. The second striking thing about Francke's society for the Study of the Bible is also connected to the timing of its emergence, not as an illustration of Spener but of Francke. According to Francke's own testimony, the formation of the Bible society took place before Francke's spiritual formation.

Francke's spiritual formation occurred two years later, in Luneburg in 1687. While preparing to deliver a sermon, Francke's own sermon made him reflect upon his life. This resulted in a feeling of emptiness. At this point Francke realized he was not a Christian, and questioned if he even believed in God. Francke earnestly prayed. Following his prayer he records "When I knelt down I did not believe that there was a God but when I stood up I believed it to the point of giving up my blood without fear or doubt. . . It was as if I had spent my whole life in a deep sleep, and everything to this point had only been a dream and I had just woken up."[6] The result was clear, for Francke later proclaimed, "All my doubts disappeared at once, and I was assured of his favor. I could not only call him God but my father."[7] His spiritual birth connected the skills that Francke developed since his youth, along with a passion that dedicated his work and life to God. Beyond the outward labors that Francke is famous for, from the fall of 1687 onward, Francke believed that his chief work was simply "to become a justified Christian."[8] With this as his primary focus, his outward work took on a new character and shaped not only his life, but the face of Prussia and by extension Germany and modernity.

6. Francke, "Autobiography," 105.
7. Francke, *Memoirs of Augustus Hermann Francke*, 32.
8. Francke, "Autobiography," 102.

Just like Saul on the road to Damascus would only regain his sight after meeting with Ananias, the scales fell from Francke's eyes only when he meet with his spiritual father, Spener. In 1688 Francke spent two months with Spener in Dresden. Interestingly enough the experiences that brought these men together at this point were not similar. Contrary to the standard formula of a conversion experience similar to Francke's, Spener had no experience. Francke's conversion experience was not yet an expectation among the Pietists, his conversion in October 1687 is one of the earliest examples of the "born again" conversion experiences within Lutheranism.

What Spener and Francke shared was not their experience of being born again, but the formation of the *collegia pietatis*, and Bible communities. By spending time in Spener's house, Francke gained practical training, and other spiritual benefits, such as council and encouragement. At the same time, such a close association with Spener at this time carried with it certain dangers as well. When Francke's time with Spener was done, he moved to Leipzig to work as a private teacher, and set up more Bible Societies. While he may have faced opposition before this time, Francke's name was now coupled with that of Spener and the two of them were unpopular with the authorities. Francke, like Perkins and Spener, faced a ban and was forced to defend himself on more than one occasion. His prime opponents were the Theology faculty at the university. "They declared that private teachers had no right to deliver theological lectures. Francke replied that he had not touched upon any of the theological controversies, but had confined himself to the explanation of the Scriptures, and the practical application of them, and that this was a right of every Christian. But notwithstanding this, his lectures were forbidden."[9] This defense and those who supported Francke did not count for much. All works deemed "Pietist" were forbidden and this included any public lectures by Francke.

To get around the ban, Francke, as well as a few others, held meetings in his house daily. The edict forbidding Pietist books, including Arndt's *True Christianity*, was simply ignored. With full knowledge that Francke flouted the law, every one of his packages of mail were confiscated. In order to prove that he disseminated banned books, the package was opened in court. Lucky for him this time it only held New Testaments. This served to benefit Francke, as all charges were dismissed.

The controversy resulted in Francke leaving Leipzig, and for the next fifteen months he resided in Erfurt. While in Erfut, the practice of Bible Societies continued, as did the persecution from the established Lutheran Orthodoxy. The Orthodox clergy called a council, which ordered him to

---

9. Francke, *Memoirs of Augustus Hermann Francke*, 48.

leave the city. It was only the petitions of many citizens (including Roman Catholics) and the Duke of Gotha that prevented his forced removal.

At some point throughout these trials Francke met and married Anna Magdalena von Wurmb, who he describes as "an amiable and pious lady."[10] By all accounts they had a happy marriage. They had three children, with only two surviving infancy. Their son also became a professor and resided at Halle. Their daughter married a pious man, Johann Anastasius Freylinghausen. The Francke household was noted for their piety and also their silence. August Hermann Francke had a daily ritual of beginning with an hour of quiet Bible study every morning. The rest of the day remained just as quiet and orderly. Amongst the rules for good order Francke states "All laughter is forbidden"[11] and this extended to his house. Everything must have a purpose and laughter, as well as all forms of leisure, either served no purpose at all or fed the impulse towards impropriety. Francke's opposition to leisure was so intense that he refused to permit any form of exercise that did not advance some pedagogical end. Oddly Francke resembles the modern notion of a Puritan far more than Perkins.

While it may be difficult to believe, the household was always described as a happy one, happy, but without laughter. Francke's home was very busy in accomplishing the multitude of tasks he believed must get done. In addition to no horseplay and no laughter, there were very few spontaneous conversations with outsiders. If Francke met with someone, it was to accomplish some task. There was no banter, no idle dialogue or futile conversations. Saying of himself "I have not time to converse long with each of my visitors. I can truly say, that when I devote an hour of my life to any one, I feel that I have made him a large present, for an hour is worth more to me, than much money."[12]

It is easy to paint Francke as an angry recluse, but this is far from the case. First it may be interesting to note that this sentiment comes partly from à Kempis who advises "DO NOT open your heart to every man, but discuss your affairs with one who is wise and who fears God. Do not keep company with young people and strangers."[13] Later à Kempis advises, "SHUN the gossip of men as much as possible, for discussion of worldly affairs, even though sincere, is a great distraction inasmuch as we are quickly ensnared

---

10. Francke, *Memoirs of Augustus Hermann Francke*. 155.
11. Francke, "Rules," 112.
12. Francke, *Memoirs of Augustus Hermann Francke*, 158.
13. Thomas à Kempis, *Imitation of Christ*, 6.

and captivated by vanity."[14] Largely Francke isolated himself as a way to purify himself.

Furthermore Francke reminds us in his *Rules for the protection of conscience and for good order in conversation or in society*, to "Honor each person in society,"[15] and never to be "sad and melancholy among people, but joyous and loving for joy and love enliven everyone."[16] While frivolous activities and laughter did not have a place, joy should accompany every interaction. Francke was free to associate with people if there was a spiritual purpose, but small talk was a vice to be avoided. So was the convention of the household built by Francke.

Until his marriage in 1691, Francke spent the first half of his life as a journeyman throughout nearly every major Protestant territory in Germany. Shortly after his nuptials the journeyman found a home for the rest of his life in Halle. Halle, from its conception, was built for an innovator like Francke. Frederick III(I)[17] of Brandenburg Prussia sought a new university to offset the overly Lutheran bias in his territory. King Frederick I, like his father the Great Elector Frederic Wilhelm (d. 1688), was a Calvinist, yet the vast majority of their territory was Lutheran. This confessional battle strengthened the Junkers and all those who opposed the Elector and King.

Beginning in the 1660s, the Great Elector opened the borders of his territory to other Calvinists and Huguenots. While this did bolster the economy of his capital, it did little to solve the theological divide over the rest of his territory. As the Lutherans were too united against the Reform, Frederic Wilhelm took measures to restrict their rights to interfere with the practices of his co-confessionalists. With the opposition continuing, the Great Elector extended his immigration policy to include Pietists as well. He hoped that they would be less hostile to the Reformed Church than the Orthodox Lutherans. This attempt was not that successful, as the training for all pastors came from the hotbed of Lutheran Orthodoxy in neighboring Saxony.

Since the divide was a theological one, the solution must be theological as well. The main problem was that until 1692 there was no university in

---

14. Thomas à Kempis, *Imitation of Christ*, 7.
15. Francke, "Rules," 112.
16. Francke, "Rules," 112.
17. Elector Frederick III, through some political maneuvers promotes himself to become the first Prussian King in 1701. As such he is identified both as Frederick III and Frederick I, one corresponding to the Electoral Title and the other of his monarchy. As he ends with the title king, and to avoid confusion with his father, I will make reference to him as King Frederick I, even though the events occurring here take place nearly a decade before the coronation of Frederick.

Brandenburg-Prussia that produced Lutheran clergy for their cities, let alone clergy that could show leniency towards Calvinism and the Reform practices of the Hohenzollern dynasty. To remedy this situation, Frederick I sought out theological minds he believed would promote union and serve as a counterbalance to his theological foes, the Lutheran Orthodox.

As Spener was the chief foe of the Orthodox Lutheran, he was chosen to found the university. In actuality, Spener did little compared to others. His greatest accomplishment was bringing Francke in as professor of Greek and Oriental Languages. This professorship was a great fit for Francke, who quickly outgrew that position and headed up the department of Theology in 1698. Halle was known for Pietistic Theology and Enlightenment Philosophy. Both departments were filled with professors that opposed the Lutheran Orthodoxy, and often each other as well. In actuality, the founding of the university was simultaneously a success and failure. Little more than a decade after its founding, the University of Halle became the largest university in Germany with a student body of fifteen hundred during the 1710s. The theological program followed Francke's pietistic and pedagogical leanings and trained up a new crop of pastors that soon would displace the old guard in Brandenburg Prussia. Unfortunately neither the Philosophy department nor the Theology department supported the theological union that the Hohenzollern's sought.

In addition to the professorship, Francke was given a post as the Pastor of St. Georges Church in Glaucha, the slums outside of Halle. Glaucha was described as a "sin resort," and for good reason. Unlike other areas of Germany, the citizens of Glaucha could all manufacture and sell spirits. While involved in the supply side, the small town was also used to strong drink. Glaucha had two hundred dwellings, of which thirty seven were taverns, often with an accompanying brothel. Infidelity was so rampant that the previous pastor was dismissed for committing adultery in the confessional. One would not think that a pursuit of piety could take root in this town, but Francke's persistence paid off.

The first thing that Francke did as pastor was to set up Biblical Societies just as he had done in Leipzig and elsewhere. Surprisingly Francke had similar results. The societies grew just as in Leipzig, but without the same degree of opposition. In his *Guide to the Reading and Study of the Holy Scripture*, Francke instructs his readers that the scripture may be the same for all, but not everyone approaches it the same. Just like Perkins, Francke categorizes his audience, and the readers of scripture. In the same work Francke outlines different modes and motivations for reading the Bible. As such, not everyone will "derive not from their labors the same advantages."[18] To fully understand the scriptures, one must come to them not only with the requisite skills of knowledge, but also appreciation for the scriptures and a drive to be close to God.

The first focus for Francke was his personal pursuit of holiness and the expectation that all men and women truly want the same thing. Francke rejected any form of predestination, as advocated by Perkins, and "maintained that God had issued a 'general call to grace,' granting salvation to whoever experienced rebirth and served his or her neighbor."[19] While grace was offered to all, there was still a problem. The problem was clear, it was sin, and the denial that sin produces.

In a letter to a friend on preaching, Francke writes that self-deceit is common. The key is to instruct hearers of their duty of self-examination. It is only after this reflection that anyone can be "awakened from their natural sleep in sin."[20] Because of the fraud perpetuated by our will, the key according to Francke was in breaking the will. Just as is the case for Tauler and Arndt, Francke asserts that the will belongs to the 'old man' and it is the fountain of sin and disobedience.

Similar to à Kempis and Arndt, Francke maintained that we can be perfect in our endeavors. "Perfection, however, was not interpreted as sinlessness; it meant definite progress in the Christian life. Such progress would be evidence of an undeviating allegiance to spiritual reality in contrast to the worldliness of the time, including that of the church and its clergy."[21] In his letter *On Christian Perfection*, Francke outlines fifteen theses concerning Christian Perfection. Throughout the work Francke conveys perfection, not only though the guise of justification and sanctification, but on the doctrine of transmuted righteousness.[22] "Perfection is nothing other than faith in the Lord Jesus and is not in us or ours but in Christ or of Christ for whose sake we are considered perfect before God and thus his perfection is ours by ascription."[23] This perfection is not a license to sin, as Francke maintains that Christians are only perfect from the perspective of God. The Christian is also not perfect, as there is always room to grow and set aside

18. Francke, *Guide to Holy Scriptures*, 17.
19. Gawthrop, *Pietism*, 152.
20. Francke, "Letter To A Friend," 118.
21. Dillenberger, *Protestant Christianity*, 122.
22. Francke, "On Christian Perfection," 114.
23. Francke, "On Christian Perfection," 114.

every evil.[24] Perfection applies to righteousness, and ongoing sanctification is required. Following the process of justification before God, the Christian is made perfect, though still has sin, but as long as they endeavor towards sanctification, the sin is not counted against them.[25]

This is both freeing, as sin does not condemn the true Christian, but is also frightening, for how can one know if they are saved. The question that is central to Perkins and Calvinism remains a question for Francke's Lutheran audience. Francke attempts to clarify this in his work, *If And How One May Be Certain That One Is A Child Of God*. Francke maintains that "you ought not to say: 'I am baptized, I go to church, I am a Christian.' The hypocrites do the same. There is many a person baptized who yet went back on his oath and was faithless and fell out of his baptismal covenant. Many people go to the Lord's Supper and misuse it and receive it to their judgment and death. You must make no decisions because you follow externals."[26] Francke takes away the external signs of grace. Taking Arndt's position even farther, the sacraments hold little value for Francke, at least when determining ones status before God. Rather what is needed is a new heart and a life that is directed toward serving God and neighbor. Francke undoubtedly was comforted by his own conversion experience, something that Spener and others lacked.

To work out ones salvation, one must also rework their life and their surroundings. Francke is best identified as a constant worker, never ceasing in his labors, believing they all come from God. Within Francke there exists very little notion that Christians are to find rest in God, as Angela da Foligno did upon her death. Likely Francke took the reports of saints dying in peace and joy to an absurd level, possibly holding that only at death can one enter into peace and joy. This life was not designed to rest but to perform one's Christian duties. Francke maintained that the duty of the Christian is to toil for God. This notion surprisingly once again comes from Thomas à Kempis, who in Book Two of *The Imitation of Christ*, states "Why do you look for rest when you were born to work? Resign yourself to patience rather than to comfort, to carrying your cross rather than to enjoyment."[27] While à Kempis used this phrase to highlight the value of the Cross for the Christian, the industrious Francke saw first toil, obligation, and fulfilling his commission as a cleric.

---

24. Francke, "On Christian Perfection," 115.
25. Francke, "On Christian Perfection," 116.
26. Francke, "How One May Be Certain," 147.
27. Thomas à Kempis, *Imitation of Christ*, 38.

It was in this manner that Francke saw his pastoral duties in Glaucha. Glaucha required a transformation from the sin resort it was known as into a city of God. As pastor Francke focused not only on the spiritual needs of his people, but also on their obvious physical needs, "a matter that he regarded as inseparable from conversion and revival."[28] While diligent and covetous of his time, Francke appears rather flexible when it comes to his parish's needs. When he perceived a need, Francke quickly and methodically sought out a solution. These solutions to the practical problems of the day are Francke's legacy, as much if not more than his theological contributions.

The most practical concern that Francke addressed was the orphans of Glaucha. The creation of an Orphan House like the endeavors that followed was simply a practical solution to a real problem. For Francke it began with the custom of the poor to arrive at stated times at the houses of their benefactors to receive alms. Quickly Franke grew tired of simply distributing alms and wanted to understand the conditions of the poor. He promptly divided the poor into three different categories. In the first category were those he believed were simply to be poor regardless of assistance, often because of love of vices more than a desire to escape from poverty. On the other end of the spectrum France knew there were many who needed assistance even though they refused to request it. This left the remainder to be his focus; those who were poor, but through education may find a way to escape poverty.

It may be interesting to note here that Francke did not share the medieval Catholic belief that there were any spiritual blessings associated with poverty, neither was wealth demonized. Wealth should never be an end in itself, which was clearly a sin, but if the "Children of God" who were financially blessed used their money for the good of their neighbors, their wealth could be sanctified. This does not mean that Francke believed that anyone should receive a high wage though, as higher wages may distract from the constant prayer that is required of the Christian and provide for "sinful, costly diversions."[29] In what became typical Puritan fashion elsewhere, wealth had a value to be accumulated but not spent. It should be given away in service to those in need and not spent on luxury items.

With the masses who could escape poverty if only given an opportunity, Francke had to figure out a means of assisting them. Francke believed the best use of his effort was to direct his energies to children rather than the adults. It began with the poor requesting alms. Francke invited them into his home and asked the children, in front of their parents, questions about

---

28. Pierard, "German Pietism as Protestant Missions," 286.
29. Gawthrop, *Pietism*, 178.

their shared Lutheran Catechism. Too often the children were ignorant of this. This served to differentiate those who failed to understand the tenets of their faith from those who were not open to receiving aid. Of course for Francke true aid included hearing the gospel. To this end, Francke instructed them in the catechism and read scripture. Only after this was money distributed.

Shortly after beginning this new educational regime, Francke received a substantial gift. This generous gift was put into solving a practical problem, a lack of books. Francke decided to purchase books for the needy, but this turned out to be mistake as most of the books were quickly lost or sold elsewhere. To fix this practical problem Francke purchased more books, but retained them in his house for the children. This quickly created a school for the poor children. Children gathered regularly at Francke's house for instruction. So many gathered that Francke's house was no longer a house but a school. This was all the more true for the orphans. The orphans were brought in but quickly they outgrew Francke's house. The orphans and the school worked together and grew together, each growing into larger buildings, and becoming greater undertakings. In 1730 Francke had 500 people belonging to his school. Beyond the students, a city grew up around the Orphan House and school houses where 3,000 people were connected in one way or the other to Francke's educational system outside of the university. Francke actually set up multiple schools, one for the sons and daughters of the Burghers and another for the poor, in addition to those specifically for the orphans. Some of the classes were directed towards practical concerns while other were focused more on spiritual education. In all Francke oversaw twenty-seven different classes intended on educating the youth of every socio-economic background.

The true purpose of the Orphan House and the schoolhouse was to produce ascetic Christians who not only received charity but would give charity to their neighbors in need. The education for both houses was intensive on a level far more ambitious than anything else in the sixteenth century. Education began with what Francke believed was the first step in becoming a Christian, namely "breaking the will." Unsurprisingly, not every student wanted his or her will broken. Often students were removed from their old enjoinment and even physically isolated from other children until their wills were broken. While the indoctrination was thorough and coercive, it was also to be done with the greatest degree of kindness possible. Francke's pedagogical theory began with, breaking the child's "natural will" as quickly as possible. This would prevent them from falling into the snares

Institutional Pietism 109

of the world and urge them toward the goal of subordination to the divine will, and internalize the Pietist's values.

At the beginning Francke was completely dependent upon gifts from various benefactors to pay for the increasing scope of his projects. While philanthropic gifts continued, much of the need for them dissipated after Francke was given the formula and rights to a specific medicine in 1698. The orphans supplied the labor and an apothecary quickly became the chief business of the Orphan House. In short order Halle became a center for medical knowledge in Germany. By 1705 the first widely disseminated manual of practical medicine, the *Kurger und deutlicher Unterrickt von dem Leibe uni naturlichen Leben des Menschen,* was written by Christian Friedrich Richter (1676-1711). People came from all around for medical treatments and a barn was converted to a hospital. The barn clinic grew into the third best clinic in Europe and saw one hundred patients per month.

Francke landed on another small business at this time, a printing press. Calling it the "Poor People's Press," the orphans at Halle set up press initially to produce printed sermons and commentaries authored by Francke. With the combination of cheap labor and a determined work ethic produced from the educational system, which comprised of a broken will and determination, the orphans quickly became a means of profitability for Halle instead of a burden. Not everything Francke touched turned into gold; many of his other entrepreneurial aims fell flat or even cost much more than they brought in. Still the apothecary and press stood as shining examples for the world.

The world quickly took note of the activities at Halle. Largely to expand the reach of helping his neighbor, Francke sent out missionaries to three continents. Sending out missionaries at the beginning of the eighteenth century was a novel idea. Very few Protestants sent out missionaries and most were opposed to this idea at the time. Francke maintained that the entire world needed reforming. Success also begat more success. As Francke sent out missionaries into new markets, the people there purchased his medicine. Those who converted also purchased works published at Francke' printing press. This grew Halle and made it more important, which only encouraged more countries to take note of the success of Halle. Peter the Great of Russia even tried to reform some of Russia on the model of Halle, including setting up Pietists in influential positions in the Russian court.

The greatest synthesis of missionary success came with Denmark. King Frederick IV of Denmark (d. 1730) was the only Lutheran ruler whose kingdom had multiple nationalities.[30] This created a great need for Denmark

---

30. Danes, Germans, Norwegians, Africans Greenlanders, West Indian Virgin

to spread the Lutheran message to places outside of Europe. Halle sent 162 missionaries to the King of Denmark who served to convert his subjects in India. The relationship between the Danish empire and Halle was renowned for their success. Very quickly the "Danish-Halle" system of missionaries became the model for the rest of Protestant Europe. Throughout the eighteenth century, the main missionary publication was the *Hallesche Berichte* (Halle Reports), a product of this symbiotic relationship. What was also new was the expectation placed on the prospective convert. True to Francke's view of the sacraments, Halle mission theory held that a convert should be baptized only after undergoing a lengthy period of instruction in Christian doctrine. While he expected a born again experience, conversion was still a process, and not a spontaneous act. To best spread the message of Christianity to foreign cultures, they first needed to be understood and the natives who converted became the leaders of the new catechumens.

Francke remained in Halle until the death of Spener in 1705. Following Spener's death, Francke suffered his own health crisis, likely due to depression. Francke was advised to travel as a means of medicine. After a quick trip throughout Germany, he returned to Halle and spent the next twenty years, give or take, with more doctor prescribed travel and fluctuating health, before his eventual death in 1727.

We find within Francke all the hallmarks of modernity, both its good and ails. Francke is rather universalistic and caring in ways that most in the late seventeenth century were not. At the same time Francke's notion of discipline was clearly oppressive, even if the oppression was covered in love and patriarchal concern. Far more emotional in his understanding of the relationship Christians are to have with God than Spener or Arndt, Francke was also far more structured in his own life. Richard Gawthrop sums it up best when he says "Francke's was a truly Promethean spirituality, an obsession with power, action, and domination fueled by the vision of an infinite challenge to be faced."[31] The struggle to help ones neighbor while not wasting any time with the minutia of life quickly transfers from Francke to Halle and from Halle to Prussia. Following Francke, the preachers produced at Halle transformed Prussia. The church officials were the means of the bureaucratic system that renovated Prussia from tough farm land into the driving force in Europe over the next few centuries.

Francke's institutionalized Pietism has lasting repercussions throughout the eighteenth and nineteenth century. It was his school that Zinzendorf would attend, and Halle transformed the Prussian ethos

---

Islanders, Bengalis, and Tamils.

31. Gawthrop, *Pietism*, 149.

from the sleeping Michael to the industrious stoic Prussia that consumes popular conceptions of Germany in the twentieth century. This Prussian industrialism is the culture that nineteenth-century romanticism reacted against. More importantly, Francke elevated experience. The conversion experience became an expectation for Pietists following Francke, to the point that anyone who failed to give evidence of this experience was held suspect. This conversion experience trumps understanding and even the sacraments. This experience took many forms and often occurred more than once. Francke also contributed to Tauler, Thomas à Kempis, and Arndt's notion of Christian perfection. By bringing this idea to the forefront, Franke provides further Pietistic justifications for the doctrine advanced by Wesley.

COUNT NICHOLAS LUDWIG VON ZINZENDORF (1700-1760)—QUASI-MYSTIC

> "Faith is the Christian's obligation; to be holy is the Christian's nature."[32]
>
> — Count Nicholas von Zinzendorf

It would be apt to say that Spener has two legitimate heirs to his Pietism, Francke and his godson and student of Francke, Nicholas Ludwig von Zinzendorf. These two heirs are two poles of the Lutheran pietistic experience. Francke's Pietism is described as a promethean spirituality filled with work, power, struggle, and strife against the established order. Zinzendorf's spirituality, on the other hand, has a far more casual and personal feel to it. While both theologians express intimacy with God in their life and letters, Zinzendorf's piety appears more natural and less forced. Zinzendorf has his own challenges with the established Lutheran Church in Saxony. Still this contest appears less of a constant struggle than what Francke faced in a friendly Prussia. Due to this ease of Zinzendorf's piety, he is often described as a mystic rather than a theologian. Francke and Francke's Pietism established the Prussian ethos for the next century, while Zinzendorf transformed the Pietist ethos and made it universal. To understand the man, the quasi-mystic, we need to understand his life.

Before we can speak of Count Nicholas Ludwig it is beneficial to briefly address the experiential spirituality of his grandfather and the ancestral journey leading to Nicholas Ludwig.[33] The Zinzendorf's were a prominent family in the Holy Roman Empire, earning the title of *Reichsgafenstand*.[34] During the early days of the Reformation, Maximilian Sinsendorf sided with Luther. This necessitated a migration not only of confessions but also territory, out of Catholic Austria and into Lutheran Saxony. The name changed at this point from Sinsendorf to Zinzendorf. Maximillian married Anna Amalia von Dietrichstein and they had two sons and three daughters. Both of Maximillian's sons George and Otto took positions in the Saxon government and both were Lutherans, but only one of them became a Pietist. That one was Nicholas's father, George Ludwig.

George was married once before he married the twenty-five year old, Charlotte Justine. He also had two daughters with his first wife before

---

32. Zinzendorf, *Christian Life and Witness*, 21.

33. It is due to his family's nobility that we have many records of his Grandfather and Father—records that are sorely lacking for most of our other Pietists.

34. This is where we get the title Count for Nicholas.

her death, but Charlotte gave the Count something the 37 year old always wanted, a son. The son arrived in Dresden on May 26, 1700 and they named him Nicholas Ludwig. Both George and Charlotte shared a pietistic outlook and were determined to raise their son a Pietist. George shared news of this blessing with his friend, the Pietists leader, Philip Jakob Spener who he also named the child's godfather. Within six weeks of the birth George died from tuberculosis. Charlotte outlived both her husband George and her son Nicholas, the latter only by three years.

Following the death of George, Charlotte took her son and lived with her mother. Nicholas's older sisters lived with his uncle Otto. Four years later, in 1704, Charlotte married Dubinslaw Gneomer von Natzmer, a Prussian Field Marshal and moved with him to Berlin, leaving Nicholas in the care of her mother in Saxony. The two saw each other only rarely from this point forward. Nicholas was in the care of his very religious grandmother, Henriette Katherina von Gersdorf (d. 1726). Henriette cared deeply for Lutz, her nickname for him, and raised him with the same pietistic zeal that she possessed. The home was a center of activity that focused on personal devotion to God in prayer, Bible reading and most important for Nicholas, hymns. The young Count's relationship with his grandmother and God had to suffice as the large estate had no other children for him to play with.

His personal devotion to God can clearly be seen in two events in 1706. The first took place when the gardener complained about repeatedly finding paper outside of Lutz's window. Upon further inspection, this was not trash, but letters composed by the young Count to Jesus. His grandmother "gently told him that the love letters to Jesus were a wonderful idea but throwing them out the window was not the way to deliver them to Jesus."[35] They were no more papers strewn out his window again.

The second event took place when the Swedish armies overran Saxony. Eager for supplies, a military unit ransacked the estate. That is until they entered Zinzendorf's room. The six year old paid no mind to the invasion of his home and continued his regular prayers and devotions. The Lutheran Swedish soldiers then paused in their assignment and listened to him speak about Jesus, they even joined in in prayer. Zinzendorf spent the next four years living with his grandmother and growing in his Pietism.

At age ten Zinzendorf was sent off to study under Francke at Halle. It is here that Zinzendorf encountered other children his age as well as some personal struggles. Zinzendorf was already rather bright and like Francke, he knew several languages. One language he did not speak was the language of his peers. While he expressed the same pietistic beliefs as his classmates,

---

35. Jacobs, *History Makers*, 5.

he had a difficult time connecting with any of them. There are multiple accounts of his poor interactions with not only his students but some of the teachers at Halle. One reason for this difficulty is accredited to a letter his mother sent to Francke. In this letter she urged Francke to "break his spirit and keep him down in order that pride not take root in his heart."[36] The other reason was his social standing. As a Count there were those at the school who envied his birth status, including a tutor who tried to destroy his reputation and have him removed from Halle.

All attempts at destroying Nicholas's reputation failed. All they did was focus his piety even more, and by the age of twelve he began writing hymns. Zinzendorf's piety and intelligence were clearly seen by all, including Francke, and he became a regular guest at his table. Some of the creative organizational skills of Francke must have rubbed off on Zinzendorf over the next few years because at fifteen Zinzendorf created his own student society within Halle. He called the society "The Order of the Grain of Mustard Seed." Zinzendorf drew on Jesus's parable in Matthew 17, of faith likened to a small mustard seed that grows into a great tree. The key to this faith can be found in the motto that they had inscribed onto rings, "No one liveth unto himself."[37] The piety required at Halle and Zinzendorf is a selfless piety. That same year Zinzendorf graduated from Halle, the valedictorian.

While Zinzendorf's heart was focused on service and personal devotion to God, where he would go next did not line up with his desires. In 1716 he began his studies at University of Wittenberg.[38] With Zinzendorf's background and family, it is odd he went to study at the main university of the Lutheran Orthodox, Wittenberg. The motivation for this becomes clear when we understand the three mains reasons why the Count attended that school. First, as a Lutheran there was an appeal to studying at the same school where Luther was a professor of the Bible. Second, Wittenberg kept Zinzendorf close to the seat of power, where he would likely find a vocation after his education. Third, and most clearly the reason why the young Zinzendorf studied at Wittenberg, was because his uncle Otto sent him there. While Zinzendorf was under the care of his very Pietist grandmother, his father's brother did have some sway over the young man's future and his uncle cared little for Pietism. As such the Count once again had a tutor who did not like him. This time his tutor had little understanding of his religious inclinations and did not care to foster them. This did not stop the young

---

36. Zinzendorf, *Christian Life and Witness*, xv.
37. Jacobs, *History Makers*, 7.
38. Jacobs, *History Makers*, 8.

Zinzendorf from handing out pietistic literature in the streets surrounding the staunchly Lutheran orthodox university.

Although Zinzendorf hoped to study theology at Luther's university in Wittenberg, his uncle directed his studies toward the practical concerns of law. Nicholas's uncle Otto was determined that the young Count receive an education for all the requisite skills of a Count, therefore the young man took classes in dancing, fencing, and horseback riding. In addition to this Nicholas was sent out on trips throughout the major cities of Western Europe. The young Count wrote of his frustrations, testifying "my uncle was obsessed to change my heart and put a different head on my body."[39]

While on this trek through Europe, he encountered a painting in the Dusseldorf museum. The painting was entitled *Behold, the Man*, by Domenico Feti. The painting was of Christ presented by Pilate, as described in John 19:5.[40] The depiction of Christ in all his suffering struck the young count. Zinzendorf intensified his focus on Christ, maintaining that Christ must be glorified in all things since Christ suffered so much for his sake. Zinzendorf was often carried away by strong vehement feelings of sorrow and joy.

Following this encounter, Zinzendorf visited a hospital in Paris and began a lengthy conversation with a Catholic cardinal. The obvious confessional differences were overshadowed by their mutual focus on the cross. Surprisingly for some the two became friends and a mutual respect grew among them. The two only had a falling out when the cardinal recanted his opposition to a papal Bull that condemned Arndt's *True Christianity*. Zinzendorf possessed none of the reflexive vitriol that Perkins, Arndt, and Spener had for Catholicism.

In 1721 Zinzendorf began a career as a lawyer in the court of King Frederick August (d. 1733) in Dresden. This was the same position held by his father before his death. Frederick August, known as August II and August "the Strong," was the electoral prince of Saxony who took the Polish throne. As such, he earned the title King, a title that usually was forbidden to princes in Germany, although we have already mentioned the exceptions to this rule in Brandenburg-Prussia at this time. Unlike the kings of Prussia, August's religion was secondary to his need for more money. In order to take the throne of Poland, August had to convert to Catholicism as well. This only served as a wedge for most of his Lutheran citizens in Saxony.

---

39. Wemmer, *Count Zinzendorf*, 52.

40. "Then came Jesus forth, wearing the crown of thorns, and the purple robe. And Pilate saith unto them, 'Behold the man!'" (John 19:5, KJV).

While officially a lawyer, Zinzendorf's public life in Dresden included the publication of an anonymous weekly paper called "The Dresden Socrates." The paper was a critique against the Christian population of the city who professed Christ but whose lives did not resemble their confession. It was not difficult to see this as an attack on his fellow nobility and even the King himself. Zinzendorf also criticized the clergy who were lukewarm at best and he believed to be negligent. For orthodox Lutherans that could be forgiven, if they were talented and bright, but Zinzendorf criticized their sermons, saying they were "repetitious, boring and wearisome."[41]

Zinzendorf gave similar critiques in his Berlin speeches, when he said, "Today it is worse, it costs more to love people who dare to say that Jesus is the Son of God and in spite of that live in the most extreme recklessness, and only take part in what belongs to external religion, but aside from [the externals] actually drift into doubt or betray unbelief in their mode of life."[42] Echoing Spener, Zinzendorf drew a clear differentiation between church attendance, even denominational confession, and what made someone a Christian. While this idea alleviated some of the critiques directed against August the Strong, it also brought new critiques against the King. Very few people found any comfort in these words and the words from the Dresden Socrates were clearly illegal.

There is little doubt that his illegal paper would be held up by the city censors. The third edition of the paper was confiscated in order to limit this critique. Reports are mixed as to what allowed the paper to continue, some mention that once the Count revealed it was his work, the paper was again permitted. Others say that Zinzendorf's identity was revealed but without a public declaration. In either account Zinzendorf acquired many enemies in Dresden.

Some of these enemies criticized his Pietism and his constant devotion. This devotion included having religious meetings in his apartment, as these conventicles were illegal. Others took a different tact, claiming that Zinzendorf was not a true Christian at all. Some, like Henry Rimius, criticized Zinzendorf's "still greater intercourse with the See of Rome,"[43] taking his affiliation with Catholic bishops as a clear sign he was a Papist rather than a Lutheran. Other Pietistic leaning Lutherans challenged Zinzendorf on the grounds that he lacked a conversion experience. Following Francke, it was an expectation that all "true" Christians have a clear conversion experience. Keep in mind that neither Spener nor Arndt had these experiences.

---

41. Wemmer, *Count Zinzendorf*, 65.
42. Zinzendorf, *Christian Life and Witness*, 94.
43. Rimius, *Supplement*, 8.

Zinzendorf could not recall a time when he lacked an intimate connection with God. In light of this there could be no conversion experience. For those Pietist Lutherans and even many Calvinists, this was a disqualification of Zinzendorf's religious claims.

While Zinzendorf held all the qualifications and intelligence for the job, his focus was never on the King's court. Most of his attention was drawn elsewhere. Nicholas's uncle secured the training and the job at court, but his Grandmother also supported Zinzendorf having the public life of a count. This included serving at court. When Zinzendorf's grandmother died in 1727, he was free from his obligations to her. Shortly after her death he resigned from his office in Dresden.

Some of the obligations that took Zinzendorf's attention away from courtly life were his wife and family. In the spring of 1720, after a few voyages throughout Europe with friends, the young Count visited his father's sister. He immediately fell in love with the Countesses Theodora von Castelle, his eighteen year old cousin. The courtship was brief and blessed by his grandmother. It appeared that the young Theodora was to be wed shortly. Unfortunately for Nicholas, Theodora had other suitors. The Count only found this out by accident, when his coach broke down in front of his friend Count Heinrich's castle. Zinzendorf and Heinrich spent the evening talking. The main topic of the evening was Heinrich's undying love for Zinzendorf's cousin, Theodora. They both resolved to talk to the Countess and find out which of the two she wanted to marry. Theodora chose Heinrich, and they were married shortly thereafter. Zinzendorf was heartbroken, but trusted that God would provide a wife for him.

At the wedding, Zinzendorf failed to notice Heinrich's sister, the Countess Erdmuth Dorothea von Reuss. It took two more years before Zinzendorf discovered this Countess. They were quickly engaged and on September 7, 1722, Zinzendorf married the Countess Erdmuth. Both held similar pietistic leanings, and the marriage was a happy though troubled one. The problems the couple faced were twofold. One concerned the troubles of childhood mortality common in the eighteenth century. The Zinzendorfs faced joy and sorrow with the birth of their first child, a son named Christian Ernest Zinzendorf. Born in August 1724, Christian Ernst was a cause for celebration, but on his dedication to God three months later the Count lifted his son in the air to God and at that very moment, the child died. The Count and Countess grew accustomed to loss as only three of their twelve children outlived Erdmuth.

The second great challenge that the Zinzendorfs faced was the single minded focus that the Count possessed for his spiritual undertakings. While others may have been happy to simply participate in church life, Zinzendorf was so fully engaged that his attention to his wife suffered. By her death on June 19, 1756 the Count was filled with regret over the little time he spent with her, and repented of the times he had not been there for her. Count Zinzendorf was so focused on a mystical union with Christ that his earthly union with his wife suffered. With this said, there are no surviving accounts from her complaining about his zeal; we simply do not know her side.

Zinzendorf married again one year later, in 1757. This time he was married to Anna Nitschmann, the head of the single sisters. As Anna was not nobility, the marriage required the Count to abdicate his noble house in favor of his nephew. This marriage lasted for only three years before they both passed away within two weeks of each other.

The Moravians

"All the young people at Herrnhut who shall confess their faith in Christ are to be confirmed, after which these statutes are to be given them for their consideration."[44]

—*Count Nicholas von Zinzendorf*

At the same time that Count Zinzendorf courted and married the Countess Erdmuth Dorothea von Reuss he also began a lifelong relationship with a group of religious refugees. In 1722, a group of ten persecuted Christians from Moravia sought aid. Zinzendorf believed they could be relocated to his father in law Count Reuss's estate, since he already had several religious refugees on his lands. Zinzendorf had no inclination to have these refugees take up permanent residence on his lands, let alone house more than the initial ten who arrived. These refugees are commonly called Moravians. In actuality the group consisted of Moravians, as well as Poles, and Bohemians. They were followers of John Hus, the pre-reformer who was killed at the Council of Constance in 1417. The denomination

---

44. Zinzendorf, "Brotherly Union," 330.

that followed the Moravians was also called the *Unitas Fratrum*, the United Brethren. Zinzendorf was moved to compassion for them and purchased some land from his grandmother in April of 1722. The land grant was only supposed to be temporary, but when Zinzendorf returned from his wedding in December and found several trees cut down and a community house built, the Count decided that the refugees should stay. They decided to name the settlement "Herrnhut" or "The Lord's watch." While Zinzendorf did not expect a permanent settlement, he had sympathies for the ecclesial structure of the Brethren, believing that their free association was far better than the dictates of a State Church. In this way, as well as several others, we see a similarity between Zinzendorf and some of the Radical Reformers, although he remained Lutheran.

From the ten men who arrived at Herrnhut in 1722, the community grew to three hundred within four years, and a decade later there were over six hundred. Originally Zinzendorf had no inclination to involve himself with the refugees from Moravia and elsewhere, and he likely expected that they would become Lutherans, just Pietist Lutherans like himself. The Moravians were not willing to abandon their historical Protestant claims, so instead Zinzendorf adopted many of theirs, creating a distinct community where Zinzendorf found himself both their patron and religious leader. The community that grew up at Herrnhut reflected both the traditions of the Hussites and Zinzendorf's Pietistic Lutheranism.

By the following year it was clear that the community at Herrnhut was not simply passing through, rather they had founded a new settlement. In order to best facilitate understanding of what both sides expected, Zinzendorf initiated what was known as the Covenant of the Four Brethren. The covenant guaranteed actions that were to be undertaken by both Zinzendorf and the Herrnhutters. They promised to preach the gospel, give testimonies, and provide for the poor primarily through schooling. This agreement stood as the basic relationship between Zinzendorf and the Brethren while he still maintained his residence in Dresden.

When Zinzendorf left Dresden in 1727, he and his wife settled in Herrnhut, building a new house, which they named Bethel. Following this, a new covenant was struck with the Moravians on May 12, 1727. The new constitution for the Herrnhutters was simply known as the "Brotherly Agreement." This contract was rather similar to the Brethren's constitution written in 1660 and covered not only religious duties but most aspects of civil life in Herrnhut as well. The agreement stressed that everyone should be theologically trained in their faith and able to defend it against theological challenges.[45] In addition to this, the agreement emphasized the conversion of souls,[46] and that superstitions relating to omens and apparitions are both fooling and destructive.[47] Furthermore, practical concerns were agreed to as well, including the maintenance of good order through brotherly love,[48] and even going so far as to require servicemen be punctual.[49] These rules were to be distributed to all members of the community following their confirmation in the faith as a prerequisite to participation in the community life.[50]

This agreement shows the development of the institution of the Moravians at this point and is rather similar to Francke's involvement at Halle. The different character of these movements increases as the role of Francke and Zinzendorf diverge. Francke always viewed himself as a professor and pastor, as a teacher and a director of the events surrounding Halle. Zinzendorf initially had neither of these qualities; he only provided a medium for a movement to grow, and a model for religious life. This eventually grew into a prophetic character. As such it should not surprise us that the Herrnhutters/Moravians relationship within Lutheranism was more factious than the Halle Pietists.

It was clear for all in Herrnhut that they were responsible for their own religious life, and that the Christian life required experience of the divine. To aid in this endeavor, Zinzendorf launched what he called the *Losung*, or watchword. The watchword was a daily Bible verse or hymn that everyone at Herrnhut was to meditate on. Each morning Zinzendorf distributed this to an elder who then visited homes bringing the daily *Losung*. The *Losung*

---

45. "Rule 8: Everyone should be careful to comprehend the true foundation of the saving doctrine on which we are all agreed, so that we may be able to give an answer to all our adversaries in meekness, yet with wisdom and power, and all may mutually defend and support one another" (Zinzendorf, "Brotherly Union," 327).

46. "Rule 12: As the conversion of souls is the chief object of most of the present inhabitants of Herrnhut, everyone must be permitted to choose those with whom he would, for the time being, be more intimately connected, than he could be with others; and to alter his choice according to circumstances without fearing to give offense" (Zinzendorf, "Brotherly Union," 327).

47. "Rule 22: All superstitious notions and practices are inconsistent with the character of true brethren; and idle tales of apparitions, omens, and so forth, must be looked upon as foolish and hurtful" (Zinzendorf, "Brotherly Union," 328).

48. "Rule 30: No one is to harbor anything in his mind against another" (Zinzendorf, "Brotherly Union," 329).

49. "Rule 31: A mechanic or tradesman ought to be most punctual in fulfilling the promises he has made" (Zinzendorf, "Brotherly Union," 329).

50. "Rule 38: All the young people at Herrnhut who shall confess their faith in Christ are to be confirmed, after which these statutes are to be given them for their consideration" (Zinzendorf, "Brotherly Union," 330).

illustrates four key points about Zinzendorf and Herrnhut. First, as they all come from Zinzendorf, he is clearly the religious leader of the community. Second, the inspiration for the meditation was not from the perspective of maintaining power but an outgrowth from Zinzendorf's private devotional life, and an extension of his mystical encounters with the divine. In many ways Zinzendorf is the prophet of the group, like Wallace explains when addressing mazeway reformulation among the Iroquois. The prophet distributes his message to a select few. Those few then bring it to the rest of the group, who are anticipating the message and then internalizing it. Third, the *Losung* is simultaneously a word from the leader, a word from God, an individual message, and a corporate undertaking. The watchword reinforces Zinzendorf as the clear leader of the Brethren and its members one to another. Finally, we see that unlike the hyper-individualism that directly follows Calvinism and possibly Perkins, and Arndt's emphasis on personal reform, the Herrnhut community corrected individualism by stressing the commonality of the faith and brotherhood. Francke's notion of service for your neighbor extended to all who were in Herrnhut. The expectation that everyone was on the same page was also very clear. This included attending morning and evening prayers.

These prayers were not short services either, as the typical Herrnhut liturgy was long. One meeting on August 10, 1727 started at noon and did not end until midnight. The conclusion of this service, as so many others, included weeping, deep repentance, and lying prostrate on the floor. Three days later the service was a "replication of Pentecost" with the outpouring of the Holy Spirit. It is even called the Moravian Pentecost. Many of these innovations can be seen today in Pentecostal services. Two weeks after that a group began "Hourly Intercession," wherein one person was required to keep a prayer vigil for an hour then passing it onto another, thereby accomplishing constant 24 hour per day prayer. The Hourly Intercession lasted from 1727 until 1827. This too is something that modern Pentecostals replicate. In Kansas City, Missouri there is a mission organization called the International House of Prayer (IHOPKC) that began doing the same thing in 1999.

Zinzendorf's role as the mystical leader of the Moravians cannot be underscored enough, as very few of the Herrnhuters were educated, and even less were ordained. Most were artisans and craftsmen who were drawn into service of one another through a mutual belief in providence and the notion of the priesthood of all believers.

While knowledge of their faith was expected, this did not come about through systematic instruction. Rather the main catechism for those at Herrnhut was church attendance and hearing directly from Zinzendorf.

The church services were lengthy and varied. Still the basic theme of them was nearly always the same. First, everything was focused on Christ. All Biblical texts, regardless of their position in the canon were clearly speaking about Christ, the need for his crucifixion, and the resultant salvation of the members of the church. Unlike the emphasis of knowing your faith that was promoted at Francke's Halle, Zinzendorf's Herrnhut emphasized feeling and affection. This message was approachable and easy to replicate for this isolated community, even with the growth they experienced.

The greatest growth for the Moravians did not take place with people migrating to Herrnhut, but with the influence they had beyond their own borders. The practice of Pietist missionaries was not an innovation, as missionaries were already sent out from Halle. Still, under Zinzendorf and the Moravians, their missionary presence is quite extensive. Familiar with the missionary work coming from Halle and Denmark, Zinzendorf's need to send out missionaries began surprisingly in Copenhagen. In 1731 the Count was attending the coronation for King Christian VI of Denmark (d. 1746). While there he met Anthony Ulrich, a freed African slave whose family in St. Thomas[51] shared Christianity with him. When Anthony heard the gospel in St. Thomas, he converted to Christianity. Ulrich communicated his desire that his brothers and sisters hear the gospel like he had, but this was not permitted.

As historian Steven Hahn points out in his work, *A Nation Under Our Feet*, there existed a tension within the slave owners in the Americas on how to "properly" treat their slaves in regards to Christianity. For some early on, it was their Christian duty to convert their slaves and they even encouraged literacy in order to permit their slaves to read the Bible. But for many, especially following the early decades of the slave trade when enlightenment ideals grew, the idea of owning a fellow Christian felt repugnant. Oddly enough the solution was not to end the practice of slavery, but to end the practice of allowing your slaves to become Christian. This, along with the fear of having an educated slave class, resulted in a population that did not largely become Christianized until the Second Great Awakening.

This exclusion of African slaves from the Christian churches extended to the Indies as well. During that era, black people were not allowed to participate in church worship in any of the main churches operating on these islands. For Zinzendorf and the Moravians, the slave trade held many problems. While owning slaves was problematic, and we do find many accounts of Zinzendorf purchasing freedom for slaves, the greatest atrocity was the exclusion of the gospel.

---

51. In the Danish West Indies.

For Zinzendorf and many of the Brethren, the lack of hearing the gospel was an outrage that needed to be fixed. The Moravians organized in August of 1732, and Moravian missionary work began in earnest to reach the whole world. Missionaries were sent out to Algeria, Amsterdam, Ceylon, Constantinople, Greenland, Georgia, Guinea Coast, Lapland, Romania, Surinam, South Africa, and the natives of North America. Overall the Moravian missions were rather successful, especially in the New World. Mission work in the West Indies alone saw over 4,000 slaves baptized.

The Moravians were some of the most successful missionaries in the eighteenth century. They possessed an evangelical energy second to none. In many ways it was easy to stand out, since outside of their fellow Pietists at Halle, most of the Protestant world still did not send out missionaries. Most of the Orthodox Lutheran and Reform Churches restrained themselves from moving outside their own territory. This energy was not accompanied with extensive knowledge. The reason for the great success was twofold. First, many of the Moravian missionaries were completely committed to the idea of the mission. Not only were they enthusiastic about the call to missions, but they were willing to pay any cost. Many of them believed that in order to preach to the slaves they might become slaves themselves, but they counted this a worthy cost.

The second reason for their success was the simple message they brought with them. Unlike other denominations that will later send out missionaries in the nineteenth century, who came with elaborate theological systems, the Moravians simply proclaimed what Zinzendorf said, that every person is "a lost, damned, but also already redeemed person."[52] This basic idea was easy to communicate and did not require extensive theological knowledge on the part of either the missionary or the convert. Zinzendorf emphasized that while we may be damned, this is not the end, for the salvation of everyone was already accomplished, "that we are already delivered."[53] Obviously this message excluded the controversies of double predestination essential to Perkins and Calvin. This idea of a simple message easy to deliver was also a hallmark of Charles Grandison Finney, Phoebe Palmer, Dwight Lyman Moody, and American frontier preaching in the nineteenth century.

The Moravians were first sent to the slaves of the Indies, but following the success they had there they moved to the continent. Here too the focus of mission work was not on the powerful but the downtrodden, the slaves and the Natives. The first wave of Moravian missionaries went to Georgia where there was moderate success. Following this many more missionaries

---

52. Zinzendorf, *Christian Life and Witness*, 58.
53. Zinzendorf, *Christian Life and Witness*, 58.

were sent to Pennsylvania. Zinzendorf himself sailed to America in 1741, bringing with him his wife, daughter Benigna, and Anna Nitschmann, the lady who later became his second wife. The purpose of going himself on a mission trip was twofold. First, he wanted to meet the Indian tribes[54] and second, he wanted to encourage the Moravians in Pennsylvania.

In many ways the trip was rather successful, and in other ways it showed the flaws of Zinzendorf's theological agenda. On the positive end Zinzendorf founded another settlement, this one in Pennsylvania. The city was named Bethlehem and today is still the center of Moravian influence in America. While in America he met with many, as well as baptized many African slaves. Many of Zinzendorf's hymns were compiled and distributed in America. Benjamin Franklin was selected as Zinzendorf's printer, and he published a collection of Zinzendorf's hymns under the title *Hirtenlieder*, Pastoral Hymns.

Zinzendorf also encountered many setbacks, including his failed attempt to create churches with no denominational titles. It would have been hard not to see the multitude of denominations in Pennsylvania at the time. Not only were there people from all over Europe, including the English, Swedish, Scotch, Dutch, and Germans, but each nationality brought with them one or more confessions.[55] Zinzendorf saw an opportunity in the midst of the religious confusion that existed among the evangelicals. Between January and June of 1741 he held seven conferences all focused on union. Instead of peace, however, the religious warfare increased.

In order to maintain the Moravians religious liberty in America it was necessary for the Count to make some agreements with the Archbishop of Canterbury and the English throne. In 1749 he set up headquarters in London, England. Eventually he secured the rights of Moravians to not serve in the military as well as liberty for the churches in America and England. While in England Zinzendorf also spread his message there with great success. His meetings in London grew large crowds; overall more than twenty thousand people attended his meetings.

The basic message from Zinzendorf and the Moravians was very simple. It is for this reason that they were so successful in their missionary

---

54. The different Indian tribes included the Iroquois, and the Mohawks, and the Shawanoes.

55. "All shades of sectarianism exist here down to open infidelity. Besides the English, Swedish and German Lutherans, and the Scotch, Dutch and German Reformed, there were Arminians, Baptists, Mennonites from Danzig, Arians, Socinians, Schwenkfelders, Old German Tunkers, New Tunkers, New Lights, Inspired, Sabbatarians or Seventh-Day Baptists, Hermits, Independents, and Free Thinkers" (Westphal, "Early Moravian Pietism," 174).

endeavors, both in Europe and abroad. As mentioned earlier concerning the church services at Herrnhut, everything came down to Christ. Zinzendorf was radically Christocentric. For him, no Scripture passage is rightly understood until it has been referred to Jesus Christ. All references in the Christian life begin by addressing Christ. Zinzendorf's theology was singularly focused as an extension of his intimacy with his subject matter. Unlike the scholars at Halle or Wittenberg, Zinzendorf did not hesitate to address Jesus as human and personal, while also addressing Christ as an imminent, incarnate, and knowable God. The first step in Zinzendorf's theology was not to understand the relation of man and sin as is the case for Perkins and Arndt, rather the first step is simply knowing "Jesus as one's own Savior."[56] For Zinzendorf all else will follow. Both the Christocentric theology and the focus on Christ the man become central for Protestant theology in the nineteenth century, including Schleiermacher's liberal theology.

Everything about Zinzendorf's theology is an extension of this first step. All of the Christian life concerns knowing Jesus and this knowledge is not a product of study but of faith, specifically experiential faith. In *Concerning Saving Faith*, Zinzendorf tells us there are two types of faith, *fiducia implicita*, and *fiducia explicit*, in other words faith directed inwards or of the heart, and faith as it is manifested to others. Accordingly, faith explicit to others is not genuine faith, and while it may possess great effects, by itself it is not genuine faith. For Zinzendorf the real focus of faith is on *fiducia implicita*. The essential character of faith of the heart surprisingly is not an expression of faith in love, rather faith in distress. While love surely is an outgrowth of faith, Zinzendorf maintains that genuine faith occurs in distress, when the Christian abandons all hope and, like the thief on the cross (Luke 23:42), pleads with Jesus for salvation. This faith is instinctual and reflective; it acknowledges sin but also sin's defeat at the cross of Jesus.

Zinzendorf expands on his notion of faith in *Thoughts For The Learned And Yet Good-Willed Students Of Truth*. In this work he expands on the notion of faith in distress by showing that all religious knowledge is based not on abstract concepts, rather on experience.[57] Just like it was the experience of the presence of Christ that led the thief to saving knowledge of Christ, our experience of Christ brings us to salvation. Unlike the thief though, we are not present with Christ except through revelation, i.e.,

---

56. Zinzendorf, *Christian Life and Witness*, 4.

57. "Rule #2: Religion must be a matter which is able to be grasped through experience alone without any concepts" (Zinzendorf, "Thoughts for the Learned," 291).

scripture. Therefore revelation is the necessary experience for salvation.[58] As not everyone chooses to accept scripture, one can choose to avoid this experience.[59] Faith is something that must be approached willingly, but once embarked upon, must be all encompassing.

To this end Zinzendorf never concerned himself with the confessional divide he found all around him. Unlike our other Pietist leaders, Zinzendorf was not that concerned with denominational labels. A century before Palmer began her call for an ecumenical movement in America, Zinzendorf had his attempt. In many ways this was a practical concern. Herrnhut possessed not only Moravians but also Bohemians. Some of them were Hussites, while others were Lutherans or even Calvinists, and each had different customs they were not eager to abandon. To facilitate harmony Zinzendorf issued a tract called "Order and Discipline" for Herrnhut that stated "All brethren should seek harmony and love with other Christians, even if they have different or divergent views."[60] As we see in his third speech in Berlin in 1738,[61] what concerned Zinzendorf was that people were Christians and devout, rather than Lutheran, Moravian, Hussite, etc.

Zinzendorf allowed for freedom in the modes of worship in Herrnhut as well as all of his communities wherever they were found in the rest of the world. What was important for Zinzendorf was not the old system, but the heart of the churches. Wallace would point out that this is typical of a successful revitalization movement. Success is dependent upon overcoming resistance and here Zinzendorf allows people to keep what they are familiar with, therefore reducing resistance to his movement and securing clear navigation through the fourth stage.[62] The umbrella of Herrnhut would allow for what Zinzendorf called "the *Tropus*" or individual historical and cultural variations. The *Tropus* principle allowed for "total freedom in regard to the mode of worship. They could keep their customs, style of worship,

---

58. "Rule #6: Revelation is indispensably necessary in human experience" (Zinzendorf, "Thoughts for the Learned," 291).

59. "All men can come to the necessary truths if only they wish to" (Zinzendorf, "Thoughts For Students Of Truth," 292).

60. Wemmer, *Count Zinzendorf*, 91.

61. "We call all people [in all denominations] Christians and truly so, the name does not belong to us only; one should name 'so-called Christians' people who support the religion and doctrine of Christ, declare their allegiance to him externally and announce they are for him; and I wish this name [so-called Christian] were not only more established than the religious title which we use daily, but had already been in common use for a long time," (Zinzendorf, *Christian Life and Witness*, 21).

62. The first three stages are conception, communication, and organization. The fourth is adaptation.

Institutional Pietism

and all non-essentials."[63] Zinzendorf believed that the *Tropus* of Lutherans, Reformed, Pietists, or Moravian each added a unique contribution to Christianity.

Zinzendorf outlined this in his work *On the Essential Character and Circumstances of the Life of a Christian*. Accordingly, Zinzendorf states that Christians are neither Lutheran nor Calvinist nor any other denomination; he even goes so far as to say that they are not Christians. Properly speaking, or properly for Zinzendorf, Christians are not Christians as much as they are "in Christ." The *Tropus* comes from the *Tropo Paedias*, or forms of doctrine, secondary to being "in Christ." It is for this reason that Zinzendorf, unlike any other reformer, was so willing to embrace not only other Protestants but Catholics, Jews, and even heathens. Of course just because he was willing to embrace them does not mean that the embrace was reciprocated.

When King August the Strong died, his son inherited the throne. The new sovereign Augustus II[64] was opposed to Zinzendorf. Zinzendorf had alienated many of the nobles by his aberrant behavior, or at least aberrant to the nobles. The Count's life and care for common refugees and the spirit of egalitarianism he promoted was a challenge to the status quo. In addition to this, Herrnhut had grown and the theology that came from the community did not resemble Orthodox Lutheranism or Catholicism. Zinzendorf was called a religious innovator, and a founder of a new sect. While we may agree with these charges, Zinzendorf rejected them, maintaining that he was a Lutheran. It was shortly before this period, in 1734, when the Tubingen faculty ordained Zinzendorf a Lutheran Minister, but this counted for little now.

The result from August III and the nobility and clergy of Saxony was clear, Zinzendorf must be exiled; he must be banned from Saxony. Officially Zinzendorf was banned for committing three great crimes. First, he introduced religious novelties, second, he founded conventicles, and finally he taught false doctrine. Zinzendorf was in an odd position that he could attempt to disprove the first and the third charge, but without a greater degree of support from the Lutheran clergy in Saxony he found himself condemned a heretic. His banishment began in 1736. This was supposed to be a lifetime ban, but the banishment was lifted ten years later. The ban was not extended to Herrnhut though. With hundreds of refugees in Herrnhut, displacing them would become a burden upon Saxony, so they were permitted to stay as long as they adhered to Luther's catechism and the

---

63. Wemmer, *Count Zinzendorf*, 141.

64. Again, like his father, he held multiple names and titles, Augustus II, Elector of Saxony, and Augustus III, King of Poland.

Augsburg Confession. The belief was that they would simply disintegrate and slowly leave Herrnhut for other territories if Zinzendorf was removed. This did not happen. If anything the exile prompted Zinzendorf to add to his credentials in order to grow the community both in Saxony and elsewhere. It also served to further separate the institutional forms of Zinzendorf's Herrnhut and promote the idea that what occurred there was not Lutheran and therefore a distinct confession or denomination.

The Count resisted this idea and traveled to Sweden, where following an examination from theology professors, he received a certificate stating that he agreed with prescribed Lutheran doctrine. Following this, Zinzendorf requested an audience with the King of Prussia, Friedrich Wilhelm I. His stepfather, the Field Marshal General Von Natzmer, assisted in his preparations to meet with the Prussian soldier King. When the Count arrived at court, he was greeted by a court jester. This was an insult Zinzendorf could not accept, and he refused the meeting until a proper servant accompanied him. Later the Count recorded in his journal "I knew the king considered me a simpleton, and the reception was so appalling that I don't want to describe it to any person. . . his inquiries were cold, abrupt and thorough. But soon he must have noted that I was not what he expected."[65] The Prussian king then opened his land to Zinzendorf and his Brethren. Zinzendorf also served as a spiritual guide for Friedrich Wilhelm. Friedrich Wilhelm wrote letters to Daniel Ernest Jablonsky, a bishop for the United Brethren. Jablonsky and Zinzendorf had an established relationship, but under the King's direction the two continued their rapport. This led to a request from Zinzendorf that Jablonsky ordain him a bishop of the United Brethren, a task completed on May 20, 1737. This ordination strengthened Zinzendorf in a number of ways. First, it served to insulate him from many of challenges directed against his Protestant credentials. More importantly, being a bishop allowed Zinzendorf to ordain members of Herrnhut, granting the community stability and legal protection in the event that the Saxon King evicted them. The Brethren were ordained as missionaries, which aided in their proselytizing, as well as other tasks, such as baptizing converts.

It is during Zinzendorf's exile that he traveled Europe and America to the greatest degree. Preceding and during his exile, Zinzendorf established many settlements and cell groups throughout Europe and America. Estimates place the total at over 500 large cells by 1748.[66] Of these cell groups and settlements, three stand out. First, and most notable, is Herrnhut, second

---

65. Wemmer, *Count Zinzendorf*, 122.

66. Wemmer, *Count Zinzendorf*, Places the number at 540 large cell groups.

was Bethlehem in Pennsylvania. The third, Herrnhag, was Germany's second great community, founded in 1738. Since Zinzendorf was exiled from Saxony, Count Ernst Casimir von Ysenburg permitted Zinzendorf and a few Moravians to build on his land in Hesse. The intention was to mirror the growth, dynamism, and spirit of Herrnhut. Even the name of this new community closely mirrored Zinzendorf's original settlement. This settlement became known as Herrnhag, or the Lord's Grove.[67]

Herrnhag and Sifting Time

"Feeling itself is something questionable."[68]

— *Count Nicholas von Zinzendorf*

The composition of both groups, as well as what took place in the settlements, were radically different. The Moravians and other refugees who arrived at Herrnhut were determined, somber, hardworking, disciplined, working class, and generally poorly educated. In short, they were religious refugees who through generations of persecution were used to finding a way to survive while maintaining their fervent religious ideology. Those who arrived at Herrnhag were nearly the opposite in composition. Not only were their countries of origin different, as they came from Switzerland, Holland, England, and France, but their ethos was also rather different. The Herrnhagers were not somber and poorly educated refugees; many were well educated and came from a higher social strata.[69] The refugees at Herrnhut were desperate and earnest, and while those at Herrnhag were pious, they had many options available to them, thus, if the community fell apart they would survive.

Not at all somber, the attitude of Herrnhag is best described as a town of frivolity. This should not detract from Herrnhag, like Herrnhut, being a town based on pietistic devotion, but Herrnhag stressed the sentimentality and sensuality inherent in the theological and mystical system supported by Zinzendorf. The extremes found within Herrnhag are consistent with the Moravian ethos, which maintains that failing to experience happiness in church suggests a spiritual disconnect. This disconnect can have several causes. The easiest cause for this separation is an insincere attempt at practicing Moravian piety. Other causes include lack of understanding for

---

67. Some sources record the city as Herrnhaag rather than Herrnhag.
68. Zinzendorf, *Christian Life and Witness*, 76.
69. Wemmer, *Count Zinzendorf*, 165.

one's own religious needs, failing to fully perform religious duties, and the pastor being ineffective. Assuming that these conditions are not present, the devotee should experience ecstasy and happiness in their Christian life. The difference is that this joy was not grounded in the selfless life that Herrnhut exemplified.

For a little over a decade the settlement of Herrnhag grew to a small city of roughly a thousand people. The chaos that became the hallmark of the city necessitated the cities demise. The beginning of the end for the community took place when the cities benefactor, Count Ernst Casimir von Ysenburg, died in 1749. The heir to Ernst Casimir was his son Gustav, who did not see Herrnhag as a model of piety, and began the process of closing the settlement down. Gustav gave them three years to vacate the property. Because many of the citizens of Herrnhag came from the higher ends of the social strata, finding a new settlement was more inconvenient than disastrous. Still some did not possess the means to relocate. Zinzendorf paid those to resettle and in 1753 Herrnhag's demise was complete.

The significance of Herrnhag was not simply an example of frivolous living for the Moravians, it is also a time of frivolous theology from Zinzendorf. Just like the excitement that animated the city, Zinzendorf was animated by the possibility to create something new, and to experiment with a new attempt at approaching the divine. Moravian historians refer to this time as the *Sichtungzeit* or "Sifting Time." The sifting time corresponds directly with the zenith of Herrnhag, beginning around 1743 and coming to an end when the settlement began to shut down in 1750.[70] The period is known as a sifting time in reference to when John the Baptist states that Jesus will gather all together and then sift the wheat from the chaff (Matt 3:12). Most theologians, including Moravians, contend that Zinzendorf during this period produced far more chaff than wheat. Outside of Zinzendorf's long standing appeal to an ecumenical Christianity, which also found a home at this time, we have two new theological innovations. The first is identified as the theology of Blood and Wounds, or the Side Wound theology. The second innovation identified the Holy Spirit as Mother.

Probably the most interesting theological innovation of Zinzendorf was the Side Wound theology. Before we can really get into the dogma connected to blood and wounds, we need to remember that theology, even innovated theology, does not emerge from nowhere, and much of this theology comes from two main sources. The first is the medieval mystical traditions that focus on Christ's body and especially his blood. Medieval

---

70. Dates for the Sifting Time range from a high of 1736–52 to a low of 1746–49, but the most common dating is 1743–50.

mystics like St. Bernard of Clairvaux and the hymns associated to him, like O Haupt voll Blut und Wunden (O Sacred Head, Now Wounded) which invite the participants to gaze deeply at the blood streaming from Christ. This hymn as well as others were sung continually by Moravians until the middle of the nineteenth century, and the imagery was not something foreign to any mystical Christian tradition in the eighteenth century. We have similar discussions on the wounds of Christ from Angela da Foligno.

The notion of Christ's wounds would also mirror Luther's theology of the Cross. Where Luther called for Evangelicals to look toward Jesus on the cross as the focal point of redemptive history, for Zinzendorf the cross remains central but the focus intensifies. It is no longer just the cross that the Herrnhager should direct their meditative focus towards, but the wounds of Christ upon the cross. For Zinzendorf it is the wounds of Christ, rather than the cross alone that is the source of redemption.

Zinzendorf borrowed the traditional Western Christian image associated with the atonement as ransom for sin, and Christ as the substitute. For Roman Catholics, and by extension the Protestants who emerged from the Latin West, Christ's death on the cross was a substitution for the death and wrath that is due all men. This theology has its roots in the West and is not common to Eastern Christians.[71] For the West, Christ's death on the cross was a substation for the death and wrath that is due all men. As the cross appeases God's wrath, it is also the source of redemption and freedom for the Christian. From this it is natural that the cross is a constant source of devotion and study for Western Christians, Lutherans as well as Moravians. This imagery is very clearly seen Zinzendorf's sermons, including this one. "We are truly paid for, as a person purchases one item from another, as one can ransom a prisoner, so are we purchased from wrath, from judgment, from the curse, from the Fall and all ruin, from sin, death, the devil and hell through a true, alone in the treasury of God, legal and complete payment, namely, through the blood of the one who tasted death for us all through the grace of God."[72]

Specifically the doctrine of the Side Wounds reaches far beyond the doctrine of Substitutionary Atonement or Luther's theology of the cross. The doctrine maintains that Christ's side wound is the dwelling chamber for sinners. Mentioned in one of Zinzendorf's main hymns on the subject,

---

71. The prevailing view for Eastern Orthodox Christianity is that Christ's death on the cross was to show his power and mastery over all affairs of human existence including death, the death is tied in with the Resurrection illustrating how Christ defeated death by death, as is sung in the Paschal Hymn, "Christ is risen from the dead, trampling down death by death, and to those who are in the tombs he has granted life."

72. Atwood, *Community of the Cross*, 99.

"Rock of Ages cleft for me, let me hid myself in Thee; let the water and the blood, from the wounded side which flowed, be of sin the double cure, save from wrath and make me pure."[73] Zinzendorf proposes that the church was birthed from Christ's side wound in a similar manner as Eve was birthed from the side of Adam. The opening of the side becomes the mystical custom of birth when God creates something new, specifically a new bride, first Eve from the first Adam, and then the church from the second Adam, namely Christ. Just like Eve belonged to Adam, following the side wound of Christ, "All true believers belong in the side of Christ."[74]

Likewise the shedding of blood acted like the breaking of a dam, but instead of water washing over a valley, Christ's blood unleashed the Holy Spirit. "When the dear Savior died and his blood poured out, when his side was opened up, then the Holy Spirit, like a dammed stream, broke out again. She burst through and made the entire earth a streambed. As a part of its surface is covered with water, so is the entire world, at least by and by, covered with the Holy Spirit."[75] Zinzendorf conflates Pentecost with Good Friday. Good Friday is the breaking of the dam and Pentecost is the arrival of the refreshing water.

In his "Litany of the Life, Suffering, and Death of Jesus Christ," Zinzendorf constantly draws the participants back into Christ's death and Christ's blood.

> So many drops of blood flowed out from you,
> So many are the voices which pray for us and plead for us.
> By your head crowned with thorns
> By your nail-pierced hands
> May your martyrdom and blood nourish us to eternal life![76]

Even the existence of this specific litany in the church service illustrates the profound impact that this doctrine has upon the Moravian communities. It is often said that Zinzendorf clarified his notion of penance and atonement as one that is different than the typical Pietist view. For the Pietist, his and her own sin are constantly in the foreground and they look towards the wounds of Christ. For Zinzendorf and his followers, the wounds are before them and they look towards the misery of their sin. As a result,

---

73. Wemmer, *Count Zinzendorf*, 166.
74. Atwood, "Zinzendorf's Blood and Wounds Theology," 40.
75. Atwood, "Zinzendorf's Blood and Wounds Theology," 37.
76. Zinzendorf, "Litany," 299.

the Pietist in his timidity is comforted by the wounds and the Moravian in his happiness is shamed by his sin.[77]

Zinzendorf finds the wounds of Christ to be liberating and freeing. Instead of immense guilt, as one may expect, meditation on the wounds connects one personally and intimately with their savior. To this point, Zinzendorf exclaims "we have indeed the great blessing that we are bathed in and swim in Jesus's blood."[78] In many ways Zinzendorf echoes St. Angela de Foligno's fourteenth step, where God ordered Angela to place her mouth on the wound in his side. For Angela the blood brought reassurance of Christ's forgiveness, which brings both joy and sadness. For Zinzendorf, the wound, rather than the blood, takes precedence as the means of birth of a repentant life. Still the shared imagery and focus on the blood and side wounds specifically as the fount of spiritual rebirth is striking, especially given the how rare identifying the wound of Christ is for the total redemptive act of the passion.

Such a departure from the established doxa of the Western Churches did face some resistance. Both George Whitefield and John Wesley break with the Moravians at this time. There are also challenges to Zinzendorf's sanity. Many critics point to this doctrine as an example of a psychological break, possibly due to the burden of his exile. Others may wish to blame this on the death of his son and heir apparent, Christian Renatus, but that would not occur until 1752, and the demonstrations of morbidity began well before this.

It is also false to conclude the Blood and Wounds Theology with the ending of Herrnhag and the Sifting Time as many Moravians attempt to do. There is evidence that the side wounds as a source of comfort existed for quite some time, including a reference to the Count "resting on the side wounds of Jesus"[79] in one of the many eulogies dedicated to Zinzendorf delivered by Pastor Burkhard George Müller.

The second theological innovation of Zinzendorf's that emerged during this Sifting Time is his defining the Holy Spirit as the Holy Mother. To be clear, Zinzendorf is not deifying and elevating the Virgin Mary to the positon of Holy Spirit, rather he is doing quite the opposite. While for many Catholics, as well as Protestants, up till this time the Virgin Mary stood as the Queen of heaven and the chief model of femininity, and of piety for women

---

77. "The former [the Pietist] has his misery before his eyes and looks toward the wounds [of Christ]; the latter [the Herrnhuter] has the wounds before his eyes and looks at the misery. The wounds comfort the one in his timidity; the other is shamed of his misery in his blessedness" (Zinzendorf, *Der öffentlichen Gemein Reden*, 349).

78. Atwood, "Zinzendorf's Blood and Wounds Theology," 37.

79. Wemmer, *Count Zinzendorf*, 230.

as well as men. Zinzendorf intentionally and unintentionally demotes Mary by raising a new exemplar of motherhood, namely the Holy Spirit.

Zinzendorf outlines his understanding of the Holy Spirit in 1746. Zinzendorf is not proclaiming a belief in a goddess or advocating goddess worship, rather he views the traditional Christian doctrine of the Trinity in terms of a holy household, with the Father, Son, and Mother, as the expression of the Holy Spirit. Specifically the doctrine of the motherhood of the Holy Spirit proclaims that she is a mother in three different ways. First, the Spirit and not Mary, is the true mother of Jesus, as it is the Holy Spirit who prepared him in the womb. Second, the Spirit is the mother of all living things as the Holy Spirit is the breath of God that animated the earth in Genesis. The Holy Spirit is also the mother that births the church through the side wound of Jesus, the womb of the church, as understood in the previously addressed doctrine of the side wound of Christ.

Since the Holy Spirit is the one responsible for the transformation of bread and wine into the Body and Blood of Christ in the Eucharist,[80] it is now the Mother's role. For the rest of the Christian churches that maintain a belief in the Real Presence of Christ in the Eucharist, it is by the Holy Spirit that the Father acts in the transformation of elements into Christ. As such, it is not only Christ who is present in the Eucharist, but the whole Trinity. A similar event occurs when water is blessed for Holy baptism; the Spirit proceeds from the Father. When Zinzendorf proclaims the Holy Spirit to be the Mother, the relationship in the Godhead changes. Following Zinzendorf, it is no longer the Father who processes the Spirit, but the Spirit as the Mother does these actions alone. Now it is a Mother, and not the Father who is the agent within the sacraments. This is all the more pertinent for Protestants who only have these two sacraments.

In none of this does Zinzendorf appeal to any established creeds of the church, but only to his own interrelation of motherhood and what he assumed the Holy Spirit's role to be in light of the missionary journeys undertaken by the Brethren. When trying to explain the Holy Spirit's activities, he found himself unable to speak about it, stating "I simply believed that she is the third person of the Godhead, but I could not say how this was properly so. Instead I thought of her abstractly.... The Holy Spirit had known me well, but I did not know her before the year 1738. That is why I carefully avoided entering in the matter until the mother office of the Holy Spirit had been so clearly opened up for me."[81] The justification for

---

80. Zinzendorf, like Luther, maintained a belief in the Real Presence of Christ in the Eucharist, but he would have rejected the doctrine of Transubstantiation.

81. Atwood, "Mother of God's People," 889.

this doctrine lies purely in Zinzendorf's mysticism and not in traditions of the church or any faith community.

Yet Zinzendorf knew full well that his proclamations as prophet in Herrnhag would not suffice. He did supply some theological justification for his view by combining two biblical verses together. He did this in a way that no one else conceived of before. The verses in question are Isaiah 66:13 and John 14:26. In John, Jesus tells his disciples that "the Comforter, which is the Holy Ghost, whom the Father will send in my name," will come. This is combined with Isaiah who also uses the term comforter and says "As a mother comforts her child, so will I comfort you; and you will be comforted over Jerusalem." Since the word comforter is used in both verses, Zinzendorf feels free to equate them, stating that the Father will send the Comforter/Mother who comforts her child. Even in the same language, combining these verses is a stretch. To make matters more difficult, these verses were written in different languages, Hebrew and Greek. The term comforter in Greek is often translated as advocate instead. All of that would not matter if there was any indication that Jesus was alluding to Isaiah, as Zinzendorf maintains, but there is no indication of this. Once again we are left with Zinzendorf's mystical union with God as the justification for a theological proclamation. This permits his followers to suspend their previous catechisms. It is also evident that if Zinzendorf submitted these doctrines to the Swedish Lutheran theology professors he faced in 1737, they would have revoked the certificate stating that he agreed with prescribed Lutheran doctrines.

An interesting juxtaposition can be observed between Zinzendorf and Tauler. Tauler always sought to minimize himself as the source of authority, choosing instead the theological language of the established church. Zinzendorf is doing the opposite, choosing to modify and even abandon the theological language of the church, utilizing his own reasoning and experience as the fount of authority instead. Both men are noted for their mysticism, but how they choose to communicate their experience is radically different.

Once Zinzendorf proclaimed this doctrine, his communities in Herrnhag, Herrnhut, and Bethlehem embraced it. The equating of the Holy Spirit with the Holy Mother was not the eccentric language of a theological renegade, rather the devotional language of a large community. In many ways this doctrine was easy to accept, as the doctrine of the trinity already used imagery of a family, namely Father and Son. The Catholic Church elevated Joseph the betrothed in icons and images of the church promoting the idea of a Holy Family, with Jesus, Mary, and Joseph, and these images are still present in Protestant Europe. Likewise Zinzendorf assumed that since everyone had a mother and was familiar with the ideal of motherhood, the language was an easy fit. For Zinzendorf a mother was a comforter and a giver of life who provided nourishment for their children. Presumably Zinzendorf acquired this understanding of motherhood from his wife, as his mother was absent for most of his life. It may even have been this absence that encouraged Zinzendorf to have the Holy Spirit as an ideal type.

Very quickly the Moravians adopted language of the Godhead as a family with Father, Son, and Mother. The community was urged to "sit on the Mother's lap." Even prayers were rewritten to include this imagery. The Trisagion (thrice holy)[82] is reinterpreted using the language of Father, Mother, and Bridegroom. In 1744, Zinzendorf wrote separate litanies based on the *Te Deum* to the Mother.

The quest to relabel the Holy Spirit as Mother was successful. In the early 1750's "the church proclaimed that the Holy Spirit was to be officially enthroned as the Mother of the Moravian Church, just as Jesus had been proclaimed the Chief Elder ten years earlier."[83] The Moravians also held *Mutterfests*, Mother feasts in honor and worship to the Holy Spirit. Bethlehem celebrated their first on in 1756.

The proclamation of the Holy Spirit as Mother is a fairly short lived phenomena for the Moravians. Once Zinzendorf died in 1760, attitudes on this doctrine began to wane. By the first synod of the Moravians following the death of Zinzendorf, held in Marenbom in 1764, the doctrine is dropped. This synod, often called the doctrinal synod, is really the time of sifting where many of Zinzendorf's doctrines are reexamined, dropped, and even a few hidden. Officially the reason to drop the language of Holy Spirit as Mother was to make it simpler for children and others to understand. Oddly enough this was the same justification that Zinzendorf used to instigate the belief in the first place.

Twenty years passed with the doctrine in place, but the experimentation of the Sifting Time was coming to an end. The litanies and hymns written by Zinzendorf that enshrined the Holy Spirit as Mother were rewritten, now simply stating Comforter instead of Mother. The older copies were either burned or permitted to go out of print. The Mutterfest was last celebrated in 1774, and with its conclusion, preserved some of Zinzendorf's legacy for the next century.

---

82. This refrain—"Holy, Holy, Holy"—is found in Isaiah and Revelation, and is used in many hymns for the Eastern and Western Church, sometimes incorporated into larger hymns and sometimes standing alone.

83. Atwood, *Motherhood of Holy Spirit*.

Institutional Pietism

While the Mutterfest was one extension of the doctrine of the Holy Spirit as Mother, Zinzendorf promoted another innovation along these lines, namely the ordination of women. Zinzendorf noticed in his missionary journey to Pennsylvania the peculiar practices of the Quakers. Writing to a friend he stated "When you visit the Quakers you will soon notice that the women will talk and preach. Rightly so. If we put women in the corner we will lose a jewel. . . . I have always encouraged our sisters to teach and preach in our congregation, and I have put gifted women in key leading positions."[84]

The role of women in Zinzendorf's communities was not one of a subject or second class citizen but as identical to men in nearly every account, including ordination. To be accurate, Zinzendorf, while ordained a priest and later a bishop, did not hold ordination in the same regard as traditional Lutherans or Catholics. It is common to receive a license to preach while not being ordained a priest. The purpose of ordination was not a license to preach, rather to administer the sacraments. Zinzendorf also did not regard ordination as anything that Luther's doctrine of the priesthood of all believers did not include. In many ways Zinzendorf was simply advancing the priesthood of all believers a further step, as interpreted by Spener.

From the time of his ordination to bishop, Zinzendorf ordained over two hundred women deacons and fourteen *Priesterinnen* (female priests). These women had the same responsibility for spiritual care as any man. Likely their roles were focused on overseeing the spiritual care of women, but they also served on decision making bodies as any male elder or deacon would. Chief among the ordained women was Anna Nitschmann. While Zinzendorf was the father of the community, Anna was the Mutter. In 1730, at the age of fifteen, she was named an eldress in Herrnhut even before Zinzendorf became a bishop. She also led the single women and would likely have been the next leader of the church after Zinzendorf's death if she outlived him by more than a few weeks.

The elevation of the Holy Spirit as Mother elevated women within the community, even to the point of women serving Holy Communion, the only Western Church[85] to do so prior to the mid-nineteenth century. While the doctrine that lent its support for the practice was reversed shortly after Zinzendorf's death, the practice of ordaining women was not.

---

84. Wemmer, *Count Zinzendorf*, 179.

85. It is permitted, but not common, for Eastern Orthodox women to be ordained to the deaconate, usually to serve to women in the congregation or nuns. These women can administer the sacrament, but—as mentioned—this is rare.

Moravians Secured

> "Nothing comes between us and him—no man, no book, no knowledge, no learning, not even the most necessary truths—but only the distress, the sinner's shame, and the faithfulness of the Shepherd."[86]
>
> — Count Nicholas von Zinzendorf

In October 1747, Zinzendorf's ban from Saxony was rescinded. Contrary to the desires of the Saxon King and Saxon clergy, Zinzendorf did not fade from prominence during his exile. Instead, the decade outside of Saxony only saw an expansion of Moravian ideals throughout Germany and the world. August III also noticed how the Pietists in Prussia aided their economy. We can posit that the rival to Herrnhut, Herrnhag, also served as a constant reminder of the lost revenues to the cash strapped Saxony. Once the exile was lifted, Zinzendorf left Herrnhag for Herrnhut and was there within three days.

Zinzendorf also secured further rights for the Brethren in Saxony. "The United Brethren have all the permanent rights of a normal Saxon citizen. They have been granted permanent religious freedom and are free to conduct their own distinctive services and determine their own spiritual leaders."[87] This secured the Moravians position in Saxony and Zinzendorf's legacy.

Once back in Herrnhut, Zinzendorf continued to face challenges. In addition to the dismantling of Herrnhag in 1750–1753, Zinzendorf endured the death of his son and heir, Christian Renatus, in 1752, and the death of his wife, the Countess Dorothea, in 1756. As mentioned earlier, he remarried, this time to Anna Nitschmann, but doing so required his abdication of his noble house and the loss of many of the lands associated with it.

Throughout this time, Zinzendorf continued to preach sermons, often as many as eight a day, but his robust leadership began its inevitable march to an end in 1758. Zinzendorf, his wife, and his household, journeyed one more time to his beloved Holland. He stayed for a year. Despite many leisurely walks, his once robust health was failing. He had frequent colds, his voice grew hoarse and he gained weight. Zinzendorf and Anna returned for the last time to Herrnhut on Christmas Eve in 1759. Both were sick and would die in May. Anna grew rather weak, as she was suffering from cancer, and visited her husband and the leader of the community shortly before his

---

86. Zinzendorf, "Nine Public Lectures," 308.
87. Wemmer, *Count Zinzendorf,* 180.

death on May 9. Early on that morning, around ten o'clock, Zinzendorf, the Bishop of the Moravians and leader to thousands around the world, but no longer the Count, lifted his head and took a few breaths before laying his head back on the pillow. In his death he was surrounded by his community leaders and missionaries, who stated that at the time of his death "His eyes were clear and discerning."[88]

Shortly after his death, Pastor Burkhard George Müller delivered a eulogy. In it he states that Zinzendorf lived in spiritual "awareness and his heart was burning. That is why he could not live without Him and he was drawn into an intimate union with Him. This union with his most Beloved was tender and childlike." More than a Count, or a bishop, Zinzendorf was the mystical leader of a movement which transformed Pietism and Protestantism. He was without question the most influential German theologian between Luther and Schleiermacher. The spiritual heirs of Zinzendorf include not only include Schleiermacher and Kierkegaard but also Johann Christoph Blumhardt, Jurgen Moltmann, Dietrich Bonhoeffer, and Karl Barth. Zinzendorf conveyed his spirituality as an intimate language of the heart, whereas Müller said in his eulogy "Christ was his other I."[89] His mysticism survives not only in the community he left, but also in the over 2,000 hymns he wrote during his life.

Zinzendorf's radical Christo-centrism was likely his lasting impact for Protestant theologians following his passing. This prioritization of Christ became the theological mission of Schleiermacher, who like Zinzendorf began and ended every theological assumption by first looking to Christ at the center of it. For both Schleiermacher and other nineteenth-century theologians—such as Soren Kierkegaard—the incarnation of Christ was the starting point in theology. Zinzendorf was one of several Pietists who promoted one form or another of female ordination, as well as ecumenicalism. Denominations and gender were of little use in light of the mystical encounter with Christ that Zinzendorf urged for all Christians. To this end, Zinzendorf was also a theological innovator, believing that theology was taken too seriously. His liberties in reconstructing basic theological assumptions, including the Godhead, gave license to other dogmatic theologians, church leaders, and lay preachers to re-contextualize, reexamine, and reconstruct all theology, making it new for themselves and for their audience.

---

88. Wemmer, *Count Zinzendorf*, 221.
89. Wemmer, *Count Zinzendorf*, 227.

INSTITUTIONS TO DENOMINATIONS

> "A revitalization movement is defined as a deliberate, organized, conscious effort by members of a society to construct a more satisfying culture."[90]
>
> — Anthony Wallace

Both Francke's Halle and Zinzendorf's Moravians are examples of Pietism asserting itself. Both the Halle Pietists and Moravians largely remained within German Lutheranism, though both began to branch outward and diminish their claims to Lutheranism for the claims of experiential Protestants and Christians. The missionary movement launched from both camps likely forced both groups to reexamine their adversaries, which increasingly was the established Lutheran Church. The *Unitas Fratrum*, the United Brethren, or Moravians, began long before Zinzendorf's involvement, but became an alternative that operated both inside and outside the Lutheranism. Zinzendorf did not truly form a new denomination, as Wesley does in the next chapter, rather he synthesized elements of Lutheran Pietism and the Lollardry of Jan Hus. The Moravians will remain an interdenominational sect for some time, contributing to Lutheranism and Reform.

---

90. Wallace, *Revitalizations and Mazeways*, 10.

IV.

Denominational Pietism
Wesley and the Impact of Institutionalized Pietism

"We know that myths transform themselves. These transformations bear sometimes on the framework, sometimes on the code, sometimes on the message of the myth, but without its ceasing to exist as such."[1]

— Claude Levi-Strauss

FOLLOWING FRANCKE AND ZINZENDORF, Pietism underwent a dramatic but expected change. This transformation was from persecuted outsiders to privileged insiders. With the growth and success of being insiders, Pietism, in its various forms, was also moving itself outside of the established denominations. The numbers of recruits to experiential Protestantism and the waning influence of scholasticism manufactured the need for Pietist denominations. While Zinzendorf's Moravians represent an early attempt at denominational formation, their success on the continent largely remained within Lutheranism and Reform Protestant Churches. England was a different matter altogether.

As mentioned in chapter two with the treatment of William Perkins, the history of English Pietism was radically altered due to the events of the Civil War and Restoration. Another blow took place following the Glorious Revolution of 1688, wherein the very nature of the English government

---

1. Levi-Strauss, *Structural Anthropology*, 2:256.

changed. No longer was the state a pure monarchy run by the dictates of a sovereign. The Long Parliament, the Cromwellian Period, the Restoration, and Glorious Revolution all ensured a place for Parliament and the subsequent bureaucratic system that grew to accommodate the diffusion of power.

The English state now lay in stark opposition to the religious enthusiasm of the Puritans and Cromwell following 1688. The single most important task of this bureaucracy was not religious, rather it sought to raise money. One of the greatest mechanisms to ensure fiscal solvency was to ensure political harmony, which necessitated pursuing a new tact in religion. Heresy was no longer defined as wavering from purity of doctrine, rather it was now chiefly characterized as opposition to the institution. The result of the earlier English attempt at institutionalized Pietism was a new religious climate marked by rationalism and agnosticism towards religious enthusiasm. While Zinzendorf's Moravians excited Germans, the Dutch, and the Danes, the English served as the saucer to cool the boiling cup of Pietism. The earlier passion for Perkins's predestination turned sour. Free will, rather than divine determinism, was the message for England in the eighteenth century.

With such a different climate for the English than Central Europe, it should come as no surprise that the surviving English variant of Pietism, while resulting in a similar expression, began from a different starting point. Since the time of Perkins, England continued to undergo changes. Unlike the German expressions of Pietism, which reacted against the rigid dogmatic neo-scholastic Protestant orthodoxy, English Pietism could not begin by rejecting the constraints of a dogmatic church, rather against the dogmatic rationalism of the state. The supreme faith in reason, not the faith in orthodoxy, was the impetus for the larger lasting impact of Pietism upon the Church of England. It is in the late eighteenth century, not the early seventeenth century, that Pietism became its own church. Both the earlier and later attempt began in England, not in Germany. It is from England that the ashes of Puritanism are mixed with the waters of Moravians that Methodism forms following the life and teachings of John Wesley.

JOHN WESLEY (1703-1791)—PERSONAL RELATIONSHIP WITH GOD

"God is holy; I am unholy. God is a consuming fire: I am altogether a sinner, suitable only to be consumed."[2]

—John Wesley

The demise of Puritanism came as a blow to the Wesleys. John's parents, Samuel and Susanna, came from a long line of Puritan ministers. Susanna's great grandfather was one of those responsible for Charles's first minister's execution by the revolutionary parliament. Her grandfather chaired the commissions into clerical abuses, publishing *The Century of Scandalous Priests*. Samuel's grandfather Bartholomew Wesley prevented Charles's flight from England and abolished not only the monarchy but the episcopacy and the House of Lords. His other grandfather, John White, was the architect of the Puritan Massachusetts settlement. Both Samuel and Susanna's fathers served as ministers for Cromwell. In 1662, two years after Charles II was restored, most Puritan ministers were expelled. This included both fathers. The legacy of Puritanism weighed heavily upon the Wesley household.

Within the household library John Wesley was familiar with not only his Puritan grandfathers but also Pietist writings from the Continent. Francke was highly esteemed by Samuel and Susanna Wesley. John's journal later records him reading Francke's *Pietas Hallensis*, specifically referencing the charitable and missionary endeavors of Halle. John Wesley grew up reading Pietistic writings that likely included Arndt's *True Christianity*, which made its way across the channel as early as 1648.

In 1703 John Wesley was born into a contentious England and a household that was much the same. Samuel Wesley, like his father, grandfather, and great grandfather before him, was a minister. Like his forefathers, he also had Puritan leanings. Not only did he need to defend his position to the state, but Puritanism grew so repugnant, that even the new muted version still resulted in outright hostility and aggression by the laity.

One notable example took place on a Thursday night in February 1709, when the wooden rectory in the Lincolnshire village of Epworth caught fire, and not by accident. In the process of burning to the ground, Samuel and Susanna gathered up their children before making a hasty escape. The escape was a bit too hasty as they overlooked their five year old son who was still sleeping in the attic. Luckily for the boy the flames woke him before they consumed him. Unfortunately Samuel could not make it up

---

2. Wesley, "His Spiritual Journey," 38.

the collapsing stairs and resigned his son to the flames. Kneeling in prayer, Samuel petitioned the Lord to accept the boy's soul. While his father was unable to save the boy, the neighbors were not. They came to the boy's aid standing on each other's shoulders. They grabbed his arms just as the roof collapsed. The five year old was John. This was a formative experience, as one may no doubt imagine. John often spoke of himself as a "brand snatched from the burning"[3]; this was not simply a reference to his eternal locale.

For the next five years John grew up in the Wesley household that was overwhelmingly female, as he had five older sisters.[4] His brother Samuel (Jr) was 12 years older than he was and was out of the house shortly after John was born. His brother Charles was only a baby when the rectory succumbed to the flames, but was often the only other male in the house. John's father Samuel was absent nearly as often as he was present in the home. His duties required regular periods of absence. When he was present he was often at fierce odds with Susanna over politics. These arguments grew to the point that they did not share a bed.

At the age of ten, John Wesley was sent off to boarding school to continue his education. Over the next six years (1714–1720), John's life at the Charterhouse in London took on a new character. While staying at the converted monastery, John enjoyed a free position at the school as one of the few poor scholars. Most of his food was taken from him by the older boys and John Wesley's devotional life also suffered. He portrays this time as a fall from grace and his time of rebellion. Likely John is exaggerating his fall from grace, as he still maintained daily Bible reading, morning and evening prayers, and there appeared to be no behavior issues recorded by the school. We have no accounts similar to Perkins's drunkenness or Francke's lack of faith. Rather the rebellion was one that only John was aware of. John claimed that he was separated from God. John Wesley characterized this time of being a spiritual slacker where he was tempted by the other boys at the school and his sins grew from thoughts to words and deeds. Largely he characterizes his sin as being negligent and weak rather than openly defiant, a terror, a drunk, or an unbeliever. Keep in mind his personal notion of salvation centered on personal intimacy with his God. The lack of intimacy in his prayers and devotional life and the permissiveness to entertain other ideas mirrored his father's absence from his mother, a relationship that needed mending.

While at the charter school, the Wesleys encountered a disturbance at their house. This disturbance grew from noises to unexplainable events,

---

3. Johnson, *Evolution of Christianity*, 149.
4. Emily, Susanna, Mary, Hetty (short for Mehetabel), and Anne.

and eventually all but Samuel Wesley believed that a poltergeist took up residence in their house. They named the poltergeist "Old Jeffrey" after the former inhabitant of the house who died there. Many of the unexplainable events committed by Old Jeffrey include levitating a bed and disturbing Samuel's prayers for the King. Most important was John's lifelong belief in the supernatural, not only a belief in God but also in the constant interaction of this world with a world populated with angels, ghosts, witches, and demons. While England was in the middle of their own Enlightenment, John Wesley rejected the rationalistic system for one which still contained mystery and intimacy with the divine.

Following the charter school John went off to Oxford. The university was large and rather conservative. He quickly graduated[5] but stayed on at Christ Church to study for his Master's degree. During this time John denounced the rebellion against God that characterized his time at the charter school and began a new focused devotion. This devotion was partly derived from a doctor's prescription that he moderate his diet, exercise and sleep. While the doctor prescribed moderation, John's view of moderation was anything but moderate. He immediately set out a program of self-discipline that dictated how he spent his day and limited every action to his understanding of how Christ would respond to that proposition.

This new program of extreme moderation suited him well. It also prepared him for the events of 1729. After his graduation and ordination, John was recalled as a tutor at Oxford. His brother Charles, admitted to Oxford just two years earlier, underwent a similar personal revival. Charles took steps to ensure the fidelity of his new level of piety by gathering a few other men around him. When John returned, he was invited to join this club. In its infancy the club was rather small, consisting of only four members. John and Charles were half of the membership; William Morgan and Bob Kirkham made up the other two. The chief aim of the club was to gather together in the evenings and study the Bible and devotional works, as well as review sermons they heard. They committed to one another that they would lead a holy and sober life. The chief practical change was the frequency they took communion. While most theology students took communion once a quarter, these four began receiving the Eucharist weekly. This practice alarmed much of the school as extreme, and as Puritan. Since no one could come up with a reason why they should not have weekly communion, the practice continued, but so did a new host of names. The two names that stuck were The Holy Club, as well as Methodists, both originally being terms of derision.

---

5. The year is now 1724.

The club grew and before long it attracted a young George Whitefield (d. 1770). Whitefield had a leading role in the development of Methodism over the next few decades. The Holy Club consumed John, who quickly became the groups de facto leader. John was the only ordained member of the club and held a deep desire to be a pastor. The group provided this. It also provided John rivals in piety that spurred one another along to new extremes. One such extreme was the obsession with fasting. John's older brother Samuel grew concerned that John was going too far. While applauding the move towards holiness, Samuel worried that John was "laying excessive burdens on himself that were liable to injure his health."[6]

It was not John's health that was injured, rather it was a different founding member of the Holy Club that bore that burden. The rule for fasting resulted in the death of William Morgan. In a letter to William's father, John Wesley states "On Sunday last I was informed that my brother and I had killed your son: That the rigorous fasting which he had imposed upon himself by our advice had increased his illness and hastened his death."[7] He clearly lacked the empathy that we would expect, and found no guilt in his part of Morgan's death since it was done out of devotion to God. Clearly John was moving past the acceptable limits of piety that England imposed upon its citizens. It is also interesting to note that John Wesley did not appeal to any mystical or personal claims to justify the death of Morgan. While a relationship with God is central to Wesley's religious outlook, he never claimed the mantle of mysticism that Zinzendorf wrapped himself in.

As Methodism has its early beginnings at Oxford, it may be prudent to look at Wesley's conception of a Methodist. According to Wesley, "A Methodist is one in whom 'the love of God has been poured out in (his) heart by the Holy Spirit who was given to (him)' (Rom. 5:5); one who loves the Lord his God with all his heart, with all his soul, with all his mind, and with all his strength (see Mark 12:30). God is the jay of his heart, and the desire of his soul, which is constantly crying out."[8] We can take a few points from this definition. First, unlike historical Christianity, Wesley does not define a Methodist along theological or even doctrinal lines, rather a Methodist is someone whose heart is filled with the love of God and who lives out this love with actions. We will get into Wesley's theology later, but central to Wesley's aim was not defining theology, but action and piety.

For most of John's early life, this piety was extremely personal. Even during his time at Oxford, the chief focus of his life was himself. We see

---

6. Tomkins, *John Wesley*, 35.
7. Wesley, "Rise of the Holy Club," 18.
8. Wesley, "Character of a Methodist," 829.

evidence of this when his father Samuel died in 1734. His family urged John to come home and become the new pastor at Epworth, taking his father's post. John refused. When his mother appealed to the good he could do for the people, John replied, "The question is not whether I could do more good to others, but whether I could do more good to myself."[9] He maintained that wherever he was most holy, more people would gather around him to become holy themselves.

Two years later, in 1736, John Wesley believed that the place to become a shining light for others to gather around was no longer Oxford, but Georgia. The Society for the Promotion of Christian Knowledge urged Wesley to take his piety to the newly formed colony of Georgia. He was going to save the Indians and purify the colony. He did neither. From the very beginning John's voyage to Georgia was a massive failure. John only succeeded in one thing, convincing his brother Charles and a few others from Oxford to join him on his doomed trek.

Once the ship set sail, it continually faced storms that terrified John Wesley. He believed on more than one occasion that the ship was going to sink. John was going to America to be the light surrounded by spiritual darkness, but on the boat his light was extinguished by the raging waters. Even his strict fasting[10] did not preserve his faith. Instead he noticed a new light, not from his own piety but from the faith of German immigrants. Many of these Germans were not Germans at all, rather they were Moravians sent by Zinzendorf. John was immediately attracted to their calm serenity on the chaotic waters. The Moravians sang hymns and did not fear death. John on the other hand was terrified of his own death.

John recalls that he could not but say to himself, "'How is it that thou hast no faith?' being still unwilling to die."[11] The Moravian leader Spangenburg confronted Wesley on just this when he later asked Wesley if he knew Christ and that Christ saved him. Wesley said he knew Christ, but believed this to be a lie. Wesley did not really understand the Lutheran theology surrounding justification by faith that was so engrained in the Moravian ethos.

The lie he told Spangenburg and himself did not stop Wesley from his mission. John believed that he could still save the people, even though he now believed he needed saving himself. Just like his time at Oxford, Wesley once again re-devoted his life to God, and like his time at Oxford,

---

9. Tomkins, *John Wesley*, 40.

10. John and Charles ate only rice and biscuits on the voyage, choosing to fast from meat while on the water.

11. Wesley, "His Spiritual Journey," 28.

the key was found with asceticism and study. It almost goes without saying that neither the Georgian colonists nor the Natives appreciated his strict demands. Wesley's mission to save anyone's soul was over before it began. John and his message were extremely unpopular.

Wesley was confronted with another challenge in Georgia. This was the decision to marry or remain celibate. John's vacillation on this issue resulted in an uproar in Savannah. In order to cover up his personal failings, John chose to defame William Williamson, one of the town's leaders. This resulted in his arrest. Ten charges were brought against him, nine of which dealt with his religious regime. He was released without bail. Some came to his aid, but not many. John did not make many friends over the year and a half he was in Georgia.

The trial was set for August but was moved back. Wesley took this as an opportunity to avoid it all together. He announced to the magistrate, a man named Causton, that "the Lord called him to return to England."[12] He told Causton he was to leave in November. In light of the debt Wesley owed and an upcoming trial, Causton forbade him from leaving and the court forbade anyone from helping him leave. In response, Wesley prayed and then shook the dust from his feet and escaped through the swamp to Charleston to gather his brother. On December 22, 1737 John and Charles Wesley fled America to head back to England. John's efforts were wasted. His year and a half in America only resulted in disaster and becoming a fugitive. This time was influential in his subsequent conversion the following year in England.

Once back in England, John looked up the Moravians and encountered Peter Böhler, a Moravian missionary who was planning on going on to Georgia. Böhler remained in England long enough for Wesley to learn a new type of theology. Böhler told Wesley that he had no saving faith. This did not shock John. Still, Böhler insisted that Wesley continue preaching. Böhler told John "to preach faith till you have it; and then, because you have it, you will preach faith."[13]

Like Francke, Welsey began his Pietist mission calling others to convert before he ever experienced his own conversion. While still growing into the faith that Böhler promised Wesley he could have, the two founded the Fetter Lane Society, on May 1, 1738. The society was a synthesis of both the Holy Club from Oxford and the Moravians. This was the first real predecessor to the Methodist societies that John formed.

---

12. Tomkins, *John Wesley*, 55.
13. Tomkins, *John Wesley*, 58.

Wesley's Moravian Methodism

"May we this life improve, to mourn for errors past; and live this short, revolving day as if it were our last."[14]

—John Wesley

The Moravians held Bible studies all over London and it was to one of these studies that Wesley attributes his religious conversion. On May 24, 1738 Wesley attended a meeting on Aldersgate Street. Here he heard the reading of Luther's Preface to the Epistles of the Romans, and at eight forty five that evening, Wesley said "I felt my heart strangely warmed. I felt I did trust in Christ, Christ alone for salvation. An assurance was given to me, that He had taken away my sins, even mine, and saved me from the law of sin and death."[15]

Even though Wesley was an ordained Anglican Priest, missionary, and founder of multiple religious societies, he describes this moment on Aldersgate as the beginning of his life as a Christian. If nothing else Wesley now accepted the Moravian view of salvation and converted to this mode of piety. It is important to note that Wesley does not break with the Church of England at this time, nor any time. His remaining within the English system was both pragmatic and essential for his understanding of what a Christian was. Faith, rather than reason or orthodoxy, defined one as a Christian. Doctrine and dogma were and would remain secondary to the personal experience Wesley promotes.

While this conversion is notable, still some scholars believe that John Wesley had already converted prior to this point. It is likely that Wesley had a gradual conversion and did not have a single moment that he could use to call others to faith. Therefore he elevated the encounter at Aldersgate. Even before this encounter Wesley was displaying signs of a converted life such as the founding of Fetter Lane and his visits to prisons. It is interesting to note that both of our English Pietists, Wesley and Perkins, begin their converted life preaching to prisoners.

If we take John's conversion narrative seriously, it immediately followed his brother's conversion. Charles Wesley experienced a similar conversion just three days before John. It is possible that both brothers chose this time to declare their theological shift. It is just as likely as not that following their experience in Georgia and their tutelage under Böhler they accepted the preeminent position of experience of the divine that is a hallmark of Pietism.

14. Wesley, "We Lift Our Hearts," 1342.
15. Wemmer, *Count Zinzendorf*, 133.

Interestingly, the next morning Wesley records in his journal that "I did grieve the Spirit of God, not only by not being watchful in prayer, but likewise by speaking with sharpness instead of tender love about one who was not sound in the faith. Immediately God hid His face, and I was troubled; and in this heaviness I continued till the next morning."[16] This new experiential relationship with God contained both highs and lows, and seemingly for little reason.

Three weeks after his Aldersgate conversion, Wesley trekked to Herrnhut to visit Zinzendorf. For the next three months Wesley further internalized the Moravian ethos and observed their communal life. Wesley retained two things from his time with the Moravians. First, they served as an example for Wesley of a community that lived by faith. Second, Wesley was greatly influenced by the hymnody of the Moravians. The hymns that Wesley wrote are largely modeled after what he saw in Herrnhut. Early Methodist hymnals basic structure consisted of three different authors of hymns, those belonging to Charles Wesley, John Wesley, and Count Zinzendorf.

When John returned from his march through Moravian lands, Methodism changed once again. Unlike its early forms in the Holy Club and Fetter Lane, Wesley matured in his theology and his mission was clear. The only problem is that as soon as he proclaimed his understanding of the gospel, no pulpit was open to him. He was too Puritan, too Moravian, and not in any way a proper English preacher. It appeared that the new mission failed before it began. Unlike the failure that was his Georgia mission, Wesley was a bit more humble and willing to look outside himself. Wesley looked towards George Whitefield and the solution he was working on, since many pulpits were closed to him as well. The solution used by Whitefield was outdoor preaching. From the establishment perspective, this was ludicrous. It was far too Puritan and was roundly condemned, but this was just the move Wesley settled on. It was also successful. Successful enough that he raised enough money to buy land and began building "the New Room," the first real Methodist meeting hall.

By 1739, Wesley's message grew large enough that many societies formed, which required many preachers. The problem came when one member, John Cennick, began to preach. While a prominent school teacher and a fellow with Wesley from Oxford, Cennick was not ordained. Wesley rejected the requirement of all preachers to be ordained, and stated that "In cases of necessity when no ordained person was available, lay Methodists

---

16. Wesley, "His Spiritual Journey," 39.

could preach."[17] While not technically a pastor or a priest, Cennick became a 'lay assistant.' Lay preaching grew far beyond Cennick as the need arose and it arose often. This use of lay preaching was consistent with previous Pietists theology, but none of our previous examples were forming a denomination in the way that Wesley was in the early stages of doing.

The emphasis on preaching was only one of the Puritan survivals that Wesley inherited from Perkins. There was an important precedent in the works of Puritan authors. While England rejected the strict Calvinism of the Puritan era, the relationship between election and fulfilling ones calling connected to justification, sanctification, and glorification remained. These stages are directly taken from Perkins's *Golden Chain*. Though Wesley rejects the doctrine of double predestination, the framework is the same. Wesley inherited Perkins framework, though he may disagree as to the particular points within that framework. Additionally, both Perkins and Wesley view the mechanism of election as coming from hearing the Bible and the efficacy of preaching, along with the style that Perkins initiated in *The Art of Prophesying*.

In addition to the preaching and preachers being radically different from their Anglican counterparts, the audience was also rather different. England was growing and its demographics shifted as the Industrial Revolution began. The Anglican Church was not growing, and was not addressing the new industrial centers. Wesley saw this as an opportunity. The audience for his preaching was the lower strata of society. In many ways this echoes the great success that Francke and Zinzendorf had before him. The working class and poor were far too long neglected by the established churches who favored the educated, cultured elites.

The greatest example of the new audience was in Newcastle. Wesley identified the city as dire, filled with workers who knew little or nothing of religion, but knew a lot of drunkenness and cursing, even among the children. In their shared depravity, Wesley's Newcastle resembles Francke's Glaucha. Large crowds of industrial workers came out to hear Wesley preach. While most of the people Wesley gathered to himself were not already attached to a church, the episcopacy and other critics of Wesley claimed he was taking Christians away from other churches. His response was harsh, saying that "These were not Christians before they were thus joined. Most of them were barefaced heathens. . . If these are Christians at all, they are devil Christians."[18]

17. Tomkins, *John Wesley*, 82.
18. Wesley, "Plain Account of Methodists," 810.

Wesley and the Methodist preachers put on a show that was novel for anyone. While Wesley did not identify himself as a mystic, this did not preclude the movement from containing ecstatic outbursts. At the Baldwin Street meeting, one woman started crying out as if in the agonies of death. This scream subsided when the congregation prayed for her. Her horror turned to joy, she and others began laughing. In many ways this prefigures the holy laughter of the Pentecostals. Wesley himself was putting on Pentecostal revivals. The parallels between his movement and those taking place in Pentecostal Churches in the twentieth century are rather clear, especially given their link to the Holiness Movement of Phoebe Palmer and Charles G. Finney. The parallels are also rather clear to spirit possession as described by IM Lewis, where the lower strata of society and other disenfranchised choose a socially acceptable way of expressing their concerns, thereby finding relief from their torments.

As Methodism grew larger, so did the organization. While originally the focus was on small class meetings that looked rather like Spener's *Collogia*, with a dozen or so in each class, these classes grew into societies. These societies each had a superintendent. Each superintendent was placed on a circuit. Pairs of preachers, including some lay assistants, were responsible for each circuit. The circuits all fell under Wesley's rule, known as the Connection. Later this Connection became the annual conference where people were assigned a position for three years. While Wesley modeled his message after the Moravians, the bureaucratic structure of Methodism resembled the efficiency of Halle and Prussia and the organization of English companies. Throughout this structure, converts were supported and received constant evangelical teaching. Circuit preaching grew and was rather successful. Initially there were seven circuits.[19] Within two years there were two more, with over 80 societies.

The operation of the circuit was very much like a franchise. As the circuits grew, preachers took John's message, even if they were not formally under his leadership. Once a preacher chose to come under Wesley's leadership, they received the benefits and costs associated with the franchise. This guaranteed them regular visits from Wesley and other preachers for support. They were expected to surrender all independence on issues of doctrine, organization, and lifestyle. As John grew in popularity, so too did the option of joining with him. Unfortunately for many preachers, the demands that Wesley placed on the Methodists were strict and many preachers wanted out after joining. Often the congregations remained with Wesley and not their initial preacher.

19. London, Bristol, Cornwall, Evesham, York, Newcastle, and Wales.

When questions arose in 1744, Wesley called for the first conference at the Foundry. The first conference was rather small; in addition to the Wesley brothers, there were four ministers and four lay preachers. They set up rules and addressed concerns. Many of these concerns were practical in nature. In 1746 Wesley began a fund to give loans to Methodists in need. He also established a free dispensary of medicine. Undoubtedly some of these practices were his attempt to replicate Halle. Unfortunately the medical dispensary only lasted a few years as the 300 or so regular patients grew too expensive for the Methodists.

Like Francke, Wesley opened schools. Francke is often criticized for the harshness and discipline of his schools. Wesley chose to imitate the intensity of Francke as well. At Kingswood, students were expected to arrive at four o'clock in the morning and stay until eight o'clock in the evening. During this time they were held to the highest discipline to maximize religious and physical development. Students would fast, but not play. "He that plays when he is a child," Wesley explained, "shall play when he is a man."[20] School life was rigid and difficult. In addition to not being allowed to play, many schools also forbade children from speaking to anyone other than their instructors, and any child who missed two days of school without permission was dropped from their rolls.

Wesley opened many schools, including ones modeled after the Orphan House at Halle, but most closed shortly after they opened. Wesley attempted to have different schools for different communities, including one set up for children of preachers and another for the poor. Most of these schools floundered because Wesley failed to understand the child mind. He expected every child to have the same level of discipline that his mother imposed on him, and that expected of himself. Despite this, Wesley and the Methodists had a tremendous impact on education, especially after his death.

Wesley's pastoral legacy includes some theological innovations as well as practical ones. Many of these innovations are entirely his own, borrowing little or nothing from Continental Pietists. Wesley, like Zinzendorf, concerned himself fairly little with doctrinal orthodoxy, believing it "but a very slender part of religion."[21] Clearly Wesley is not borrowing from Tauler's concern to remain within any established theological system, choosing instead to break from ecclesial and theological conventions.

Practically the only theological innovation that Wesley did borrow was his view of the church. Like Zinzendorf, Wesley maintained an

---

20. Tomkins, *John Wesley*, 123.
21. Campbell, *Methodist Doctrine*, 30.

ecumenical spirit, and held that there existed an invisible church which all true believers belonged to in all ages and among all nations. For both Zinzendorf and Wesley this ecumenical spirit extended to the point that denominational membership accounted for very little other than serving as a practical association. Like other Pietists, Wesley's gathering of people out of their church, or making churches out of churches, was viewed as nothing but the most economical way of providing a means for individuals to work out their own salvation. In a surprising twist, Wesley, who cared little for denominations, ended up forming his own.

Other views Wesley held concerning the church were his own.[22] One example is his view of the "primitive church." Wesley often appealed to his associations at Oxford and others as the examples of being "Bible Christians." Wesley defines Bible Christians as "Christians taking the Bible, as interpreted by the primitive church and our own, for their whole and sole rule."[23] The only problem with this is that Wesley knew little to nothing about the primitive or ancient church. To begin with, Wesley gives no time table as to what period we are covering. We know from other mentions that Wesley defined primitive as being before the time of Constantine, but his lack of mentioning any early church fathers, as Perkins did, may place the primitive church to only the time of the Apostles. Oddly enough, the church fathers and councils that provide not only the creeds but also the Christian canon are excluded from being examples of the church.

We know that Wesley denies any real value of apostolic succession. Methodists today likewise reject the value of the practice. Wesley also makes reference to the "Constantinian fall of the church."[24] This is the belief that sometime around Constantine (272–337), and the patronage of the Roman Empire, the church was compromised and corrupted. With all the problems Wesley saw in the church, it is odd to follow what he says in a 1783 Sermon called "The Mystery of Iniquity," where he blames Constantine for inflicting "the greatest wound true Christianity ever received."[25] This is peculiar, as Wesley's knowledge of the early church largely came from supposition and imagination, and his claims about its operation came to him upon reflection. With this said, he tried to mimic some practices that he read about, including the Wednesday and Friday Fasts.[26]

---

22. Many were taken from other theological trends popular in England at the time, such as Baptists and other non-conformists, but were not common among Pietists.

23. Wesley, "Short History of Methodism," 804.

24. Buchan, "Wesley and the Constantinian Fall," 146.

25. Buchan, "Wesley and the Constantinian Fall," 148.

26. These fasts are still held for the Eastern Orthodox Christians.

Central to Wesley's view of Christianity is that it is divided. The divide is between real Christians and false Christians. These false Christians are sometimes referred to as "almost" Christians. The hallmark of an almost Christian is not any outward act. Indeed they may perform every rite and every practice of the "true" Christian, but they lack sincerity. "By sincerity I mean, a real, inward principle of religion, from which these outward actions flow."[27] They lack the type of faith that becomes so central for Wesley. Wesley would likely categorize himself as an almost Christian before his Aldersgate experience.

Along with the transformation of the Church and Christianity, Wesley also develops a new version of the Sacraments. Like many Reform Protestants, the sacraments lose their sacerdotal character. As with most Protestants in the eighteenth century, the number of sacraments is limited to the Eucharist and baptism. Wesley, following the model of Calvin and Perkins, will actually allude to a new sacrament while simultaneously demoting the only two surviving sacraments.

To begin with, Wesley, like Zwingli, did not hold the doctrine of the Real Presence of Christ in the Eucharist. Coming closer to Calvin, Wesley holds to a notion of a spiritual benefit, or spiritual presence, but like Calvin, did not go into too much detail on his beliefs. Wesley held that communion "was an outward means by which God conveyed to our souls spiritual grace purchased for us by Christ, and the mystical relation which the bread by consecration had to Christ's body was sufficient to give it the name of his body."[28] For this reason he urged regular communion, since his times at the Holy Club.

Baptism is also minimized for Wesley. Wesley denies any connection between baptism and justification or the new birth. Stating rather clearly that "baptism is not the new birth"[29] in his sermon called the new birth, he attempts to prove this from the English catechism. His conclusion is contrary to his deduction, as the catechism states that the inward part is cleansed in baptism, then states that it is not the new birth. Wesley, like many Calvinists and Francke, demand a born again experience to prove salvation; baptism is rejected as this experience.

Interestingly enough Wesley promotes a different Christian practice, Bible reading, to the level of a sacrament. This is similar to Calvin and Perkins treatment of the Bible as a sacrament. Bible reading becomes the central rite and practice for the Methodist Church, and is the only action that

---

27. Wesley, "Almost Christian," 173.
28. Nagler, *Pietism and Methodism*, 83.
29. Wesley, "New Birth," 221.

truly gives a Christian a spiritual blessing. While not named a sacrament, practically this is the only one that Wesley truly maintains.

A new command is also given by Wesley. Wesley actually gives many commands dictating life and practice, but he explicitly states that a "true Christian" is one who is happy. Regardless of the other constraints, such as forbidding laughter, Christians are to be happy. They should have within themselves "a fountain of water springing up into everlasting life, and overflowing soul with peace and joy."[30]

Wesley's Perfection

"This is to be a perfect man, to be sanctified throughout, even to have a heart so all-flaming with the love of God."[31]

—*John Wesley*

Central to Wesley's theological innovations is his notion of Sinless Perfection, or Christian Perfection. This doctrine is often confused and distorted by both followers and opponents of Wesley. In many ways the doctrine is rather straight forward, but in other ways it is not. Confusion is understandable, as Wesley was confused also. To truly understand this central doctrine we need to understand Wesley's theological starting point. This is a modified version of Luther's salvation by faith, and parts of it resemble the Pietist interpretation of man held by Arndt and Spener. With this said, Wesley's expression of this doctrine is wholly his own and Luther, Arndt, and Spener would all take umbrage at parts of this doctrine, which at times resembles Pelagianism, Donatism, and Manicheism.[32]

The theological starting point for Wesley is threefold. First, that all men by nature are dead in sin, therefore children of wrath. Second, that justification is by faith alone, and finally, that faith produces inward and outward holiness. In the first case we see that Wesley maintains the Western notion of Original Sin. But unlike even Augustine, Wesley maintains that in man's fallen state, "No one loves God."[33] Furthermore no one can have any knowledge of God, and man bears the image of the devil. This view is borrowed wholly from Perkins and Calvin. Man in this state is blind and

---

30. Wesley, "Character of a Methodist," 829.

31. Wesley, *Plain Account of Christian Perfection*, 75.

32. It may be fair to number quite a few other heresies that Wesley flirts with, but these are the main ones.

33. Wesley, "Original Sin," 129.

deaf to the nature and reality of God; spiritually he is dead. Wesley in this case maintains an extreme Calvinist and Puritan position. Wesley is also borrowing from à Kempis, who in the *Imitation of Christ*, states that without God, "We have eyes and do not see."[34]

Unlike Perkins and Calvin, Wesley maintains that man can be saved by grace. Wesley maintains the notion of total depravity as held by Calvinists, but rejects the doctrine of election and predestination. Here he resembles Luther, but only in words. The meanings are rather different. Wesley interprets Luther's doctrine of salvation by faith to two separate but related notions. First, justification, that is to say that God justifies man's fallen nature. Second, Wesley holds the notion of the new birth. This resembles Arndt, but only superficially. Wesley's notion of the new birth /new creation includes a notion of perfection that Arndt did not. For Wesley "the new birth is absolutely necessary in order to eternal salvation."[35]

Since Wesley's beginning point is that man is spiritually dead, the new birth is in all aspects new. Man is made alive through Christ's life. Faith is the agent of love, and "when a man is justified he is born of God."[36] This leads to conformity to the will of God. This conformity is not partial, rather Wesley explicitly states that "being born of God, he does not sin."[37] This new birth is a metamorphosis, not simply a modification of the old life. Oddly, Wesley holds that this change occurs all at once at the moment of conversion, but the Christian may not even know of their justification until long after it has transpired.[38]

Maintaining a Pauline duality verging on Manicheanism between flesh and spirit, Wesley holds that upon justification the spirit is born. Still the degree to which the person is spirit verse flesh is not yet resolved.[39] In this spirit man is sanctified, not only justified. This is necessary, for according to Wesley, Christ cannot reign where sin is present, nor dwell where sin is allowed. If the Christian is to maintain a relationship with Christ, they cannot have sin. Only to confuse this doctrine more, while Wesley

---

34. à Kempis, *Imitation of Christ*, 3.
35. Wesley, "New Birth," 221.
36. Wesley, "Principles of a Methodist," 843.
37. Wesley, "Principles of a Methodist," 843
38. "I believe that conversion is an instantaneous work; and that the moment he is converted, or has living faith in Christ, he is justified: which faith a man cannot have, without knowing that he has it. Yet I believe he may not know that he is justified (that is, that he has living faith) till a long time after" (Wesley, "Principles of a Methodist," 843).
39. "Thus, although even babes In Christ are *sanctified*, yet it is only in part. In a degree, according to the measure of their faith, they are spiritual; yet, in a degree they are carnal" (Wesley, "On Sin in Believers," 350).

often conflates the notions of justification and sanctification, stating that both happen at the same time in order to allow room for Christ, he also separates them, claiming that the new birth is an instantaneous and gradual practice. In a few places Wesley places sanctification as complete and whole, occurring at the same time as justification. They occur as one event that takes place immediately. In other places Wesley states that sanctification is a process only beginning at the moment of justification. Contrary to Luther, Wesley also views justification not as the moment when, trusting in the merits of Christ alone man is made just, rather it is a process of trusting in Christ until sanctification is complete. From a Lutheran perspective these terms are confused and distorted. While Arndt and other Pietists we have addressed used these terms, their meanings were different, if not the complete opposite of how Wesley used them.

This is important because of what Wesley really means when he addresses sanctification and the new birth. Specifically Wesley addresses sanctification as "as *entire sanctification* or *Christian perfection.*"[40] Christian perfection is often synonymous with sinlessness, or being one with Christ. Here we must also define Wesley's notion of sin. For Wesley, sin is any "temper, passion, or affection; such as pride, self-will, love of the world in any kind or degree; such as lust, anger, peevishness; any disposition contrary to the mind that was in Christ."[41] Nearly always, Wesley links the term sin with either the adjective inward or outward. Wesley is far more concerned with addressing outward sin as real sin that separates man from God, implying that inward sin is the same as a temptation. Outward sin, as real sin, is dangerous since Wesley and all Methodists agree and earnestly maintain, "He who sins is of the devil."[42] Therefore those who sin are not Christians.

This is one issue that Wesley does not leave open to debate or interpretation, proclaiming that "Whoever has been born of God does not sin, for His seed remains in him; and he cannot sin, because he has been born of God"[43] Wesley does not permit the interpretation that the believer sins but not habitually, as the word habitually is absent from the text. "*Habitually!* Where is that? I do not read it. It is not written in the Book. God plainly says, 'He does not sin'; and you add, *habitually!* Who are you

---

40. Campbell, *Methodist Doctrine*, 68.
41. Wesley, "On Sin in Believers," 342.
42. Wesley, "On Sin in Believers," 342.
43. Wesley, "Marks of the New Birth," 229.

that *mends* the Word of God."[44] Sin is a state where man is at enmity with God and a True Christian cannot be a Christian if he is at enmity with God.

If Christians cannot sin, then it logically follows that Christians are sinless, or as Wesley defines it, perfect. Wesley defines Christian Perfection as "loving God with all our heart, mind, soul, and strength. This implies that no wrong temper, none contrary to love, remains in the soul; and that all the thoughts, words, and actions are governed by pure love."[45] In other words, "Perfection is living in the presence of Christ and sin is failure to live in the fullness of that presence."[46] Once again, we see how Wesley interprets Christianity through the lens of relationship rather than specific dogmas, or even rational declarations.

Wesley also states what he does not mean by perfection. Since he is addressing man in his current state, his definition of perfection excludes Adamic perfection, as well as the perfection of angels. Perfection excludes other common traits that are characteristic of humanity. Christian perfection is not perfection in knowledge, error or mistakes. Christians are also not free from bodily infirmities or temptation. Oddly enough, temptation is counted as an error in humanity. Wesley overlooks Christ's temptations, leading one to believe that Wesley fell into the seventh-century heresy of monothelitism, believing that Christ had only one will. Christians are perfect only as it relates to matters of salvation, as perfection is equated to love of God.

Wesley also holds that perfection does not include perfect knowledge. There is no certainty that one is saved from all sin unless God chooses to endow the believer with that as a blessing, a blessing that Wesley may not have received himself, as in 1767, in a letter to Lloyd's Evening Post, Wesley himself states, "I have told all the world I am not perfect."[47] Although one should assume his Aldersgate experience counted for something.

Finally, Wesley leaves us with one other question pertaining to Christian salvation. Is a Christian always perfect or can a Christian lose perfection? Wesley maintains that Christians can fall from grace, therefore losing salvation and losing perfection. They can also recover from the loss and become perfect once again. This striking notion likely emerges due to Wesley's peculiar view of justification and sanctification, and his desire to leave room for free will.

---

44. Wesley, "Marks of the New Birth," 229.
45. Wesley, "Plain Account of Christian Perfection," 1053.
46. Dillenberger, *Protestant Christianity*, 132.
47. Tomkins, *John Wesley*, 158.

This doctrine differs wildly from the notion of perfection held by earlier mystics and Pietists like Thomas à Kempis, Arndt, and Tauler. Thomas à Kempis viewed perfection as something that was never complete until death, but something worth striving for. Arndt maintained that perfection was a "denial of one's own will."[48] When Tauler speaks of perfection, he states "A perfect will is an abandonment of all that is not God. If a man hath not done this in works, he must do it in will if his will be perfect."[49] Thomas à Kempis, Arndt, and Tauler define perfection as abandoning one's own will, rather than a transformative state where one cannot sin. All four likely would agree that this state of perfection, whatever it looks like, would only be temporary, lasting as long as one has surrendered their will to God. Wesley, Arndt, and Tauler never believed that this state was a permanent one while in this life, and à Kempis went so far as to state "Every perfection in this life has some imperfection mixed with it."[50]

In summation, the problem with this central doctrine for Wesley is that while he made many attempts to clarify his position, he often equated the words "perfection," "sanctification," and "holiness" to mean essentially the same thing. He also put different emphasis on perfection when the mood struck him; sometimes it implied spiritual notions, while other times it largely resided with ethical considerations of love for one's neighbor. The Christian also becomes incapable of sin, yet perfection can be lost, assumedly when love of God or neighbor wains and the Christian sins. Wesley here is a semi-Donatist. Here the notion of new birth is different than perfection, but otherwise it is one and the same. Still, in no way does Wesley apply either the new birth or sanctification to any sacraments, but all are a result of man's effort, resulting in a Pelagianism that somehow works with Wesley's Calvinist view of total depravity. All of this is held together as both the hope of a Christian and also the first step for a Christian. All of it is the work of the individual with Christ, and not the church, yet all salvation leads to works that presumably happen in the individual and the communities they find themselves in.

We should also note that while Francke addressed notions of perfection as well, Francke never equated perfection as sinlessness. Rather for Francke it was always progress in the Christian life, and was equated with faith. Again Wesley used much of the language of the Pietists concerning his doctrine of perfection, but not their meanings.

---

48. Arndt, *True Christianity*, 224.
49. Tauler, *Following of Christ*, 136.
50. à Kempis, *Imitation of Christ*, 3.

One clear example where Wesley was not perfect is in regards to women. It is seemingly odd, or perfectly appropriate, that a man who spent most of his life as a professed celibate preacher had so many difficulties with women. Then again, his father and mother were not the example of a high functioning marriage, and it would not be difficult for any Freudian psychoanalyst to diagnose Wesley with a strong Oedipal complex. When considering marriage in 1749, the first objection to marriage he had was his long held belief that he should not ever find a wife "as such a woman as my father had."[51]

Wesley's mother, Susanna was an exemplary woman by many respects. Not only did she possess the proper pedigree for any devoted Puritan living in England during the eighteenth century, but her intellect was as strong as anyone else's. She was also determined and possessed the management skills that any Fortune 500 CEO would admire. Married at nineteen, she gave birth to somewhere between 17 and 19 children.[52] Only nine survived to adulthood. She managed the house in all its affairs, including the first decade of each of her children's education. Her methodical style in teaching and her strong discipline are likely the models of Christian living that John envisioned when creating schools, classes, and the mechanisms of Methodism in general.

Wesley's first real love other than his mother occurred on his dismal journey to Georgia. As mentioned earlier, he ran into difficulty when he wavered on the issue of marriage. Her name was Sophy Hopkey and at fifteen this devoted young woman tempted John away from the celibate life that he had envisioned for himself. Sophy attended the churches that Wesley was in charge of. Wesley also took special daily attention to her lessons and spiritual development. During that cursed year, John chose to throw off his vow of celibacy and proposed to Sophy. The problem was he did not do so clearly and Sophy was ignorant of John's proposal. Reasonably Sophy and those responsible for her chilled to the notion of marriage. After all, who would want to plan a marriage with someone who was not certain they wanted to enter into marriage at all. Further problems arose when John chose to propose again, and again. These subsequent times John was far more clear and forceful with his proposals of marriage, but so was Sophy's response. She issued a clear and direct no. The failed proposal was the origin of the charges against Wesley. Once rejected by Sophy, John was rejected by Georgia and fled back to England with the charges still pending.

A decade later John once again was tempted with giving up the celibate life. As the leaders of a charismatic movement, it should not surprise us that

---

51. Tomkins, *John Wesley*, 130.

52. A larger number of children than we find with other Pietist leaders but not irregular for Susanna who was likely the twenty-fifth child of her father.

John and his brother Charles were constantly "dangerous snares to many young women,"[53] as a friend described. John was snared this time by Grace Murray. Grace was 32 years of age, attractive, senior in the faith, but lower in class, and a widow. Grace nursed John back to health after he fell ill in August of 1748. John's love for this lowly woman destroyed all objections he held for the estate of marriage. Unfortunately John learned nothing from his proposals to Sophy Hopkey. When John proposed to Grace, it was equally opaque. Wesley's vague proclamations that "if I were ever to marry you would be the one,"[54] were not a picturesque proposal. She responded kindly but failed to comprehend she had accepted his proposal.

In order to further distort the proposal, if one could even call it that, John immediately took off on a preaching circuit. Grace then took interest in a Methodist preacher named John Bennett and the two of them were engaged. Grace was so far from understanding that Wesley believed they were betrothed, she told others she was not even aware that Wesley had any feelings for her. The botched proposal created a rift between Wesley and Bennett, as well as John Wesley and his brother Charles. Charles believed that John should remain celibate. Grace married Bennett shortly thereafter, and a larger rift occurred between the brothers. John was heartbroken and his trusted brother would not console him.

As luck had it John's broken heart would not last long. Within eighteen months of Grace's marriage to Bennet, Wesley was married as well. He likely learned how to be direct with his proposals and he chose a woman whose social standing could not be challenged. Molly Vazeille came from strong Protestant stock. Her family were Huguenots and she was wealthy. The 41 year old widow had four children, and she ensured that her wealth was set aside for their care and not for John. The courtship was brief. John tells us nothing of this in his copious journals. Equally surprising is the complete absence of the marriage from the journals as well.

At the time of the wedding Charles was also absent, in that he was not even invited to the wedding. It is doubtful that he would have attended if invited. While the proposals to Grace served as a rift between the brothers, the marriage served as a break between Charles and John. Charles believed that John should not get married, not to Grace, Molly, or any woman. Charles believed that marriage would hinder John's preaching. In actuality preaching hindered John's marriage. Charles was right in his assessment that John could only do one well, and the marriage would suffer.

53. Tomkins, *John Wesley*, 121.
54. Tomkins, *John Wesley*, 123.

Molly was not prepared to become Mrs. Wesley. John expected Molly to travel the circuits with him, but his voyages were grueling. Molly attempted to keep up, but found the ordeal to be a bit much. Molly complained about the weather, the road, the beds, and the food. John complained about his wife, muttering "to have persons at my ear fretting and murmuring at everything is like tearing the flesh off my bones."[55] Other times John simply left Molly behind. At least once when waiting for a coach Molly was running late, John counted the minutes on his watch. Once she was ten minutes past, he climbed aboard and left her behind.

The marriage was quickly falling apart. Molly complained that John paid too much attention to those under his instruction, especially the women. Molly seriously suspected John of adultery. These accusations were not simply the thoughts of an ill-treated and overly mistrustful wife. John wrote many letters to women with far more romantic claims than he used in his proposals to Sophy Hopkey and Grace Murray.

Molly first discovered these letters in 1755, only five years into their troubled marriage. The first letter was to Mrs. Lefevre. Unsure what she should do, Molly turned to John's brother Charles. Charles refused to speak to her about the matter. Two years later Molly's suspicions grew again. John developed another overly close relationship with a woman. This time it began when John appointed Sarah Ryan as the new housekeeper. Sarah was ill suited for the job; she lacked the education and organizational skills needed for the job. The only thing that her resume supplied was bigamy. Technically she was married to three men at this time. Molly believed that that John's motives were not pure. Molly discovered a letter John wrote Sarah saying "I love your simplicity, conversing with you, either by speaking or writing, is an unspeakable blessing to me. I cannot think of you without thinking of God."[56] These words are far kinder than anything John was saying to his wife at the time. The only thing he ever praised Molly about was "I still love you. . . . for your uncommon neatness and cleanliness."[57] Wesley was the one who coined the phrase that cleanliness is next to godliness. Molly had enough of this and called John on his likely adultery during the 1757 annual conference at Bristol. John then barred Molly from communion for several years.

Molly wanted clearer proof of John's involvement with Sarah Ryan or Mrs. Lefevre, so she broke into his bureau and took letters that he wrote. She found only suggestive passages, but Sarah Ryan was not the only woman he was writing to at this time. John also wrote alluringly to Sarah Crosby, a

55. Bufford, *John Wesley and Marriage*, 119.
56. Tomkins, *John Wesley*, 153.
57. Tomkins, *John Wesley*, 165.

class leader at the Foundry. Clearly this was too much even for John's friends, who advised him to stop writing, as his letters were far too suggestive. John refused. Instead he declared "as long as I can hold a pen, I assert my right of conversing with whom I please. . . . If the unbeliever (Molly) will depart, let her depart."[58] In addition to declaring his wife an unbeliever John took steps to prevent her from finding his correspondence and commissioned a new bureau built, this one with secret compartments.

While Molly's evidence of John's promiscuity was largely limited to letters, she did record that in December of 1560, John left a meeting one night with Betty Disine, only to be found in her company the next morning. Molly told her husband that he should "desist from running after strange women, for your character is at stake."[59]

The marriage was clearly doomed. While remaining married, they saw very little of each other. Every few years Molly suspected John's indiscretion and proclaimed she was leaving him, but would then return. John continued his preaching and Molly remained at home with her children in London. When Molly grew sick, John went to visit her in 1768. Having heard of her recovery, he left for Bristol in the middle of the night, without seeing her. In 1771 Molly declared she was leaving John again. This time it likely stuck. John responded "I did not leave her: I did not send her away: I will not call her back."[60] We have no record of the two even seeing each other after 1776. Molly lived the last five years of her life without her husband. She died on October 8, 1781. John did not attend her funeral. He also only received a ring from her vast estate, as the rest went to her daughter.

Aside from his wife, it appears that John quite admired women. This extended to laying the groundwork for ordination by allowing women to preach. As Methodism was largely a lay religious movement and John already permitted lay preachers, the notion of women preaching was not much of a stretch, especially given Zinzendorf's work on that front already. John decided to take that next step in 1761, when Sarah Crosby went to encourage other women outside of her class in Derby. A crowd of 200 showed up and she decided to share her own story in front of the church. When this was brought to Wesley, he surmised that if it benefited the people, God could not object. The advice for her was, "When you meet again, tell them simply, 'You lay me under a great difficulty. The Methodists do not allow of women preachers; neither do I take upon me any such character.

---

58. Tomkins, *John Wesley*, 154.
59. Tomkins, *John Wesley*, 159.
60. Tomkins, *John Wesley*, 174.

But I will just nakedly tell you what is on my heart.' . . . I do not see that you have broken any law. Go on calmly and steadily."[61]

The rule was not for Sarah alone, John then encouraged Grace Walton to give a short exhortation. Within a decade, John began to create new rules for women preachers, telling Sarah Crosby in 1769 to preach, but to avoid the form of preaching. The sermons were to be short and interlaced with prayers so she could call the services a prayer meeting. Two years later the façade of Crosby's sermons began to crack and it was obvious to most that she was delivering sermons. Mary Bosanquet and other women were doing the same, leading many male preachers to complain. In response, Wesley refused to ordain the women but gave them license to operate as any lay male preacher. Sarah and Mary traveled the circuit just like Wesley and his other preachers.

Wesley and Methodism on Their Own

"By Methodists I mean, a people who profess to pursue holiness of heart and life, inward and outward conformity to all things to the revealed will of God."[62]

— *John Wesley*

One may suspect that John was intent on breaking with the established Church of England. After all he promoted the notion of lay preaching, including women, and his classes grew into their own churches, with their own government and rules. Methodism, like many forms of continental Pietism was, de facto, a church within the church. With the growing success and ever increasing levels of hostility of the church to it, it was only a matter of time before it became a church outside the church. But the time for its break would not occur until after Wesley's death. In the conference of 1755, many hoped to break with the Church of England, but John convinced them to remain. Even more striking was that Wesley permitted a lay preacher, Charles Perronet, to give communion in London. Charles Wesley was appalled, but John's response was to further blur the lines that ordination imposed, stating that "We have in effect ordained already."[63]

John clearly saw little value in the Church of England, and in the boundaries of ordination. Yet he was not willing to allow for schism. John maintained that "When the Methodists leave the church, God will leave

---

61. Tomkins, *John Wesley*, 160.
62. Wesley, "Advice to Methodists," 849.
63. Tomkins, *John Wesley*, 150.

them."[64] After his death, the meeting of 1795 put in place the Plan of Pacification, which allowed individual churches to break from the Church of England if they desired. It only took two years before churches in England began to break away.

Churches in America had already done so. This was as a result of the Revolutionary War. It became increasingly difficult for Americans to have an American ordained by the Episcopacy in England. The solution was to appoint a bishop for the United States. John was in an odd position of ordaining men priests, while not a bishop himself, and remaining under the Archbishop of Canterbury. Wesley's response was to again blur the lines between presbyter and bishop, claiming that priest and bishop were of the same order and that he was as much a Christian bishop as the Archbishop of Canterbury, even though he was in no way a bishop.

Wesley did decide to break with the Moravians though in 1749. Wesley was disenchanted by some of the Moravian revivals he witnessed in London. These Moravians grew too extreme, even for Wesley. Wesley urged all who had been fooled into joining the Brethren to desert them. The great error that the Moravians perpetuated was not that extreme. It came down to the totality of faith. Moravians contended that faith became an all or nothing proposition. Wesley maintained that while that was possible, often it came by degrees. Oddly enough, Wesley makes similar propositions as the Moravians as we already addressed with his doctrine of Christian Perfection. Wesley did take the missionary spirit with him from the Moravians and continued to send out missionaries, not only to the Americas but the whole world. The Moravians taught John Wesley to say "The world is my parish!"

Wesley had similar breaks with Whitfield, and his brother Charles. John Wesley owes quite a debt to Whitfield, who was one of the early members at Oxford and provided Wesley with the means of his early preaching career in the field. But Whitfield's fidelity to Calvin's notion of predestination was not one that Wesley could accept. As we have seen in many instances, John believes in free will. Beyond the theological difference, there was also a practical one. Whitfield was content with being a preacher while Wesley was a preacher, a pastor, administrator, and creator of a new religious movement. Whitfield believed that delivering sermons would be the means that the Elect should accept Christ. Wesley, not believing that the Elect were predestined, needed to build an organization around them to facilitate salvation.

Two other issues separated the two preachers. First, Whitfield laughed. For Wesley laughter was needless and dangerous to one's salvation. While

---

64. Tomkins, *John Wesley*, 188.

Whitfield believed in freedom to laugh, Wesley believed in freedom from slavery. Whitfield spent far more time in America than Wesley and came to the conclusion that slavery was necessary for the economic life of the Southern colonies. He was even responsible for overthrowing Oglethorpe's ban on slavery in Georgia and owned 25 slaves himself. Wesley came to the conclusion of many in the Enlightenment, that slavery restricted freedom and was an oppression that must be stopped.

The greatest champion and challenger to John's career was not Whitfield, but John's brother Charles Wesley. Charles began the Holiness Club that John then took over; he also produced the majority of the hymns that are used for the Methodists. Charles was also willing to challenge his brother when seemingly no one else could. Charles, while less theologically minded than his brother, believed that fidelity to doctrine was far more important. Sometimes this fidelity encouraged Methodism to remain within the bounds of the English Church, other times Charles supported breaking from the church. Charles also wanted to have strong preachers, while John permitted poor preaching from time to time. Charles was clearly the heir to his brothers movement, but he was always more comfortable correcting his brothers abuses than leading such a movement on his own. When John fell ill in 1753, Charles refused to succeed his brother as the leader.

John recovered and lived for nearly another forty years. Before his death in 1784, John drew up the Deed of Declaration. The Deed established the Conference as the leading body of the Methodists and outlined the requirement of annual meetings with election for members every three years. John died on March 2, 1791.

With membership based not on theological fidelity or rational proofs, Wesley created the Methodist Church. By many respects, this is the single largest institutional result of Pietism. Wesley's religion fit well within the dictates of Kantian philosophy that emerged during the same time, namely Kant's belief that religion was primarily about ethics. Wesley's Pietism focused on reforming the ethical life, not just doctrines. Wesley's greatest impact in the nineteenth century was within the Methodist Church. Methodism grew to become a ledge protruding from the edifice of Pietism that other movements built off of, including the Holiness Movement, Pentecostalism, and fundamentalism. Wesley provided the mantle for Palmer. She remained a Methodist, while birthing the Holiness Movement, advancing Wesley's doctrines of Christian Perfection and living the life of a Bible Christian.

Wesley and Zinzendorf also combine to pave the way for female ordination. Both called women to serve in the church in positions usually held only for men. Significantly, this came from Spener, whose *collegia* promoted an egalitarian spirit, allowing women prominent roles. Zinzendorf then advocated for greater notions of equality and Wesley eliminated all divisions of gender through eliminating the ecclesial division between bishop and presbyter, as well as priests, and the laity.

Conclusion
Success and Impact of Halle, Moravians & Methodists through the Eighteenth Century

> "A Monster is whatever we are not, so as monsters change form so do we, by implication."[1]
>
> —*Zakiya Hanafi*

WHILE INITIALLY AN OPPRESSED minority, Pietism for most in the eighteenth century was empowering. The oppression proved fealty to God and only served to encourage the group. This encouragement took place in spiritual autobiographies as addressed by Van Leiburg, the *collegias* set up by Spener and Francke, Methodist meeting halls, and the Moravian enclaves in Herrnhut, Herrnhag, and the Americas. The Pietists were a group within the larger group. Through the eighteenth century those small groups began to dominate the whole.

By the conclusion of the eighteenth century, Pietism was clearly a force that was not going away, and it was not going to remain subordinate to the Orthodox elements within the confessions of Lutheranism, Reform, or Anglicanism. It is even argued that in Germany the Pietist attitude represents the default religious standpoint at the dawn of the nineteenth century. Pietism, emerging from Halle, Herrnhut, and Holiness Clubs, grew to dominate the cultural landscape. The critiques from these communities grew into attacks against the Protestant establishments. No longer were the Pietists simply distressed outsiders, rather they fashioned themselves the liberators of Christendom. The Pietist offensive naturally produced

---

1. Hanafi, *Monster in the Machine*, viii.

polemics against them. Possibly the strongest anti-Pietist tract was written by Valentin Ernst Loscher, who penned *Malum Pietisticum*.[2]

Pietisms earliest success came at the University of Halle, with the Pietist network that it created. What many consider a fortuitous happenstance was anything but. Once Francke received the charge of creating a theology department, he immediately planned out the course advancement he foresaw for the institution in his work *Der Grosse Aufsatz*[3] in 1704. Francke conceived of the university as the manufacturing plant for the spiritual needs of Prussia, Germany and the world. The Pietist leaders coming out of the school advanced Francke's vision of a renewal for all areas of society. At Halle, catechism lessons taught the poor to read and write as well as how to be pious Christians, disciplined workers, and obedient subjects.

The University of Halle was also known as one of the centers for the German Enlightenment, the *Aufklärer*. As noted earlier, Pietism and Enlightenment rationalism were not always antithetical to each other. From the lifelong friendship of Leibniz and Spener, to the shared drive to investigate individual experience, Halle shaped both impulses in the eighteenth century, often shaping one by the other. It should not be a surprise that the university hosted rationalist Christian Wolff, or created the educational system that fashioned Immanuel Kant, as well as Friedrich Schleiermacher.

In addition to reforming the educational system of Pietist as well as Rationalist schools, Halle also became the model of eighteenth-century orphanages throughout all of Europe. Halle set the example first for Protestant Germans, with up to 25 percent of the orphanages founded between 1695 and 1806 modeled directly after Halle's success. The orphanages succeeded because they were less burdensome than others. Not only did they remove the orphans from the street, but they were also manufacturing centers. Today many of us may find the idea of orphans as a source of labor objectionable. Yet in the eighteenth century, this relationship between care and work was viewed as symbiotic, not exploitative. Orphans came out of the Halle system and spread throughout Europe, internalizing the Pietist message, as well as the promethean ethic of Francke, applying it to other ventures as well.

Johann Henrich Schulze and Anna Hedwig Petersin illustrate success stories from the orphan system. Schulze began attending the orphan house after the death of one of his parents. Immediately he attended the Latin school and became an accomplished linguist, teaching at the Halle Padagogium

---

2. "The Pietistic Evil."
3. "The Great Project."

Conclusion

and university, and becoming a professor of medicine and Greek in Altdorf. Anna Petersin was given an education excelling in arithmetic and writing. She even worked in Francke's home, caring for the children. Halle's orphans included both men and women, educating both. We have already seen the significant roles women played in early Pietism in Frankfurt with Anna Elisabeth Kissner, Johanna Eleonora von Merlau, and Maria Juliana Baur von Eyseneck.

Possibly the world's most famous Halle orphan was Georg Friedrich Handel. Following his father's death, Handel attended Halle before ultimately making his home in London in 1711. Handel still visited Halle from time to time. The message and model of the orphanage was internalized by Handel. When the London Foundling Hospital was established in 1749, Handel composed hymns for the occasion. Sitting on the board of governors, Handel shaped the hospital from what he saw during his youth at Halle. Also his music was used as a fundraising endeavor for the hospital. Every year the performance of *the Messiah* generated revenue for the hospital.

The Moravians were not quite as successful as the University at Halle early on. Unlike Halle, which sought to reform the pedagogy of Christendom, the Moravians sought to plant settlements which Zinzendorf and others hoped would impact the world around them. Herrnhut provided a great example; Herrnhag less so. In the New World, the settlements were equally mixed. Georgia, the Moravians first attempt at settlement outside of Germany, was largely a failure. It was short lived once the English and Spaniards began fighting over the territory between Spanish controlled Florida and English held Georgia. The foreseeable conflict was the reason why the Moravians were permitted to settle in Georgia by the English. By 1740 the settlement dwindled to a dozen people. Other efforts to evangelize to the Germans and slaves at Purysburg, South Carolina were also unsuccessful.

Pennsylvania was somewhat more positive, but only slightly. Zinzendorf hoped to bring inter-denominational dialogue with the Moravians and the others, including Lutherans, Reformed, Quakers, Mennonites, Dunkers, Ephrata monks, the Inspired, and separatists who were all there. The ecumenical spirit inherent in Moravian piety fell to the necessary theological contentions inherent in all but Pietist theology. Success for Pennsylvania came only with the settlement of Bethlehem and the mission work that grew out of it.

Further success for the Moravians in America came after the American Revolution, not in settlements, but in schooling. Early American education was still closely tied to church schools, which restricted attendance to those who shared denominational ties. The Moravians, being more ecumenically minded that others, opened their schools to outsiders, beginning with their reorganization in 1785. Moravian education impacted non-Moravians, undoubtedly shaping their theology and views of education.

Perhaps the greatest significance of the Moravians in America and Europe was their impact on John Wesley and the entire Methodist tradition. Wesley began an eighteenth-century English revival. The conventional understanding of the English Evangelical revivals starts with Wesley, and for good reason. Wesley synthesized Perkins and Zinzendorf into a renewed English Pietism which provided an answer to the needs of the industrializing centers of England.

Even after Wesley's opposition to the Revolution, the Methodists found success in America as well. After plummeting attendance, on the eve of the Revolution by 1790, participation exceeded 60,000 Methodists in America, only slightly less than the 70,000 in England.[4] The Revolution untied the hands of the Methodists, allowing them to promote their own clergy, including their own bishops, apart from the wishes of Canterbury, and even Wesley. The Methodist Episcopal Church and the American Methodists had their own bishops decades ahead of their English counterparts, who remained connected to the Anglican Church until after Wesley's death.

The expansion of America and the increased need to provide preachers fueled further growth for Methodists in America. Lay preachers and circuit preachers adapted well to the frontier. These extraordinary ministers celebrated the sacraments apart from a higher ecclesial body. Many operated largely independent from one another, with local elders determining who was eligible to celebrate. The local decisions continued to promote local preachers as well as lay preachers, and even consecrated women as deaconesses. In America today there are four related major Methodist denominations that grew from the Methodist Episcopal.[5]

Outside of denominational formation, the success of these movements impacted Christian societies at large, primarily in three areas, Prussianism, Missionary Movements, and the Great Awakenings in the United States. These advancements grew out of Halle, Herrrnhut, and the Holiness Clubs and came into their own in the late eighteenth and early nineteenth centuries.

Prussianism is often defined as the monomaniacal devotion to the interests of the state over all other concerns of life, the fulfillment of the

---

4. 61,811 in America (six times more than a decade earlier) and 71,463 members in England.

5. The African Methodist Episcopal (AME) Church, The African Methodist Episcopal Zion (AME Zion) Church, The Christian Methodist Episcopal (CME) Church, and The United Methodist Church (UMC).

needs of the state over the needs of any individual citizen. The mechanism of Prussianism is usually tied to the bureaucratic state as a function of the military apparatus, to the point that many observed that "Prussia was not a country with an army, but an army with a country."[6] The discipline of the army is the discipline of the state, which requires centralization and control, and produces hegemony, homogeny, and industrial harmony with the interests of the state.

Prussianism is more than the process of German advancement. The advancement led to the collision with England, producing the First and Second World Wars, as described by Friedrich Meinecke in *The German Catastrophe*. It was the slow shift from Germany as the old Sleeping Michael to the industrious reputation Germans gained by the end of the nineteenth century described by historian David Blackbourn. The German nation took their character from Prussia, who took its character not only from the Hohenzollerns, and the bureaucratic military structure, but from the Pietists at Halle.

Beginning with the ascension of Fredrick Wilhelm I to the Prussian throne in 1713, ascetic Christianity found a dynastic champion. Fredrick Wilhelm and his decedents demanded military discipline of themselves and their state. The church served as the mechanism to inculcate the populace along the monarch's disciplinary desires. Fredrick Wilhelm's sense of duty and obligation was only rivaled by one man, August Hermann Francke. Both promoted an ambitious campaign to remake Brandenburg-Prussia. The new ascetic attitude, once internalized, was no longer simply a monarchical decree, but a divine command. Hartmut Lehman argues that Pietism, applied in service to the state, created "an 'inner fatherland,' constituting in fantasy what was missing in the reality of late eighteenth-century Germany."[7] The Hohenzollerns and Francke agreed that civic duty was synonymous with the Christians duty.

With these objectives aligned, all Lutheran pastors in Brandenburg-Prussia following 1729 were required to study at least two years at the University of Halle. Given the opportunity, Francke reordered the society to ensure the success of his brand of Pietism. Not only did the school educate Pietists rather than Scholastic Lutherans, but the rejection of idleness and the self-discipline imposed was alluring and unescapable. Francke set up a patronage network that controlled all appointments to the Prussian army chaplaincy. This patronage system favored Halle graduates, not only in the military, but in all areas of the Prussian bureaucracy. Pietist control over

---

6. Blackbourn, *Long Nineteenth Century*, 23.
7. Lehmann, "Pietism and Nationalism," 40.

patronage was not only about promoting their own people, but also about excluding outsiders. Pietism and Halle education became the litmus tests for promotion to political appointments. As a result of Halle's influence, Pietist leaders such as Baron Carl Hildebrand von Canstein grew so powerful that they manipulated Frederick Wilhelm and even blocked his agenda.

Halle Pietists were not simply cooperating with Hohenzollern ironfisted discipline, they were going beyond their perceived function. The Prussian Pietists appeared to be cooperating or even allied with Frederick Wilhelm, when in reality they were really subverting the King's religious agenda. Fredrick Wilhelm wanted his Calvinism to thrive against the Lutheran Scholasticism. This was the aim of promoting Pietism, not the consequence. Frederick Wilhelm wanted religious toleration. This toleration produced a level of intellectual freedom and an openness in Brandenburg-Prussia not seen in most other German states. What the ideological power vacuum actually produced was a theocracy masquerading as a monarchy. By the end of the eighteenth century, Halle Pietists were the Prussian state. Even Johann Christoph Woellner (1732–1800), the confidant to Frederick Wilhelm II and champion of the *Aufklarung*, was educated at Halle. According to Michael J. Sauter, the Edict on Religion of 1788 and the Enlightenment views that the edict supposedly represented, were in actuality politically and socially exclusive, rather than emancipatory.

The austere living required from Prussianism could not have succeeded in the relatively short time it did by the decrees or ambitions of the Hohenzollerns alone. It was the religious goals of the Pietists that broke down provincial isolation and fostered centralization. They also gave an internal motivation to the subjects of the Hohenzollerns that advanced the Brandenburg-Prussian ideology known as Prussianism.

The expansionist aim of the Pietists not only reformed the Prussian state, but sought to do so for the entire world through the formation of missionary movements. Eighteenth-century Pietism gave birth to the Protestant missions. These missions began as an inner mission to save the souls of Protestants, but this inner mission expanded to an outer mission, with a strong feeling of social responsibility for the disinherited people.

As already addressed, this began with the Halle-Danish missions. The Danish empire sought Halle trained missionaries Bartholomaus Ziegenbalg (1682–1719) and Heinrich Plutsckau (1677–1747). These two founded a mission school for Tamil boys and girls in Tranquebar, using the curriculum and educational methods found in Halle. This expanded through schools

Conclusion

set up throughout the world,[8] as well as the medical missions and print missions selling sermons and Biblical commentaries.

Halle and the Moravians shared in this task. Both were focused on linguistic training and analysis, which afforded them the flexibility and curiosity to approach the peoples around the world with eager inquisitiveness, along with evangelical zeal. The result, beyond their spiritual aims, was a remarkable production of scholarly treatises in linguistics and ethnography.

The Methodists joined the Moravians in their attempts to convert the natives of America. With the greater emphasis on lay preaching, the Methodists lacked the pedagogical resources of Halle and the Moravians. The Methodists found limited success missionizing the natives in the Americas, rather their greatest triumph was found in the industrial centers in England.

The Methodist message, as well as the surviving Puritan missive, resounded among the colonials in North America. The result was the First and Second Great Awakenings. The Puritans legacy of the First Great Awakening of the 1730s and 1740s is easily seen with the contributions of Cotton Mather and Jonathan Edwards. Both Cotton Mather and Jonathan Edwards were greatly influenced by Perkins and Ames. Mather set the stage as a pre-revivalist for the Great Awakening, and Edwards was the main theologian of that revival. Though English and in America, Mather was still aware of the events in Europe and was known to have sent bags of gold to Francke for his work with orphans, Jewish-children, and foreign missions. Mather also called for an "outpouring of the Holy Spirit" in a similar manner as Zinzendorf before the "Moravian Pentecost."

Edwards is the main preacher of the American revival. Throughout his sermons, the impact of Perkins is clear, and the margins of his copy of Ames's *Marrow of Theology* were filled with notes. The Pietist impulse is also abundantly clear in Edwards's sermon "The Reality of a Divine and Supernatural Light." In it, Edwards describes two modes of understanding. The first one is speculative. The other is "that which consists in the sense of the heart."[9] This creates a fundamental difference when one approaches God. Edwards holds that God is observed, not from the head as a rational judgment, but felt in the heart, sensing God's beauty and living in appreciation of it.

Fifty years later, the Second Great Awakening began in North America. The remnant of American Puritans lit the flame, but the Methodists and Moravians fueled the fervor, and the Methodists gained more from it than

---

8. Including England, Denmark, Hungary, Estonia, Siberia, and India.
9. Edwards, "Divine and Supernatural Light," 14.

anyone else. Generally viewed as a rural revival, Methodists took advantage of their relative flexibility to scoop up members and grow churches on the frontier. The view that the Awakening was primarily a rural and frontier revival has recently been challenged though. New recent attention is paid to the success the evangelical message had in major urban centers like New York. While a debate exists about how one should characterize the greatest success of the Second Great Awakening, it is clear that it was widespread and impacted both the rural frontier and major urban centers. The impact is found in the reformation of American Protestantism along a more Pietist direction.

What we see through the Great Awakenings, as well as the early Missionary movements and Prussianism, is the expansion and growth of the Pietist impulse. While Protestant scholasticism and rationalism had their successful institutional forms at the beginning of the Reformation, Pietism developed these later in the eighteenth century. The development into institutions and the relative flexibility the experientially focused Pietists had allowed them a diverse impact on the world. Through both its own culture and expansion, Pietism, now in an institutional form, left its mark on nearly every establishment, tradition, and ideology it ran up against.

Conclusion

WHAT SUCCESS BRINGS

There must exist an intimate connection between social organization and religious belief.[10]

—Bronislaw Malinowski

With the success of institutional Pietism through political participation and denominational formation, Pietism finds itself at odds with the very reason for its emergence at the dawn of the Reformation. Specifically, Pietism is now an institution, like the various strains of Protestantism that it developed in reaction to. After three hundred years railing against the established church and the culture at large, Pietism created its own churches and formed schools, states, and other institutions. These shaped modernity at the beginning of the nineteenth century.

While the Pietists succeeded at least in part in shaping their own destiny and preserving the Protestant emphasis on experiential religion, they did so at a cost. Becoming the establishment was the very thing they were opposed to. The existing habitus for the Pietists came from the position of outsiders. Institutionalization emerged from the eschatological need for success. Pietists retained the belief in a calling, being elect, and somehow remaining set apart from the larger community. There still remained a theological and internal need for Pietists to remain outsiders. These two opposing forces worked together in the eighteenth century, largely because success was not final. By the conclusion of the century, Pietists needed to reconcile these tendencies. For many Pietists, success and institutionalization was preferable, but the drive to remain outside, to be a critic not only of society but also Christendom remained a strong force. Again, J. Z. Smith put it "the most basic sense of the 'other' is generated by the opposition in/out."[11] The theological notions attached to election and chosenness required being set apart from the larger community. If one is in the larger community, they are out of the community of God.

This is the legacy that Pietism leaves at the dawn of the nineteenth century and not surprisingly we have the same discussions of Christianity in general, and Protestant Christianity specifically, in relation to the nineteenth century as we have throughout our discussions of modernity. Namely that Christianity is simultaneously in a period of great decline, that its attempts at shaping the thoughts of Europeans and Americans are so miniscule as to not warrant mention. Others contend that this was the period of great

---

10. Malinowski, *Magic, Science, and Religion*, 21.
11. Smith, *Relating Religion*, 230.

advancement, remarking at the numerical and geographical expansion. It is after all the nineteenth century which is the crest of European and American colonialism that now embraced a multitude of missionary movements, expanding the various Protestant worldviews throughout the globe. While church member rolls are always a difficult way to explain piety, we do see a drastic jump in the American population, as church members "rose from less than 10 percent in 1800 to over 40 percent in 1910 (and to 58 percent in 1951)."[12] Mission churches, Methodist circuit-riders, Christian student societies, Sunday Schools, the YMCA/YWCA, and the decay in denominational identity become the normative practices for both Protestant Christians and the nations that they find themselves in. Each of these practices have their rationale in both the culture of the nineteenth century, as well as the theological systems and thoughts of the Pietists.

We see a similar advancement in the realm of philosophy on the European Continent. Terry Pinkard, in his work *German Philosophy 1760–1860: The Legacy of Idealism,* argues that Pietism, with its emphasis on looking inward rather than at established theological systems, laid the groundwork for German Philosophy. This self-reflection is much more in line with Leibniz and Christian Wolff than Voltaire. If we take this claim seriously, the groundwork for the philosophical revolutions that began in Germany at the conclusion of the eighteenth century is far more indebted to Pietism than rationalism, although the *Aufklarung* is a product of both. Kant, the philosophical behemoth that shaped the nineteenth century, has feet in both worlds. Pietism grew from a church within a church, to a church in and of itself, but also to an ideology that shaped the European and American mind through Kant and his philosophical predecessors. In treatments of philosophy alone, Schleiermacher and Kierkegaard are inheritors of Kant and the shared background of Pietism. Hegel is also indebted to Kant and his antagonistic interactions with Schleiermacher in shaping his own theological system.

One variant of Pietism tended towards philosophy, other variants to continued theological speculation. Still, an institutionalized Pietism existed, but its impact was making way to the other two manifestations of the ethos of the Pietistic spirit. Success in theology, philosophy, state governance, and institutional reality predicated the requirement that Pietism must shift again or forever be condemned as the dead religion that Perkins, Arndt, Spener, Francke, Zinzendorf, and Wesley were so opposed to. The solution is rather counterintuitive, but nonetheless obvious. Experiential Protestantism must once again reimagine itself. This time the label Pietism may still apply, but

---

12. Dillenberger and Welch, *Protestant Christianity*, 163.

it causes as much difficulty as it did centuries earlier. This is why identifying Pietism becomes so diverse in the nineteenth century, including to the point that some scholars believe it to be everywhere or nowhere. It is also why theologically speaking Pietism remains within confessions as well as departing from them, promoting heterodox practices and theology, and is often at odds with other Pietists as well. Pietism truly shows the booms and busts of unrestrained theology. Schisms grow and heresies are flirted with but this is largely to be an expected result of the Protestant reformations. What is profound is the success the Pietists had in reaching beyond themselves and bringing diverse people and ideas together. Pietism succeeded in forming the Western world, not only through the theological debates internal to Protestantism, but also in politics and governance, touching nearly every aspect of society. It is striking how broad reaching Pietism, a movement which emphasized an individual's experience of the divine, had at reaching outside itself and drawing not only God in but also the rest of the world.

Bibliography

Ackerley, Chris. "Samuel Beckett and Thomas a Kempis: The Roots of Quietism." *Samuel Beckett Today* 9 (2000) 81–92.
Alvis, Robert E. *Religion and the Rise of Nationalism: A Profile of an East-Central European City.* Syracuse: Syracuse University Press, 2005.
Ames, William. *The Marrow of Theology.* Translated by John Dykstra Eusden. Grand Rapids, MI: Baker, 1968.
Angela of Foligno. *Complete Works.* Edited by Paul Lachance. Classics of Western Spirituality. Mahwah, NJ: Paulist, 1993.
"Anna Magdalena von Wurmb." Geni.com. https://www.geni.com/people/Anna-Magdalena-von-Wurmb/6000000023983334161.
Antoun, Richard T. *Understanding Fundamentalism.* Second edition. Lanham, MD: Rowman & Littlefield, 2008.
Arndt, Johann. *Garden of Paradise: or, holy prayers and exercises: whereby the Christian graces and virtues may be planted and improved in man, Pursing the design of the famous treatise of True Christianity by John Arndt.* Translated by Anton Wilhelm Bohm. London: J. Downing, 1716.
———. *True Christianity.* Mahwah, NJ: Paulist, 1979.
Athanasius of Alexandria. *Life of St. Anthony of Egypt.* n.p.: Pantinos Classics, 2016.
Atwood, Craig D. *Community of the Cross: Moravian Piety in Colonial Bethlehem.* University Park, PA: University of Pennsylvania Press, 2004.
———. "The Mother of God's People: The Adoration of the Holy Spirit in the Eighteenth-Century Brüdergemeine." *Church History* 68.4 (1999) 886–909.
———. "Motherhood of Holy Spirit in Eighteenth Century." April 7, 2011. https://theflamingheretic.wordpress.com/2011/04/08/motherhood-of-holy-spirit-in-18th-century.
———. "Understanding Zinzendorf's Blood and Wounds Theology." *Journal of Moravian History* 1 (2006) 31–47.
Balmer, Randall. *Mine Eyes Have Seen the Glory: A Journey into the Evangelical Subculture in America.* Oxford: Oxford University Press, 2006.
Beeke, Joel R., and Jan van Vliet. "The Marrow of Theology by William Ames (1576–1633)." In *In The Devoted Life: An Invitation to the Puritan Classics*, edited by Kelly M. Kapic and Randall C. Gleason, 52–66. Downers Grove, IL: InterVarsity, 2004.
Beeke, Joel R., and Stephen Yuille. *William Perkins.* Grand Rapids: Evangelical, 2015.

Benedict XVI. "Blessed Angela of Foligno." October 13, 2010. https://w2.vatican.va/content/benedict-xvi/en/audiences/2010/documents/hf_ben-xvi_aud_20101013.html.

———. *Holy Women*. Huntington, IN: Our Sunday Visitor, 2011.

Berger, Peter L., and Thomas Luckmann. *The Social Construction of Reality: A Treatise in the Sociology of Knowledge*. New York: Anchor, 1966.

Blackbourn, David. *The Long Nineteenth Century*. Oxford: Oxford University Press, 1998.

Bourdieu, Pierre. *The Logic of Practice*. Stanford, CA: Stanford University Press, 1990.

———. *Outline of a Theory of Practice*. Cambridge: Cambridge University Press, 1977.

Brewer, John. *The Sinews of Power: War, Money, and the English State 1688–1783*. Cambridge: Harvard University Press, 1988.

Brook, Benjamin. *Lives of the Puritans*. Vol. 2. Pittsburgh: Soli Deo Gloria, 1997.

Brown, Dale W. *Understanding Pietism*. Nappanee, IN: Evangel, 1996.

Buchan, Thomas. "John Wesley and the Constantinian Fall of the Church: Historiographical Indications of Pietist Influence." In *The Pietist Impulse in Christianity*, edited by Christian T. Collins Winn, et al., 146–60. Eugene, OR: Pickwick, 2011.

Campbell, Ted A. *Methodist Doctrine: The Essentials*. Nashville: Abingdon, 2011.

———. "The Way of Salvation and the Methodist Ethos Beyond John Wesley: A Study in Formal Consensus and Popular Reception." *The Asbury Journal* 61.1 (2008) 9.

Coe, Bufford. *John Wesley And Marriage*. Bethlehem, PA: Lehigh University Press, 1996.

Collins Winn, Christian T., et al., eds. *The Pietist Impulse in Christianity*. Eugene, OR: Pickwick, 2011.

Crouter, Richard. *Friedrich Schleiermacher Between Enlightenment and Romanticism*. Cambridge, England: Cambridge University Press, 2005.

Dillenberger, John, and Welch, Claude. *Protestant Christianity: Interpreted Through Its Development*. New York: Scribners and Sons, 1954.

Dreher, Rod. "Purgatorio, Canto XIX." March 23, 2014. http://www.theamericanconservative.com/dreher/purgatorio-canto-xix.

Drummond, Andrew Landale. *German Protestantism Since Luther*. London: Epworth, 1951.

Duffy, Eamon. *The Stripping of the Altars: Traditional Religion in England 1400–1580*. New Haven and London: Yale University Press, 1992.

Durkheim, Emile. *The Elementary Forms of the Religious Life*. New York: Free Press, 1915.

Edwards, Jonathan. "A Divine and Supernatural Light, Immediately Imparted to the Soul by the Spirit of God, Shown to be Both a Scriptural and Rational Doctrine." In *The Works of Jonathan Edwards*, edited by Edward Hickman, 31–45. Vol. 2. 1834. Reprint, Peabody, MA: Hendrickson, 2004.

Erb, Peter, ed. *The Pietists: Selected Writings*. Mahwah, NJ: Paulist, 1983.

Francke, August Hermann. "Autobiography, 1692." In *The Pietists: Selected Writings*, edited by Peter Erb, 99–107. Mahwah, NJ: Paulist, 1983.

———. *A Guide to the Reading and Study of Holy Scriptures*. Philadelphia: David Hogan, 1823.

———. "If And How One May Be Certain That One Is A Child Of God, 1707." In *The Pietists: Selected Writings*, edited by Peter Erb, 145–48. Mahwah, NJ: Paulist, 1983.

———. "A Letter To A Friend Concerning The Most Useful Way Of Preaching, 1725." In *The Pietists: Selected Writings*, edited by Peter Erb, 117–27. Mahwah, NJ: Paulist, 1983.

———. *Memoirs of Augustus Hermann Francke*. Philadelphia: American Sunday School Union, 1830.

———. "On Christian Perfection, 1690." In *The Pietists: Selected Writings*, edited by Peter Erb, 114–16. Mahwah, NJ: Paulist, 1983.

———. "Rules For The Protection Of Conscience And For Good Order In Conversation Or In Society 1689." In *The Pietists: Selected Writings*, edited by Peter Erb, 108–13. Mahwah, NJ: Paulist, 1983.

Gawthrop, Richard L. *Pietism and The Making of Eighteenth-Century Prussia*. Cambridge: Cambridge University Press, 1993.

Gonzalez, Justo L. *The Reformation to the Present Day*. Vol. 2 of *The Story of Christianity*. New York: Harper Collins, 1985.

Hahn, Steven. *A Nation Under Our Feet: Black Political Struggles in the Rural South from Slavery to the Great Migration*. Cambridge, MA: Belknap Press of Harvard University Press, 2003.

Hambrick-Stowe, Charles. *The Practice of Piety: Puritan Devotional Disciplines in Seventeenth-Century New England*. Chapel Hill: University of North Carolina Press, 1982.

Hammond, Geordan. "John Wesley's Relations with the Lutheran Pietist Clergy in Georgia." In *The Pietist Impulse in Christianity*, edited by Christian T. Collins Winn, et al., 135–45. Eugene, OR: Pickwick, 2011.

Hanafi, Zakiya. *The Monster in the Machine: Magic, Medicine, and the Marvelous in the Time of the Scientific Revolution*. Durham: Duke University Press, 2000.

Hsia, R. Po-Chia. *Social Discipline in the Reformation Central Europe 1550-1750*. London: Routledge, 1989.

Hughs, Michael. *Early Modern Germany, 1477–1806*. Philadelphia: University of Pennsylvania Press, 1992.

Hutton, J. E. "Edict of Banishment, 1729–1736." *Zinzendorf: The Ecumenical Pioneer*, November 2011. http://zinzendorf.com/pages/index.php?id=edict-of-banishment.

International House of Prayer. "About the International House of Prayer." *IHOPKC.org*, 2019. http://www.ihopkc.org/about.

Irvin, Dale T. *Christian Histories, Christian Traditioning*. Maryknoll, NY: Orbis, 1998.

Jacobs, Linda. *History Makers: Count Nicholas Ludwig von Zinzendorf*. Pensacola, FL: Christian Life, 2004.

James, William. "The Varieties of Religious Experience." In *William James: Writings 1902–1910*, edited by Bruce Kuklick, 1–478. New York: Library of America, 1987.

Johnson, Marshall D. *The Evolution of Christianity: Twelve Crisis that Shaped the Church*. New York: Continuum, 2005.

Kapic, Kelly M., and Randall C. Gleason. *The Devoted Life: An Invitation to the Puritan Classics*. Downers Grove, IL: InterVarsity, 2004.

Kolb, Robert, and Timothy J. Wengert. *Book of Concord*. Minneapolis: Fortress, 2000.

Langer, Susanne K. "The Logic of Signs and Symbols." In *A Reader in the Anthropology of Religion*, edited by Michael Lambek, 131–39. London: Blackwell, 2008.

Lehmann, Hartmut. "Pietism and Nationalism: The Relationship between Protestant Revivalism and National Renewal in Nineteenth-Century Germany." *Church History* 51.1 (1982) 39–53.

Levi-Strauss, Claude. *Structural Anthropology*. Vol. 2. Chicago: University of Chicago Press, 1976.

Lewis, I. M. *Ecstatic Religion: An Anthropological Study of Spirit Possession and Shamanism*. Middlesex: Penguin, 1971.

Lossky, Vladimir. *The Mystical Theology of the Eastern Church*. London: James Clarke & Co., 1957.

Lovelace, Ricard F. *The American Pietism of Cotton Mather: Origins of American Evangelicalism*. Grand Rapids: Christian University Press, 1979.

Malinowski, Bronislaw. *Magic, Science, and Religion—and other essays*. Long Grove, IL: Waveland, 1992.

Marschke, Benjamin. "Halle Pietism and the Prussian State: Infiltration, Dissent, and Subversion." In *Pietism in Germany and North America 1680–1820*, edited by Jonathan Strom, et al., 217–28. Farnham: Ashgate, 2009.

Marx, Karl. "German Ideology." In *The Marx–Engels Reader*, edited by Robert C. Tucker, 146–203. London: W. W. Norton & Company, 1978.

Massey, James A. "The Hegelians, the Pietists, and the Nature of Religion." *The Journal of Religion* 58.2 (1978) 108–29.

Mauss, Marcel. *A General Theory of Magic*. London: Routledge Classics, 2007.

Meinecke, Friedrich. *The German Catastrophe: The Social and Historical Influences which led to the Rise and the Ruin of Hitler and Germany*. Boston: Beacon, 1964.

Mullen, Shirley A. "The 'Strangely Warmed' Mind: John Wesley, Piety, and Higher Education." In *The Pietist Impulse in Christianity*, edited by Christian T. Collins Winn, et al., 161–74. Eugene, OR: Pickwick, 2011.

Nagler, Arthur Wilford. *Pietism and Methodism: or, the Significance of German Pietism in the Origin and Early Development of Methodism*. Nashville: Ulan, 1918.

Nathan, Samuel. *Moravian Mafia: Religous Greed and Dictatorship*. New York: iUniverse, 2009.

Noll, Mark A. *The Rise of Evangelicalism: The Age of Edwards, Whitfield, and the Wesleys*. Downers Grove, IL: InterVarsity, 2003.

Nuttall, Geoffrey F. *The Holy Spirit in Puritan Faith and Experience*. Second edition. London: University of Chicago Press, 1992.

Obeysekere, Gananath. *Medusa's Hair: An Essay on Personal Symbols and Religious Experience*. Chicago: University of Chicago Press, 1981.

Oddie, William. "Pope Francis Is Under Attack For Saying That Outside The Church There Is No Salvation: It's A 'Poke In The Eye' Says One Presbyterian. Here Is Why He's Wrong." *Catholic Herald*, June 3, 2013. http://www.catholicherald.co.uk/commentandblogs/2013/06/03/pope-francis-is-under-attack-for-saying-that-outside-the-church-there-is-no-salvation-its-a-poke-in-the-eye-says-one-presbyterian-why-hes-wrong.

Oschlies, Wolf. *Die Arbeits- und Berufspädagogik A.H. Franckes (1663–1727). Schule und Leben im Menschenbild des Hauptvertreters des Hallischen Pietismus*. Vol. 6 of *Arbeiten zur Geschichte des Pietismus*. Witten: Luther-Verlag, 1969.

Packer, J. I. *A Quest for Godliness: The Puritan Vision of the Christian Life*. Wheaton, IL: Crossway, 1994.

Perkins, William. *The Art of Prophesying and the Calling of the Ministry.* Carlisle, PA: Banner of Truth Trust, 2011.

———. *The Foundation of Christian Religion Gathered Into Six Principles.* 1591. Reprint, Scotts Valley, CA: CreateSpace, 2010.

———. *A Golden Chain or The Description of Theology.* Edited by Greg Fox. Edinburgh, IN: Puritan Reprints, 2010.

———. *A Reformed Catholic: Or, A Declaration Shewing How Near We May Come To The Present Church Of Rome In Sundry Points Of Religion: And Wherein We Must Forever Depart From Them With An Advertisement To All Favorers Of The Roman Religion, Shewing That The Said.* 1598. Reprint, Ann Arbor, MI: Text Creation Partnership, 2004. http://quod.lib.umich.edu/e/eebo/A09453.0001.001?rgn=main;view=fulltext

Pierard, Richard V. "German Pietism as a Major Factor in the Beginnings of Modern Protestant Missions." In *The Pietist Impulse in Christianity*, edited by Christian T. Collins Winn, et al., 285–95. Eugene, OR: Pickwick, 2011.

Placher, William C. *The Domestication of Transcendence: How Modern Thinking About God Went Wrong.* Louisville: Westminster John Knox, 1996.

Plantinga, Harry, ed. "Thomas à Kempis: Ascetical Writer." *Christian Classics Ethereal Library.* http://www.ccel.org/ccel/kempis.

Potts, James Manning. *Prayers of the Middle Ages: Light from a Thousand Years.* Nashville: Upper Room, 1954.

Prout, William Cardwell. "Spener and the Theology of Pietism." *Journal of Bible and Religion* 15.1 (1947) 46–49.

Reetzke, James. "A Community at Hernnhut." *Count Zinzendorf*, 2002. http://countzinzendorf.ccws.org/community/index.html.

Rimius, Henry. *A Candid Narrative Of The Rise And Progress Of The Herrnhuters.* London: ECCO, 1753.

———. *A Supplement To The Candid Narrative Of The Rise And Progress Of The Herrnhuters.* London: ECCO, 1755.

———. *A Supplement To The Candid Narrative Of The Rise And Progress Of The Herrnhuters, Commonly Called Moravians, Or Unitas Fratrum. In Which Among Other Things, The Political Scheme And Artful Proceedings Of Their Patriarch Are Disclosed.* London: A. Linde, 1755.

Robinson, Paschal. "Bl. Angela of Foligno." *New Advent*, 2017. http://www.newadvent.org/cathen/01482a.htm.

Rogers, Richard Lee. "The Urban Threshold and the Second Great Awakening: Revivalism in New York State, 1825–1835." *Journal for the Scientific Study of Religion* 49.4 (2010) 694–709.

Ryken, Leland. *Worldly Saints: The Puritans as They Really Were.* Grand Rapids: Zondervan, 1986.

Sauter, Michael. *Vision of the Enlightenment: The Edict on Religion of 1788 and the Politics of the Public Sphere in Eighteenth-Century Prussia.* Leiden: Brill, 2009.

Shantz, Douglas H. *An Introduction to German Pietism: Protestant Renewal at the Dawn of Modern Europe.* Baltimore, MD: Johns Hopkins Univeristy Press, 2013.

Smith, Helmut Walser. *Continuities of German History.* Cambridge: Cambridge University Press, 2008.

Smith, Jonathan Z. *Relating Religion.* Chicago: University of Chicago Press, 2004.

Spener, Philip Jacob. *Philip Jacob Spener and His Work*. Philadelphia: Lutheran Publication Society, 1897.

———. *Pia Desideria*. Eugene, OR: Wipf and Stock, 1964.

Staniforth, Maxwell, ed. *Early Christian Writings: The Apostolic Fathers*. London: Penguin Classics, 1987.

Stark, Rodney. *The Victory of Reason: How Christianity Led to Freedom, Capitalism, and Western Success*. New York: Random House Trade Paperbacks, 2006.

Stoeffler, F. Ernest. *Continental Pietism and Early American Christianity*. Eugene, OR: Wipf and Stock, 2007.

———. *The Rise of Evangelical Pietism*. Leiden: E. J. Brill, 1971.

Strom, Jonathan. "Problems and Promises of Pietism Research." *Church History* 71.3 (2002) 536–54.

Styers, Randall. *Making Magic: Religion, Magic & Science in the Modern World*. Oxford: Oxford University Press, 2004.

Tauler, Johannes. *The Following of Christ*. Edited by Paul A. Boer Sr. Translated by J. R. Morell. n.p.: Veritatis Splendor, 2012.

———. *The Inner Way*. Translated by Arthur Wollaston Hutton. London: Aeterna, 2015.

———. *Sermons*. Translated by Maria Shrady. Classics of Western Spirituality. Mahwah, NJ: Paulist, 1985.

Thomas à Kempis. *The Imitation of Christ*. Translated by Aloysius Croft and Harold Bolton. Mineola, NY: Dover, 2003.

Tillich, Paul. *A Complete History of Christian Thought*. New York: Harper & Row, 1968.

———. *Perspectives on Nineteenth and Twentieth-Century Protestant Theology*. New York: Harper & Row, 1967.

Tomkins, Stephen. *John Wesley: A Biography*. Grand Rapids: Eerdmans, 2003.

van der Veer, Peter. "The Moral State: Religion, Nation, and Empire in Victorian Britain and British India." In *Nation and Religion: Perspectives on Europe and Asia*, edited by Peter van der Veer and Hartmut Lehmann, 15–43. Princeton, NJ: Princeton University Press, 1999.

van Voorhis, Daniel. *Johann Arndt: A Prophet of Lutheran Pietism*. Irvine, CA: 1517, 2018.

Wallace, Anthony. *Revitalizations and Mazeways*. Vol. 1 of *Essays on Culture Change*. Lincoln: University of Nebraska Press, 2003.

Weber, Max. *The Protestant Ethic and the "Spirit" of Capitalism*. London: Penguin, 2002.

Wemmer, Paul. *Count Zinzendorf and the Spirit of the Moravians*. Maitland: Xulon, 2013.

Wesley, John. "The Almost Christian." In *The Essential Works of John Wesley: Selected Books, Sermons, and Other Writings*, edited by Alice Russie, 171–78. Uhrichsville, OH: Barbour, 2011.

———. "The Character of a Methodist." In *The Essential Works of John Wesley: Selected Books, Sermons, and Other Writings*, edited by Alice Russie, 827–34. Uhrichsville, OH: Barbour, 2011.

———. "Christian Perfection." In *The Essential Works of John Wesley: Selected Books, Sermons, and Other Writings*, edited by Alice Russie, 397–414. Uhrichsville, OH: Barbour, 2011.

———. "His Spiritual Journey." In *The Essential Works of John Wesley: Selected Books, Sermons, and Other Writings*, edited by Alice Russie, 27–40. Uhrichsville, OH: Barbour, 2011.

———. "The Marks of the New Birth." In *The Essential Works of John Wesley: Selected Books, Sermons, and Other Writings*, edited by Alice Russie, 227–36. Uhrichsville, OH: Barbour, 2011.

———. "The New Birth." In *The Essential Works of John Wesley: Selected Books, Sermons, and Other Writings*, edited by Alice Russie, 215–26. Uhrichsville, OH: Barbour, 2011.

———. "On Early Methodism: A Short History of Methodism." In *The Essential Works of John Wesley: Selected Books, Sermons, and Other Writings*, edited by Alice Russie, 803–6. Uhrichsville, OH: Barbour, 2011.

———. "On Perfection." In *The Essential Works of John Wesley: Selected Books, Sermons, and Other Writings*, edited by Alice Russie, 415–28. Uhrichsville, OH: Barbour, 2011.

———. "On Sin in Believers." In *The Essential Works of John Wesley: Selected Books, Sermons, and Other Writings*, edited by Alice Russie, 341–52. Uhrichsville, OH: Barbour, 2011.

———. "On Working Out Our Own Salvation." In *The Essential Works of John Wesley: Selected Books, Sermons, and Other Writings*, edited by Alice Russie, 323–30. Uhrichsville, OH: Barbour, 2011.

———. "Original Sin." In *The Essential Works of John Wesley: Selected Books, Sermons, and Other Writings*, edited by Alice Russie, 125–36. Uhrichsville, OH: Barbour, 2011.

———. *A Plain Account of Christian Perfection*. Edited by Frank Banfield. Vancouver: Eremitical, 2009.

———. "A Plain Account of Christian Perfection." In *The Essential Works of John Wesley: Selected Books, Sermons, and Other Writings*, edited by Alice Russie, 1025–102. Uhrichsville, OH: Barbour, 2011.

———. "A Plain Account of the People Called Methodists." In *The Essential Works of John Wesley: Selected Books, Sermons, and Other Writings*, edited by Alice Russie, 807–26. Uhrichsville, OH: Barbour, 2011.

———. "The Principles of a Methodist." In *The Essential Works of John Wesley: Selected Books, Sermons, and Other Writings*, edited by Alice Russie, 835–48. Uhrichsville, OH: Barbour, 2011.

———. "Prologue." In *The Essential Works of John Wesley: Selected Books, Sermons, and Other Writings*, edited by Alice Russie, 1359–60. Uhrichsville, OH: Barbour, 2011.

———. "The Rise of the Holy Club." In *The Essential Works of John Wesley: Selected Books, Sermons, and Other Writings*, edited by Alice Russie, 17–26. Uhrichsville, OH: Barbour, 2011.

———. "We Lift Our Hearts to Thee." In *The Essential Works of John Wesley: Selected Books, Sermons, and Other Writings*, edited by Alice Russie, 1341–42. Uhrichsville, OH: Barbour, 2011.

Westphal, Milton C. "Early Moravian Pietism." *Pennsylvania History* 3.3 (1936) 164–81.

Yannaras, Christos. "Pietism as an Ecclesiological Heresy." In *The Freedom of Morality*, by Christos Yannaras, 119–36. Crestwood, NY: St. Vladimir's Seminary Press, 1984.

Zinzendorf, Nicolas Ludwig von. "Brotherly Union And Agreement At Herrnhut, 1727." In *The Pietists: Selected Writings*, edited by Peter Erb, 291–95. Mahwah, NJ: Paulist, 1983.

———. *Christian Life and Witness: Count Zinzendorf's 1738 Berlin Speeches*. Edited by Gary S. Kinkel. Eugene, OR: Pickwick, 2010.

———. "Concerning Saving Faith." In *The Pietists: Selected Writings*, edited by Peter Erb, 304–24. Mahwah, NJ: Paulist, 1983.

———. *Der öffentlichen Gemein Reden im Jahr 1747. Zweyter Theil*. n.p., 1749.

———. "The Litany of the Life, Suffering, and Death of Jesus Christ." In *The Pietists: Selected Writings*, edited by Peter Erb, 296–300. Mahwah, NJ: Paulist, 1983.

———. "On the Essential Character and Circumstances of the Life of a Christian." In *The Pietists: Selected Writings*, edited by Peter Erb, 304–24. Mahwah, NJ: Paulist, 1983.

———. "Thoughts For The Learned And Yet Good-Willed Students Of Truth, 1732." In *The Pietists: Selected Writings*, edited by Peter Erb, 291–95. Mahwah, NJ: Paulist, 1983.

www.ingramcontent.com/pod-product-compliance
Lightning Source LLC
Chambersburg PA
CBHW051742230426
43670CB00012B/2131